Essays on the History of Contemporary
Praise and Worship

# Essays on the History of Contemporary Praise and Worship

EDITED BY
LESTER RUTH

PICKWICK *Publications* · Eugene, Oregon

ESSAYS ON THE HISTORY OF CONTEMPORARY PRAISE AND WORSHIP

Copyright © 2020 Wipf and Stock Publishers. All rights reserved. Except for brief quotations in critical publications or reviews, no part of this book may be reproduced in any manner without prior written permission from the publisher. Write: Permissions, Wipf and Stock Publishers, 199 W. 8th Ave., Suite 3, Eugene, OR 97401.

Pickwick Publications
An Imprint of Wipf and Stock Publishers
199 W. 8th Ave., Suite 3
Eugene, OR 97401

www.wipfandstock.com

PAPERBACK ISBN: 978-1-5326-7901-8
HARDCOVER ISBN: 978-1-5326-7902-5
EBOOK ISBN: 978-1-5326-7903-2

*Cataloguing-in-Publication data:*

Names: Ruth, Lester, editor.

Title: Essays on the history of contemporary praise and worship / edited by Lester Ruth.

Description: Eugene, OR : Pickwick Publications, 2020 | Includes bibliographical references.

Identifiers: ISBN 978-1-5326-7901-8 (paperback) | ISBN 978-1-5326-7902-5 (hardcover) | ISBN 978-1-5326-7903-2 (ebook)

Subjects: LCSH: Public worship. | History.

Classification: BV15 .E75 2020 (print) | BV15 .E75 (ebook)

Manufactured in the U.S.A.        03/05/20

# Contents

List of Contributors | vii

Acknowledgment | ix

Introduction: The Importance and History of Contemporary Praise & Worship | 1
—Lester Ruth

1 James F. White, Grady Hardin, and Methodist "Contemporary" Worship in the 1970s: The 11:00 a.m. Cox Chapel Service at Highland Park | 13
—R. Matthew Sigler

2 John Wimber and the Vineyard Influence on Charismatic Catholic Worship | 34
—Billy Kangas

3 The Path to a Second Service: Mainline Decline, Church Growth, and Apostolic Leadership | 55
—Glenn Stallsmith

4 Sounding God's Enthronement in Worship: The Early History and Theology of Integrity's Hosanna! Music | 74
—Adam Perez

5  Robert Webber: Preserving Traditional Worship through Contemporary Styles | 95
   —Jonathan A. Powers

6  Forerunning Contemporary Worship Music: The Afro-Pentecostal Roots of Black Gospel | 116
   —Wen Reagan

7  Nashville and Sydney Are Not the World: The Transnational Migration of Sources for Chinese Contemporary Praise & Worship Songs | 146
   —Lim Swee Hong

8  The Rise of the Worship Degree: Pedagogical Changes in the Preparation of Church Musicians | 160
   —Jonathan Ottaway

9  Methodological Insights for the Historiography of Contemporary Praise & Worship | 176
   —Lester Ruth

# Contributors

*(listed in alphabetical order)*

**Billy Kangas** is a doctoral student at Catholic University of America.

**Lim Swee Hong** is the Director of the Master of Sacred Music Program and the Deer Park Associate Professor of Sacred Music at Emmanuel College of Victoria University in the University of Toronto.

**Jonathan Ottaway** is a doctoral student at Duke Divinity School.

**Adam Perez** is a doctoral student at Duke Divinity School.

**Jonathan A. Powers** is the Assistant Professor of Worship at Asbury Theological Seminary.

**Wen Reagan** is the Associate Director of the Center for Worship and the Arts and Visiting Assistant Professor of Music and Worship at Samford University.

**Lester Ruth** is the Research Professor of Christian Worship at Duke Divinity School.

**R. Matthew Sigler** is the Assistant Professor of Wesleyan Studies at Seattle Pacific University and Seminary.

**Glenn Stallsmith** is a doctoral student at Duke Divinity School.

# Acknowledgment

We would like to thank the Calvin Institute of Christian Worship and its director, Dr. John Witvliet, for the encouragement and support to complete this volume.

# Introduction

## The Importance and History of Contemporary Praise & Worship

— Lester Ruth —

I venture a guess: when an image has gained enough automatic recognition that it is *the* visual emblem for something, then the thing imaged has really become a *thing*. And such it is for the way of worship that this book will call Contemporary Praise & Worship. Look for books on Evangelicals or Pentecostals and one is very likely to find on the front cover a picture of people worshiping. And the image is not of just any way of worship but one characterized by hands lifted up, faces caught in the ecstasy of contemplating God, dramatic light streaming through the space, and instruments drawn from the world of popular music.[1] All these visual elements hint at Contemporary Praise & Worship and suggest that this way of worship has become representative for both wider Evangelicalism and Pentecostalism. Of course, one should expect to find such images on the covers of books dedicated to studying this way of worship,[2] but the scene is more ubiquitous than that. This image graces, among others, books on the history of youth ministry, an anthropologist's assessment of evangelical and pentecostal spirituality, a political scientist's assessment of current dynamics between Evangelicals and politics, and even a sociological analysis of violence against Christians in India.[3] The widespread use of this liturgical image suggests that Contemporary Praise & Worship has indeed become a *thing*.

---

1. For a fuller list of characteristics normally found in this way of worship, see Lim and Ruth, *Lovin' on Jesus*, 2–7.

2. For examples see recent works from ethnomusicologist Monique Ingalls: *Singing the Congregation*, and (with Amos Yong as coeditor) *Spirit of Praise*.

3. See, respectively, Bergler, *Juvenilization of American Christianity*; Luhrmann, *When God Talks Back*; Wong, *Immigrants, Evangelicals, and Politics*; and Bauman, *Pentecostals, Proselytization, and Anti-Christian Violence*.

And it has become a thing globally. Travel around the world and one can hear reference to the phenomenon's name as a technical term (actually "praise and worship" is the more common expression). In Spanish-speaking Christianity the way of worship is known as Alazbanza y Adoración. In Portuguese the label is Louvor e Adoração. Travel to Asia and one will participate in 敬拜赞美 in Mandarin-speaking congregations.

(As a parenthetical note, the reader will see the following approaches to naming the phenomenon within this current volume. When an author is speaking of the entire phenomenon, "Contemporary Praise & Worship" [notice the ampersand] will be used as a comprehensive term. "Praise and Worship" will designate those manifestations associated with the pentecostal and global settings, while "Contemporary Worship" will designate the worship largely associated with mainline denominations and some mainstream evangelical denominations. "Contemporary Worship" is a term that is mainly American and white.)

And the numbers (even just for the United States) bear out the spread of the phenomenon. Education-related numbers are just one indication. By one estimate given at a recent consultation on worship curriculum—such a consultation itself a sign of growing importance—there are in the United States 130 programs in worship as of 2018, which includes any college, seminary, or graduate degree program with the word "worship" in the title.[4] (Compare chapter 8 in this volume.) Many, if not most, of these programs aim to prepare musicians to be worship leaders, the key position in a Contemporary Praise & Worship service. Other non-degree programs, often affiliated with influential megachurches known for their worship, supplement the opportunities for worship leaders. That so many educational programs exist is not surprising given the number of congregations globally utilizing the music of Contemporary Praise & Worship. The website for Christian Copyright Licensing International (CCLI) states that more than 250,000 churches and other institutions worldwide hold licenses to use this music without having to seek permission from each copyright holder. In addition, CCLI says it has registered over 300,000 songs from over 3,000 publishers.

Numbers associated with the technological aspect of Contemporary Praise & Worship also confirm the spread of this liturgical phenomenon. For example, the annual WFX (Worship Facilities Expo) conferences focusing on this aspect have grown into large events occupying convention centers in large cities. The 2017 WFX conference in Dallas had 3,500 people in attendance at that city's downtown convention center; 219 booths filled the exhibition hall and over one hundred speakers offered information on a wide variety

---

4. Joshua Waggener, e-mail message to Lester Ruth, September 28, 2018.

of topics. Formal sociological studies confirm the spread of worship-based technology. A recent report from the National Congregations Study, based on information from over 3,800 congregations in the United States, indicated a 23 percent increase in the number of congregations utilizing projection equipment during worship, one of the largest shifts in the various items documented in the study.[5] This increase is a sure sign of the spread of one of the most common architectural features of Contemporary Praise & Worship.

Indeed, so much has Contemporary Praise & Worship spread that scholars can allude to its growing influence and pervasiveness by speaking in shorthand ways about its impact. A common shorthand is to speak about a "pentecostalization" of mainline and evangelical congregations. For example, C. Eric Lincoln and Lawrence Mamiya as early as 1990 were labelling as "neo-pentecostal" the liturgical changes associated with the adoption of Contemporary Praise & Worship in black congregations.[6] Since then Mamiya has continued to identify the advancement of band-based worship as the pentecostalization of worship among black, middle-class Baptists and Methodists, especially in megachurch settings.[7] Indeed, to draw attention to the adoption of Contemporary Praise & Worship as a kind of pentecostalization of worship has become a way to identify it as well as imply its wide extent. James Earl Massey takes this exact approach in speaking about black megachurches: "These churches, with their neo-pentecostal emphases and their high-energy entertainment-mode services led by praise teams using music adopted from the pop culture, have deemphasized denominational affiliations, rejected religious traditions, and dismissed many doctrinal constraints."[8]

And so, whether by ubiquitous image, by a technical term that stretches across continents, by the numbers, or by a shorthand identification used by scholars, Contemporary Praise & Worship has become a global phenomenon. And yet it has not been exhaustively or thoroughly studied with respect to its history.

## Current Historical Narratives for Contemporary Praise & Worship

That lack of exhaustive or thorough study does not mean that historical narratives are not available. Several are common in the secondary literature on this liturgical phenomenon.

5. Chaves and Eagle, *Religious Congregations*.
6. Lincoln and Mamiya, *The Black Church*.
7. Mamiya, *River of Struggle, River of Freedom*.
8. Massey, "Doctrinal Imperative," 35.

One narrative emphasizes the major plot line as being the growing influence of culturally-derived forms of pop and rock music on worship.[9] Notwithstanding the rejection by (white) Evangelicals of this sort of music in every sphere in the 1950s, developments starting in the 1960s bit by bit opened the door for this music into congregations' sanctuaries. Foremost among these developments was the Jesus People movement that successfully evangelized among hippies, especially in Southern California, and led to churches using the music these new Christians loved and composed. By the start of the 1980s the creation and distribution of this music had brought about several different companies that accelerated and standardized appropriation of this music. Many churches that did so in the 1980s and 1990s did so under the influence of the pragmatism of the Church Growth movement as well as of megachurches that modeled this new way of worship. A variation of this plot line notes African-American contributions to the new music post-1960s along with African-American adoption of the same in black megachurches of the 1980s and beyond.[10] Another variation of this plot line interprets these developments theologically as God's means of renewing the church.

Another narrative also has music as a central feature of the historical plot line but places it within a larger framework of the church's desire to be attractive to youth.[11] The desire itself derived from a wider cultural perception of the mid-twentieth century that the future lay with the youth and a concomitant fear that older generations and their ways had lost touch with youth. Thus, starting in mid-century, various churches and parachurch organizations began experimenting with new forms of worship—including and especially music—in order to maintain attractiveness to a growing youth subculture. The 1960s accentuated this longstanding process so that eventually a "juvenilized" way of worship featuring standard features of Contemporary Praise & Worship had become commonplace.

A third kind of historical storyline has emphasized the phenomenon's connection with "frontier" revivalism of the nineteenth century.[12] Thus, in contrast with the plot lines noted above, this historiography reaches further back historically and places a stronger emphasis on the motivation for liturgical change (to conduct successful evangelism) than the music-centered

---

9. See, for example, Reagan, "A Beautiful Noise," or Ingalls, "Awesome in This Place." Cf. Ingalls, *Singing the Congregation*, 1–11.

10. For example, Johnson, "'Oh, For a Thousand Tongues to Sing.'"

11. See especially Bergler, *Juvenilization of American Christianity*.

12. This plot line is a favorite one of liturgical historians as they have been influenced by the writings of James F. White on the Frontier tradition of worship. See White, *Protestant Worship*, 171–91.

narratives. Scholars utilizing this storyline portray a similar historical trajectory to explain the rise and dissemination of a new way of worship: a launching by the frontier camp meetings of the Second Great Awakening at the beginning of the nineteenth century; standardization by the well-known evangelist Charles Finney in the mid-nineteenth century; resurgence in the Church Growth Movement of the 1970s and 1980s; and then new expressions in exemplary megachurches of the same period, and finally mainline adoption in the 1990s.[13]

## Historical Overview: A Tale of Two Rivers and Their Confluence

Notwithstanding the useful information found in these earlier histories, especially that provided by musicologists, no one has yet provided a satisfactory comprehensive framework that seeks to embrace the breadth of the phenomenon's origins and developments. It is not that prior historiographies are wrong as much as they are incomplete. I offer the following as an attempt to provide a more comprehensive account.

I and my research colleague, Lim Swee Hong, have found it helpful to use an analogy from rivers. Rather than force the history into a single narrative we have found it best to speak of two parallel rivers, each with its own channel, to explain the history of the first fifty years or so (late 1940s to late 1990s). Each river is best identified by the technical term that predominates within that line of development: "Praise and Worship" and "Contemporary Worship."[14] Within each river were multiple currents, a fact that increases the complexity of the historical narrative. For example, within the historical development of "Praise and Worship" it is possible to identify currents associated with the independent pentecostal churches connected to the Latter Rain revival of the 1940s as well as the ways of worship developed from the Jesus Movement in California a generation later. Each current will contribute something to the larger river, reinforcing its character and strengthening its power.

Broadly put, the Praise and Worship river channel moved along on the sense of pursuing a new approach of worship as a fulfillment of the revelation of God, especially as seen in a scripturally grounded theology of worship focused on experiencing God's presence through praise. Churches in this channel worshiped in this way because God had given this way of

---

13. For a fuller review of this historiography and citations of those who utilize it, see Ruth, "Divine, Human, or Devilish?" 296–99.

14. To distinguish these phrases as technical terms, I will employ capitalization throughout.

encountering the divine; it was a gift. The critical, oft-cited Scripture was Psalm 22:3 from which worshipers in this channel believed God inhabits or is enthroned on the praises of his people. This channel was overwhelmingly pentecostal, charismatic, and/or non-white in makeup.

In contrast, the Contemporary Worship river channel flowed from an anxiety that societal and cultural changes had caused the church's worship to be out of sync with people. This channel, largely associated with mainline denominations and classic evangelical groups and churches (and usually white in its makeup), sought a new, more thoroughly inculturated way of worship to overcome the gap that had developed between culture, people, and prior forms of worship. Its purpose was to read the people desired in order to adapt worship practices to meet them. Churches in this second channel worshiped in this way because it was necessary to bridge the gap that existed between worship and people; the driving concern was this divide. The critical Scripture, if one was cited, was 1 Corinthians 9:22 from which was derived a vision of becoming all things to all people in order to win some.

The fluvial analogy has two additional features necessary to explain both the complexity of historical development over the years along with the complexity of the situation since the late 1990s. The first feature is to acknowledge a flood plain between the two river channels, a plain in which individual examples or currents occasionally spill over to share characteristics more common to the other river of development. A clear example is the ongoing tactical pragmatism found in John Wimber, a critical leader in the early Vineyard Fellowship denomination, from his prior experience in the Church Growth Movement. However, the heart of the Vineyard ethos of worship, i.e., an encounter with God in music-driven worship expressed under the category of intimacy, is solidly within the Praise and Worship channel even as Wimber's pragmatism about how to reach people was a common aspect of the Contemporary Worship channel.

The second additional feature is to imagine a confluence of the two rivers since the late 1990s. In other words, the previous channels have fused as this way of worship has gained broad acceptance, settled into the ecclesiastical landscape, and had a multi-dimensional infrastructure created to support it and maintain it. There has been a blurring of the boundaries of both channels as both sets of original motivations have decreased and original distinctives of each channel have waned. The two channels have flowed together and created a new global reality.

Having laid out the metaphor to explain the history of the entire phenomenon, let us examine the details, beginning with the Praise and Worship channel.

## Historical Overview: The Praise and Worship Channel

In 1946 Canadian pentecostal minister Reg Layzell began teaching an interpretation of Psalm 22:3 that emphasized corporate praise as the means by which God becomes manifestly present in worship. Soon Layzell had linked up with the Latter Rain revival, which had started elsewhere in Canada in 1948. This revival provided the platform by which this teaching on praise spread widely across the continent and around the world, especially in independent pentecostal churches. Further dissemination occurred as certain preachers (including Layzell), churches, and institutions (e.g., Elim Bible Institute in New York) emphasized the centrality of praise, leading an increasing number of pentecostal churches to alter previous ways of worship.

Starting in the late 1960s a surge of published literature offering biblical theologies for underpinning an emphasis on praise began to emerge. This literature reinforced a praise-centered way of worship within the Latter Rain network of churches which bled over to charismatic renewal movements and some other Pentecostals. This literature increasingly made a technical distinction between praise and worship based on biblical worship studies. Combined with the increasing musicalization of praise in the same time period (i.e., an understanding that the praise in which God becomes present is congregational singing), this distinction between praise and worship led to early types of worship "sets" of extended times of congregational singing with good flow and guided direction from praise to worship. Concurrently, the emergence of Jesus People brought about an additional current of developments within this channel, particularly with reference to the writing of new songs and the widespread introduction of guitars and bands into the instrumental mix. This period also saw the publishing of the first how-to guides and the holding of the first instructional conferences.

The mid-1980s saw an explosion in the number and range of churches doing Praise and Worship. The period also evidenced an explosion in the supports for pursing it in terms of explanatory literature and conferences. By the late 1980s the key music companies, Maranatha! Music, Vineyard/Mercy Records, and Integrity, had been established and stabilized. The pieces and the motivations were in place to support intentional "exporting" of this way of worship across the continent and around the world, including large-scale conferences to teach the theology behind and musical techniques of Praise and Worship. In addition, non-white expressions of Praise and Worship began to be seen, especially through Marcos Witt and CanZion (Spanish-speaking), the West Angeles Church of God in Christ's *Saints in Praise* CDs (African-American), and Asian sources for music, each with their own sphere of impact.

Through the 1990s what had started as a singular emphasis in 1946 on the priority of praise had swollen to a massive movement. Across the pentecostal landscape and in many evangelical congregations, a major overhaul of Sunday worship was occurring as previous forms of worship gave way to a normalizing of Praise and Worship. This spread among congregations was reinforced in several ways. The Promise Keeper rallies, for example, gave a large-scale, public introduction into this way of worship for many men, including pastors and church musicians, while the dissemination of media such as music cassette tape subscriptions and worship magazines resourced congregational adoption.

## Historical Overview: The Contemporary Worship Channel

The story of Contemporary Worship begins around the time of World War II as churches and parachurch organizations appropriated the wider cultural sensibility that the future lay with youth. Fearing the loss of a generation of young people who found worship boring and out of touch, concerned Christians adopted a mentality—paralleling developments in business marketing—that targeted youth and the developing youth subculture by using music and other parts of worship to reach and attract those targeted. This targeting established elements that would define Contemporary Worship for the next several decades: a concern for authenticity and fittingness; an attraction to creativity and novelty; and a reliance upon generational thinking with an emphasis upon youth and young adults.

The angst about the disconnection between people and the church's worship sparked in the late 1960s a period of liturgical experimentation in mainline congregations, sometimes under the name of "contemporary worship" and sometimes under alternative names. One example is the Methodist church in Washington that developed a new service known as "Church-O-Theque" (think discotheque in church). Similarly evangelical congregations were busy building generational bridges with youth musicals from Ralph Carmichael and others. While this initial use of the term "contemporary worship" had faded by the mid-1970s, the traits developed in these experimentations (contemporary language, contemporary concerns, and contemporary music) continued as anxiety about the gap between worship and culture persisted in haunting mainline and evangelical denominations.

The propensity toward attempts to overcome the perceived gap between worship and people received a jolt of energy from the Church Growth Movement. Although Church Growth thought had originally developed as a missiological theory about non-American evangelistic efforts, advocates of this movement began to apply its insights to an American context. The result was a resurgence of a form of worship pragmatism that raised the appeal of liturgical experimentation and targeting, beginning with the advocacy for multiple services within congregations. Beginning in the late 1970s and throughout the 1980s, a pragmatic approach to worship became widespread. This development helps explain how the eventual rise of Contemporary Worship by that name would become attractive to many pastors and denominational leaders since it played on their anxiety about numerical decline and a perceived gap between church and culture.

Critical for the mainstreaming of Contemporary Worship were several megachurches who modeled the pragmatism advocated by the Church Growth Movement. In addition to modeling, these churches facilitated the spread of new ways of worship by serving as centers to teach other churches a seeker-driven mind frame and the method to revolutionize sanctuaries with a contemporary style of worship. Key among these churches were Saddleback Church (California), Ginghamsburg United Methodist Church (Ohio), Prince of Peace Lutheran (Minnesota), and Willow Creek Community Church (Illinois) congregations.

Consequently, by the early 1990s many pastors and musicians in mainline congregations—and in evangelical mainline denominations like the Baptists—had become aware that something liturgically new was astir. Eager to find tactical ways to bridge the gap and anxious about numeric decline, congregations began to adopt Contemporary Worship, often by starting a new service at a new time in a new space. Denominational officials, publishing houses, and events resourced those willing to build the liturgical bridge.

## Historical Overview: The Confluence

Around the start of the new millennium the two channels of Praise and Worship and Contemporary Worship began to flow into each other, establishing a new liturgical reality, a kind of confluence. This new form of worship became increasingly widespread but lost much of its novelty as it spread. Each of the prior channels began to lose their original distinctiveness as the various currents mingled and shared. Whereas both channels' early literature was breathless with a sense of novelty or a sense of urgency about this new thing in worship, by the early 2000s both senses had begun to fade. Authors no longer wrote as if their readers would have no familiarity with the phenomenon. Neither did they argue vehemently the well-worn rationales that had characterized both channels for decades. Instead authors moved on to a new task: fine tuning a way of worship that they assumed was a given in the broader liturgical landscape.

A particularly important feature of this liturgical confluence of shared reality was the development of a globally-based musical infrastructure that gave music to the whole phenomenon. This common musical infrastructure shared several features: an international sourcing of music starting with the "British Invasion" of the late 1990s; the role of Christian Copyright Licensing International (CCLI) to facilitate use of music; the purchasing and consolidation of earlier music companies; and the rise of worship leader "celebrities."

Several other infrastructures developed to support Contemporary Praise & Worship in the confluence. One was national conferences that drew participants from across a range of churches. Another was advancements in technology that made recent services significantly more sophisticated that worship in either of the two prior channels. Another critical infrastructure was the expansion of degree programs to educate people to be worship leaders and church support staff for Contemporary Praise & Worship.

A new way of worship had arrived.

## The Chapters in This Book

This historical overview can help place this volume's chapters into a larger framework. Four of them highlight significant developments within the Praise and Worship channel. Billy Kangas's "John Wimber and the Vineyard Influence on Charismatic Catholic Worship" documents the cross influence of currents within this channel as the Vineyard approach to worship impacted the Catholic Charismatic movement. The chapter by Adam Perez, "Sounding God's Enthronement in Worship: The Early History and Theology of Integrity's Hosanna! Music," describes how the Latter Rain Movement, perhaps the largest current within the Praise and Worship channel, shaped the company, Integrity, whose products introduced Praise and Worship music to innumerable people and congregations. This introduction was a major factor in the expansion of Praise and Worship in the 1980s and 1990s. Wen Reagan's contribution, "Forerunning Contemporary Worship Music: The Afro-Pentecostal Roots of Black Gospel," explores the historical parallels between black gospel and Contemporary Praise & Worship music. Lim Swee Hong's chapter, "Nashville and Sydney Are Not the World: The Transnational Migration of Sources for Chinese Contemporary Praise

& Worship Songs," helps us see the global musical links between Chinese congregations within the Praise and Worship channel.

Three chapters represent the Contemporary Worship channel. Sigler's work on Methodist liturgists, James White and Grady Hardin, entitled "James F. White, Grady Hardin, and Methodist 'Contemporary' Worship in the 1970s: The 11:00 a.m. Cox Chapel Service at Highland Park," uses their liturgical experiments of the late 1960s and early 1970s as a case study in the mainline concern for the gap between people and the church's worship. This concern serves as a major motivator in the history of the Contemporary Worship channel. Glenn Stallsmith's chapter, "The Path to a Second Service: Mainline Decline, Church Growth, and Apostolic Leadership," takes the history of this channel forward a generation by documenting how the missiological movement known as Church Growth tapped this mainline anxiety to lead many congregations to amplify the number of services they offered, usually divided by style. This amplification became a major venue for the introduction of Contemporary services. Powers's labor on the popular writer and speaker Robert Webber, entitled "Robert Webber: Preserving Traditional Worship through Contemporary Styles," shows how Webber attempted to bring some historical direction and rooting to the liturgical flux of the Contemporary Worship channel among mainline and evangelical congregations.

As noted above, the two channels eventually form a kind of confluence in which Contemporary Praise & Worship has become a standard aspect of the broader liturgical landscape. Jonathan Ottaway's investigation, "The Rise of the Worship Degree: Pedagogical Changes in the Preparation of Church Musicians," documents a major element that both reflects the settling into this new worship reality and, in turn, reinforces its standardization: the development of educational degree programs for training worship leaders. The speed by which these programs developed indicates how solidly this new way of worship has become an institution in the American church.

A concluding essay, "Methodological Insights for the Historiography of Contemporary Praise & Worship," brings this volume to a close but, hopefully, not further historical study of this liturgical phenomenon. It is our hope that these essays will launch further work, not cut it off.

## Bibliography

Bauman, Chad M. *Pentecostals, Proselytization, and Anti-Christian Violence in Contemporary India.* Oxford: Oxford University Press, 2015.

Bergler, Thomas E. *The Juvenilization of American Christianity.* Grand Rapids: Eerdmans, 2012.

Bradshaw, Paul F. *The Search for the Origins of Christian Worship: Sources and Methods for the Study of Early Liturgy*. 2nd ed. Oxford: Oxford University Press, 2002.

Chaves, Mark, and Alison Eagle. *Religious Congregations in 21st Century America*. Durham: Duke University Department of Sociology, 2014.

Ingalls, Monique. "Awesome in This Place: Sound, Space, and Identity in Contemporary North American Evangelical Worship." PhD diss., University of Pennsylvania, 2008.

———. *Singing the Congregation: How Contemporary Worship Music Forms Evangelical Community*. Oxford: Oxford University Press, 2018.

Ingalls, Monique, and Amos Yong, eds. *The Spirit of Praise: Music and Worship and Global Pentecostal-Charismatic Christianity*. University Park, PA: Pennsylvania State University Press, 2016.

Johnson, Birgitta Joelisa. "'Oh, For a Thousand Tongues to Sing': Music and Worship in African American Megachurches of Los Angeles, California." PhD diss., University of California Los Angeles, 2008.

Lim, Swee Hong, and Lester Ruth. *Lovin' on Jesus: A Concise History of Contemporary Worship*. Nashville: Abingdon, 2017.

Lincoln, C. Eric, and Lawrence H. Mamiya. *The Black Church in the African American Experience*. Durham: Duke University Press, 1990.

Luhrmann, T. M. *When God Talks Back: Understanding the American Evangelical Relationship with God*. New York: Knopf, 2012.

Mamiya, Larry. *River of Struggle, River of Freedom: Trends among Black Churches and Black Pastoral Leadership*. Pulpit & Pew Research Reports. Durham, NC: Duke Divinity School, 2006.

Massey, James Earl. "The Doctrinal Imperative: A Word about Megachurches." *The African American Pulpit* 10 (2007) 31–35.

McKenzie, Robert Tracy. *A Little Book for New Historians: Why and How to Study History*. Downers Grove: IVP Academic, 2019.

Reagan, Wen. "A Beautiful Noise: A History of Contemporary Worship Music in Modern America." PhD diss., Duke University, 2015.

Ruth, Lester. "Divine, Human, or Devilish? The State of the Question on the Writing of the History of Contemporary Worship." *Worship* 88 (2014) 290–310.

White, James F. *Protestant Worship: Traditions in Transition*. Louisville: Westminster John Knox, 1989.

Wineburg, Sam. *Historical Thinking and Other Unnatural Acts: Charting the Future of Teaching the Past*. Philadelphia: Temple University Press, 2001.

Wong, Janelle S. *Immigrants, Evangelicals, and Politics in an Era of Demographic Change*. New York: Russell Sage Foundation, 2018.

# 1

## James F. White, Grady Hardin, and Methodist "Contemporary" Worship in the 1970s

*The 11:00 a.m. Cox Chapel Service at Highland Park*

— R. MATTHEW SIGLER —

"Millions Avoid Church" read the headline from the *Dallas Morning News* on July 17, 1965.[1] The article, which was filed under a section labeled "Young Adult Culture Found," relayed the discoveries of a commission tasked by the Methodist Church with exploring the needs of young people.[2] Central to the findings relayed in the article was that there existed a growing gap between "young culture" and "older culture"—a gap that led young adults to abandon faithful attendance at church. "How to reach this big segment of the population is an urgent concern of all denominations," remarked the author.

The article continued by offering several observations made about young adults of the baby boomer generation. First, they love questions and "meet change with excitement." Second, they "value relationship and openness." Relatedly, the study concluded that young adults of the 1960s "are more tolerant, more willing to accept and relate to people whose way of life differs from their own, than their elders." Finally, young people are "non-joiners" who are suspicious of institutions. The author concluded that young people too often find the church irrelevant.

---

1. "Millions Avoid Church," 3.
2. Thomas E. Bergler traces the emerging focus on youth during the 1950s and 1960s in his book *Juvenilization of American Christianity*.

Concerns about the relevancy of worship for young adults of the late 1960s led many to adjust their worship practices in attempts to connect with the changing culture. In this chapter, I will introduce two pastor-scholars who engaged in liturgical experimentation in the Dallas area during this time period. After considering some of the changes they implemented I offer a summary of the core liturgical values that guided their efforts. Finally, I will provide a brief retrospective on this period of experimentation, drawing from the later writings of one of the men leading these endeavors.

## Liturgical Scholars and Experimenters: James White and Grady Hardin

It is quite likely that James White[3] and Grady Hardin—two members of the Perkins School of Theology faculty—were reading the very same article on that Saturday morning in 1965. Both White and Hardin were members of Highland Park Methodist Church where the findings of the commission had been presented. Hardin had taught preaching and worship at Perkins since 1957, and White joined the faculty in 1961 to teach courses in the same area. The work of both professors in the early 1960s reflected the crest of a post-war return among Protestants to liturgies of the Reformation. In addition to embracing the Elizabethan verbiage of the English Reformation, many Protestant liturgies reclaimed a more overtly penitential emphasis in worship and a focus on God's transcendence. White, whose research had centered on church architecture, penned several articles stressing this latter point.[4] The bulk of Hardin's writings demonstrated a similar emphasis.[5] These early emphases would soon change for both men.

In the Methodist Church, this post-war trajectory emphasizing Reformation era liturgies found its paradigmatic expression in the 1965 *Book of Worship for Home and Church*. However, by the time of its publication, the liturgical sensibilities of White and Hardin had begun to shift. In his review of the 1965 Book of Worship, White noted with irony that the work on the worship book had been completed simultaneous to the promulgation of the Second Vatican Council: "evidently, liturgical revisers need as much insight into the future as into the past!"[6] Not only had the changes brought about by the Second Vatican Council led to a shifting perspective on liturgical

---

3. For more on James F. White, see Westerfield Tucker, *Sunday Service of the Methodists*, and Sigler, *Methodist Worship*, 139–96.

4. See, for example, White, "God Whom We Worship," 29–32.

5. See Hardin, Review of *Let Us Pray*.

6. White, "New American Methodist Communion Order," 559.

values, but so too did the growing sense of generational disconnect. For both of these reasons Hardin and White were keen on engaging in liturgical experimentation at the local and denominational levels as the 1960s drew to a close. Hardin would serve on the Executive Committee of the United Methodist Church's Commission on Worship from 1968 to 1972. As chair of the Committee on Alternate Rituals, he tasked White in 1970 with writing an alternate text for the Lord's Supper. The rite would eventually become "Word and Table I" for the United Methodist Church.

Grady Hardin's and James White's work on liturgical revision at the denominational level was rooted in their liturgical practices at a local level. Both pastor/scholars were involved in designing worship on the campus of Southern Methodist University. White chaired the student worship committee at Perkins and was frequently experimenting with new liturgical practices in that setting.

In addition, Hardin and White both attended Highland Park (United) Methodist Church.[7] Located on the campus of Southern Methodist University (and literally just across the parking lot from Perkins School of Theology), Highland Park was among the largest American Methodist congregations at the time. Highland Park's intimate familiarity with university life brought a heightened attention to the generational disconnect highlighted above, a dissonance that grew as the decade came to a close.

What had begun as an isolated news article in the mid-1960s had crescendoed to an alarm at the close of the decade: the church must address the widening gap between the older and younger generation or it would wither in the future. In fact, the *Dallas Morning News* was peppered with similarly-themed articles following the 1965 report. A year later the paper ran a multipage article featuring yet another study of young people's changing attitudes toward the church. This ecumenical project identified a demographic of young "apartment dwellers" living in the Dallas metroplex. Rev. Doug McLean, a Methodist pastor involved in the study, summarized the findings this way:

> The biggest need of many young apartment dwellers is for a new sense of identity. The formal traditions of many churches fail to offer this . . . Something different needs to evolve for the spiritual nourishment of people who have left the church. What will it be?[8]

---

7. The Methodist Church merged with the Evangelical United Brethren Church in 1968 to form the United Methodist Church.

8. "Teams Study Changing Attitudes," 11.

By the early months of 1970, Highland Park was making plans to offer "something different" in the form of a new worship service: "Maybe you have seen the signs—the signs of the times, that is. There's something new, something different, something distinctive that is coming to Highland Park. It begins April 5 at 9:30 a.m. in Cox Chapel."[9] This announcement, which ran in the church's newsletter, *The Tower*, continued by describing the service as being designed "with the needs of today's young adult in mind."[10] The service "is contemporary—in thought, in language, in format, in setting," read the announcement.[11] Later issues of *The Tower* also made clear that the goal of this new "contemporary" worship service was to bridge a generational gap: "The desire of the Commission on Worship [at Highland Park] was to reach out and deal creatively with worship, and attract youth and young adults who find the sanctuary services unappealing."[12] While no extant order of worship survives for the inaugural service, announcements in subsequent newsletters revealed that the time for the initial service was changed to 11:00 a.m. because "it was felt that more adults and youth would participate at this later hour."[13] Records also indicate that "Holy Communion" was offered and Grady Hardin likely preached the first sermon.[14]

The service caught the attention of *The Dallas Morning News*, which ran an article two weeks after its launch, highlighting several churches in the area who had made new attempts "to communicate with youth who are said to be 'more and more interested in religion and less and less interested in the church.'"[15] Hardin, who was interviewed for the article, confessed that the "rather traditional service in the sanctuary" was not meeting the needs of everyone in the congregation.[16] The "contemporary service in-the-round" was an attempt to create "new forms of community in our times."[17] In launching the "contemporary" worship service in Cox Chapel, Highland Park was venturing into the unknown in the hopes of connecting with a younger generation.

9. "New Contemporary Worship," 2.
10. "New Contemporary Worship," 2.
11. "New Contemporary Worship," 2.
12. "New Worship Service Begins," 1.
13. "Grady Hardin to Lead," 1.
14. "New Worship Service Begins," 1.
15. "Some Dallas Churches 'Tuning In,'" 1.
16. "Some Dallas Churches 'Tuning In,'" 1.
17. "Some Dallas Churches 'Tuning In,'" 1.

## Experimentation

While Grady Hardin officially was hired as the minister of the new service, worship design for the services was unapologetically democratic. In addition to several notices in *The Tower*, extant bulletins from the Cox Chapel service were brimming with solicitations for feedback or invitations to make suggestions for changes; indeed, Hardin included his home phone number in several bulletins for this express purpose.[18] Eventually a worship committee was formed for the service, a group that included James and Marilynn White.[19] The committee met monthly to plan services for the upcoming month. Hardin and the rest of the committee placed a premium on liturgical experimentation. Marilynn Atkinson (formerly Marilynn White) recalls: "people would come from the sanctuary . . . stand in the back of Cox Chapel, and look in to see what crazy thing they're doing today."[20] This penchant for experimentation was revealed in four main areas of the worship service.

## Space and Media

First, the liturgical space was reimagined drawing heavily from some of the values of the Second Vatican Council. Cox Chapel was constructed in 1950 and first opened for services in 1951. While the chapel was designed in the neo-gothic style of the rest of the church, it was envisioned as a more intimate setting than the larger sanctuary.[21] By 1970, however, the divided chancel was seen as inhibiting "full, conscious, and active participation" by the laity.[22] And, when the "contemporary" worship service was launched, Hardin was determined to adjust the seating configuration. The *Dallas Morning News* noted that the service featured "a rustic cross with railroad spikes . . . mounted in the center of the chapel, with the seating arranged around it."[23] Other experiments with the liturgical space were made. Banners, for example, were frequently crafted and used within the service. Some of these banners were constructed by children's Sunday School classes while

---

18. An example was the Cox Chapel 11:00 a.m. Order of Service for September 6, 1970.

19. Atkinson, Interview.

20. Atkinson, Interview.

21. See *Building for Service*, a pamphlet presented to members of Highland Park in November 1945.

22. The language of the Second Vatican Council's *Constitution on the Sacred Liturgy* was deeply influential in White's and Hardin's work.

23. "Some Dallas Churches 'Tuning In,'" 1.

others were designed by members of the worship committee.[24] Atkinson recalls making a banner for Easter out of sheer, blue material with multicolored butterflies sewn onto the fabric.[25]

More experimental installations included suspending multicolored, sparkling, string-starched balloons from the ceiling in a disco-ball effect.[26] In December 1971 a "scrim sheet" was purchased through donations from the United Methodist Men's Group and installed in the chapel. A write up of one service relayed that the scrim sheet, which allowed for projection from front and back of the curtain, presented "colored slides of Christmas cards . . . to visually represent the different portions of the service of worship."[27] Other "multi-media presentations" were utilized in the service, although the content and purpose is not always clear in remaining sources.[28] White wrote about one experimental use of multi-media in his book *New Forms of Worship*. The service was entitled "Joyful Noise" and likely took place in Perkins Chapel. He explained that the service overlaid three distinct items: the Communion service "exactly as normally performed," a series of tape recorded sounds (including a jet airplane, a football game, a rooster crowing, a baby crying, a ping-pong game, traffic, sea gulls, an ambulance, and a train passing), and slides that were projected on a scrim sheet and set to change every eight seconds.[29] The audio, images, and words of the Communion rite comprised the entirety of the service. While it is unclear if "Joyful Noise" was ever used at Cox Chapel, it is quite likely that similar approaches to multi-media were encouraged. As a member of the Cox Chapel worship committee, White certainly was influential in promoting the use of multi-media in the service. Such experiments with space and media would have been incredibly novel and no doubt account for the gawkers in the back of the chapel.

## Structure and Language

If the "contemporary" worship service at Cox Chapel pushed the envelope with regard to space and media, it displayed a bit more consistency in its

---

24. This information is found in the Cox Chapel 11:00 a.m. Order of Service for June 18, 1972.
25. Atkinson, Interview.
26. Atkinson, Interview.
27. "Methodist Men Enhance Worship," 2.
28. The Cox Chapel 11:00 a.m. Order of Service, March 11, 1973, simply included the note "B. T. Williamson will direct the multi-media presentation."
29. White, *New Forms of Worship*, 147.

basic pattern for the order of service. The services typically followed the rhythm of the Christian Year, but also included vestiges from the Methodist calendric rhythm of the first half of the twentieth century. "Kingdomtide" as well as national holidays, like Thanksgiving, were regularly observed in the service.[30] With some notable exceptions that will be considered later, the Sunday service followed a four-fold structure of Gathering, Word, Response, and Sending. Both White and Hardin were deeply aware of ecumenical liturgical developments; while the Lord's Supper was not celebrated every Sunday at the service, the basic pattern often assumed the normativity of Word and Table in that it typically included a response that mirrored the eucharistic focus of the Liturgical Renewal movement. Another way in which the typical order of service reflected broader ecumenical sensibilities of the time was in the breadth of Scripture that was publically read at the service. In addition to utilizing the Psalms, services often included readings from the Old and New Testaments.[31]

The design of the 11:00 a.m. "contemporary" service at Cox Chapel also demonstrated the influence of the Liturgical Renewal movement in its attempt to recover the offertory as an act of the entire congregation. Especially in the first few years of the service, the order of worship made much of the bringing of gifts that included bread, wine, and monetary offerings. The service held on September 6, 1970 encouraged participants to place "symbols of our work" in the chancel area prior to the service in an attempt to connect the offering with the weekly labor of the congregation. Following the presentation of the gifts, the service included this prayer of dedication: "Lord God, we bring you the ordinary things of life tools of our work, food and drink and money. We want them to represent the gift of ourselves. Take these things from us, transform them, and help us to do your work and be fed with your love. Amen."[32]

One of the most interesting dynamics of this service was the way in which it provided a venue for experimenting with what would become the primary eucharistic rite for the United Methodist Church. The "contemporary" worship service launched around the same time that James White began drafting texts for the Committee on Alternate Rituals. In fact, both White and Hardin understood their work in liturgical revision to be an endeavor in contemporizing worship. In the first place, the experimental rite drew upon the ecumenical liturgical recoveries sparked by the Second

30. The Cox Chapel 11:00 a.m. Order of Service for September 3, 1972, evidences this season.

31. The essentiality of reading from the Revised Common Lectionary was a point of conviction for James White. See White, "Our Apostasy in Worship," 842–45.

32. Cox Chapel 11:00 a.m. Order of Service, September 6, 1970.

Vatican Council and, in doing so, deviated for the first time from a basic pattern inherited from John Wesley via his revision of the 1662 *Book of Common Prayer*. White argued that this more ecumenically informed eucharistic text broke free of a centuries-old pattern and in doing so was truly "contemporary."[33]

The "Sacrament of the Lord's Supper" text went through several drafts, many of which were field tested in Cox Chapel and Perkins Chapel. Some of the distinguishing features of what would become "Word and Table I" appeared in these early services at Cox Chapel. For example, the service on September 6, 1970 included "words of pardon" that were spoken in alternating voices, first from the "lectern side" then secondly from the "pulpit side."[34] By January 1972, the absolution was pronounced first by the pastor and then echoed back by the entire congregation, a characteristic of the current UMC rite.[35] These innovations likely emerged from both parish level suggestions and field testing the texts authored by both White and Hardin.[36] Such innovations were enacted with concern for "contemporary" needs of the congregation.

Not only did White understand the recovery of patristic liturgical patterns to be an endeavor in contemporizing worship insofar as such updates reflected broader ecumenical developments, but he also sought to update the language used in the service. Hardin was equally committed to the need to utilize contemporary language in experimental rituals. In their work with denominational liturgical revision, for example, both White and Hardin utilized the contemporary translation of Scripture from *Today's English Version* (1966) on occasion.[37] The emphasis on updating liturgical language is even more apparent in surviving bulletins from the Cox Chapel service. For example, the names given to each part of the service illustrate this core value. The five main movements in the service from March 11, 1973 were entitled: "Coming In," "Discovering God's Word," "Confronting Life's Limits," "Embracing Life's Possibilities," and "Going Out."[38]

---

33. White, "Sacrament of the Lord's Supper," 13.

34. Cox Chapel 11:00 a.m. Order of Service, September 6, 1970.

35. Cox Chapel 11:00 a.m. Order of Service, January 2, 1972.

36. In reviewing extant copies of bulletins from Cox Chapel it is clear that Hardin also introduced some of his own liturgical preferences into the service. In fact, in the summer of 1971, Hardin had offered his own draft of the Eucharist service to the Committee on Alternate Rituals, unbeknownst to White. See Peiffer, "How Contemporary Liturgies Evolve," 34.

37. Peiffer, "How Contemporary Liturgies Evolve," 33.

38. Cox Chapel 11:00 a.m. Order of Service, March 11, 1973.

Other liturgical texts used within the service also demonstrated a concern for contemporary language. While the words of confession employed in the service would vary greatly, one commonality was the rejection of Elizabethan language among all the texts. An early confession used in the service at Cox Chapel, labeled "Recognizing Ourselves Before The Lord," was presented as follows:

> Our Father, we see in Jesus Christ the
> Perfection of Your truth and love and
> Ourselves as we ought to be and are not.
> Even at our best, our pride makes us quick
> To defend our disobedience to Your will
> At our worst we give our full commitment
> To things that pass away.
>
> We have loved errors more than truth,
> We have loved neither You nor our
> Brothers, we have disobeyed Your will
> And are satisfied in our own pride or
> Miserable in our own guilt.
>
> In Jesus, our Father, You identified
> Yourself with our condition and know
> Our sin. Help us to now receive again Your
> Love for us, Your acceptance of us, and
> The new life of obedience which is true
> Freedom, through Jesus Christ our Lord.
> Amen.[39]

Those tasked with worship design for the "contemporary" service at Cox Chapel also utilized "modern" language for other classic liturgical elements such as the "Lord's Prayer" and the "Affirmation of Faith." In the case of the latter, "A New Creed," written in 1968 for the United Church of Canada, became the one most frequently utilized creeds at Cox Chapel. While there does not appear to have been significant focus on avoiding gender-specific language in the service, one surviving bulletin—likely

---

39. Cox Chapel 11:00 a.m. Order of Service, September 6, 1970.

used by a presider—includes a circle and accompanying question mark around the word "men" in the text of the Great Thanksgiving.[40] Apparently, there were some who raised questions about the use of exclusively masculine pronouns in the service.

Finally, source material also indicates a remarkable interest in incorporating poetry into the service, yet another effort at amplifying "contemporary" idioms. The poetic works of Edna St. Vincent Millay, T. S. Elliot, and Carl Sandburg were featured at various times, often accompanied by other creative mediums like music and drama. "'God, Eliot and the Faith' will be presented and will include poetry from T. S. Eliot and music from Leonard Bernstein's Mass," read one announcement from *The Tower* in early November of 1972.[41]

## Music

As in the case of space and language, the music employed at the 11:00 a.m. Cox Chapel service also sought to bridge a cultural gap through liturgical experimentation. Leaders of the service utilized two primary means for providing the lyrics for congregational singing: *The Methodist Hymnal* (1966) and song sheets that were included weekly as inserts to the bulletin. The latter was an innovation in itself at the time of the launch of the "contemporary" worship service. James White often spoke glowingly of the flexibility that was afforded by the photo copier.[42] Using printed song sheets allowed those tasked with leading the service to inject a wide variety of new songs not included in the 1966 hymnal. Oftentimes songs from Roman Catholic folk masses were included. "Take Our Bread," written in 1966 by Roman Catholic musician, Joe Wise, was used regularly as the offertory. Other songs like "Kumbaya" and "We are Climbing Jacob's Ladder" that were popularized by the folk music movement of the 1960s were often featured in the service.[43] Congregational songs were also drawn from the hymnal, including the occasional Wesleyan hymn such as "O for a Thousand Tongues to Sing."[44]

Various forms of service music were also featured each Sunday. In some instances, responsorials and antiphons were used in the service. More often, extant bulletins show that "folk anthems" were regularly utilized. For example, the service held on June 18, 1972 incorporated a folk-styled

---

40. See Cox Chapel 11:00 a.m. Order of Service, June 3, 1973.
41. "Contemporary Poetry and Music," 1.
42. White, "Worship in an Age of Immediacy," 229.
43. See Cox Chapel 11:00 a.m. Order of Service, August 6, 1972.
44. Cox Chapel 11:00 a.m. Order of Service, December 31, 1972.

anthem entitled "If There is a Holy Spirit" which had just been released on vinyl early that year. The album, *Hymns Hot And Carols Cool*, included a variety of original folk songs from a calypso version of the "Doxology" to a song entitled "Put Down Your Guns and Listen!"[45] While surviving bulletins are unclear at times as to the instrumentation used—they often simply denoted instrumentalists as "musicians"—music was most often provided on the organ, guitar (sometimes more than one), and through the use of a "folk choir."[46]

Other musical innovations emerged after the first year. One service in early 1973 used the secular folk rock song "Get Together," popularized by The Youngbloods, as the offertory. The song was accompanied by two guitars and the lyrics were provided for the congregation in the bulletin.[47] Songs from the Stephen Schwartz musical *Godspell* often found their way into the service. Schwartz's "Day by Day" was sung as a closing song in June of 1972 as the song reached #13 on the *Billboard* pop singles chart that same summer. A year later, one entire service would consist of songs from *Godspell*. During this same time, James White's writings showed particular interest in electronic/synthesized music. In *New Forms of Worship* (1971) he spoke glowingly of Richard Felciano's experimental, electronic piece named "Pentecost Sunday: Double Alleluia."[48] The avant garde composition used an array of sounds like wind effects and other more melodic tones to create sonic dissonance. In some live performances, chapter 2 of Acts was read by a choir amidst the synthesized sounds. While there is no evidence that Felciano's piece was performed in Cox Chapel, White certainly encouraged similar types of electronic music as part of liturgical experimentation. Such innovations demonstrate, yet again, attempts to connect with the "youth culture" of the early 1970s.

---

45. Avery and Marsh, *Hymns Hot and Carols Cold*. Avery and Marsh, both Presbyterians, had long-standing musical careers that launched with the publication in 1967 of the songbook *Hymns Hot and Carols Cold*. Selections from the songbook were later recorded in 1972. See Van Marter, "Don Marsh is Dead at 86."

46. For example, see Cox Chapel 11:00 a.m. Order of Service for June 18, 1972 and "Some Dallas Churches 'Tuning In,'" 1.

47. Cox Chapel 11:00 a.m. Order of Service, January 28, 1973.

48. See White, *New Forms of Worship*, 135. The score and recording of "Pentecost Sunday: Double Alleluia" may be found here: http://www.richardfelciano.com/completechoralsacredworks.html.

## Kinesthetic Engagement

Perhaps the area in which the greatest experimentation took place centered on kinesthetic engagement in the service. Fifteen months after the new worship service was launched, the *Dallas Morning News* ran an article with the headline, "Highland Park Holds Unusual Chapel Service." The author struggled to characterize the service, other than the fact that it is a "different kind of worship experience than that of the more traditional one" held in the main sanctuary at the same time.[49] After noting that the new service had enjoyed "wide acceptance," the article continued by describing the upcoming service, one in which "dance will interpret and enhance the meaning of the preached word."[50] Indeed, by this point in the Cox Chapel experimental worship service dance and drama troupes had been regularly featured as part of the service all in an effort to emphasize the role of the body in worship. Hardin, for example, once referred to dance as "a means of grace" and seems to have encouraged greater use of the art form in the service.[51]

Drama was also featured prominently in the 11:00 a.m. Cox Chapel service. Beginning in late 1971, performances by the Alpha-Omega players were showcased at the Sunday worship service. The drama troupe was formed in 1967 by Drexel H. Riley, a member of Highland Park, and toured nationally for several decades. Their performances in Cox Chapel were seldom overtly biblical or theological in content but were encouraged, nonetheless, as yet another means of connecting to a new generation. Prior to the troupe's first performance, *The Tower* offered this note (likely written by Hardin) on why the stage presentation "The World of Carl Sandburg" was appropriate for the service:

> It may seem unusual for drama to be the vehicle for bringing the morning message, but the nature of this particular play confronts us with the truth of our lives before God as it is revealed through the poetry of the artist, Carl Sandburg. Presented will be the varied aspects of life from birth through death. The prose, the poetry, the humor and folk songs are woven together in a fast-paced presentation of strong social comment and just plain fun.[52]

---

49. "Highland Park Holds Unusual Chapel Service," 16.
50. "Highland Park Holds Unusual Chapel Service," 16.
51. Hardin, Review of *Leave It to the Spirit*, 43.
52. "Alpha-Omega Players in Cox Chapel," 1. The play was written in late 1959 and originally starred Bette Davis.

The emphasis on "humor," "social comment," and "just plain fun" highlights some of the qualities that Cox Chapel leadership sought to instill in the "contemporary" service.

While participation in drama and dance seems to have been limited to trained performers, presiders incorporated other elements into the service. Vibrantly colored chasubles, or what Grady Hardin called "halleluia ponchos," were worn on occasion.[53] At a Communion service held in Perkins Chapel around this time, James White presided in a janitor's uniform in an attempt to emphasize "how sharing in bread relates us to all humanity."[54] Such efforts were a part of a larger emphasis on reconnecting with the full senses in the worship service.

All of these efforts in liturgical experimentation were part of a broader, ecumenical emphasis on inculturation sparked by the reforms of the Second Vatican Council. "Many [Protestant] pastors have taken their youth groups to mass, and the young people have come back wondering out loud why the Catholics should be having all the fun," wrote White in 1972.[55] In mainline congregations like those of Highland Park, the awareness of such ecumenical developments merged with the growing concern of connecting with the youth culture of the late 1960s and early 1970s. It also appealed to young families. Marilynn Atkinson recalls how much her young children enjoyed attending the service because they could relate to many of the elements within the service.[56] At the two-year anniversary of the launch of the first 11:00 a.m. "contemporary" service two hundred and eight people were in attendance.[57] Given the seating configuration of Cox Chapel, such numbers would have meant the worship space was nearly full.

## Liturgical Norms

In February 1968 James White published an article in *The Christian Century* sounding a clarion call for liturgical experimentation. "We face today a crisis in Protestant worship, one that seems certain to increase in intensity in the years ahead," wrote White in "Worship in an Age of Immediacy."[58] Drawing heavily from Marshall McLuhan's work, White made clear that a

---

53. Atkinson, Interview.
54. White, *New Forms of Worship*, 119.
55. White, "Sacrament of the Lord's Supper," 13.
56. Atkinson, Interview.
57. The number is written in pencil on the surviving bulletin from August 6, 1972. No numbers for attendance are recorded in other bulletins.
58. White, "Worship in an Age of Immediacy," 227.

fault line had opened between a "radio generation" and a "television generation." Because mainline Protestant worship of the mid-twentieth century was designed by and for a radio generation, the crisis, said White, was not felt by the adults of the 1960s: "we expect others to supply words for us—and this is what we get in worship."[59] On the other hand, the "television generation" rejected the nearly exclusive verbal forms of perception characteristic of the older generation and thus found "the present forms of worship so intolerable."[60] Taking a phrase coined by McLuhan, White summed up his diagnosis of the crisis this way: "the chief problem, then, is that the medium is wrong and, consequently, so is the message."[61] A year later Grady Hardin offered equally high praise for Marshall McLuhan's "medium is the message" trope: "This rather appealed to many of us because we really dreaded next Sunday anyway. Perhaps there was more validity in Simon and Garfunkel with several slides on each wall."[62]

In his 1967 book, *The Worldliness of Worship*, White made a similar case, encouraging a recovery of the body in worship, particularly the senses and physical movement. Throughout the book, White highlighted some of the qualities that would eventually become key values of the 11:00 a.m. Cox Chapel service. He lauded dance for its ability to remind the worshipers of their own bodies in worship. White also encouraged a reconsideration of how music might facilitate greater participation in worship: "Some contemporary foot-tapping music might be a great help in being more true to our daily world."[63] *The Worldliness of Worship* drew broadly from contemporary liturgical scholars and theologians such as Odo Casel, Edward Schillebeeckx, and, most frequently, Paul Tillich.[64]

In addition to calling for experimentation of new "mediums" within Christian worship, White also identified multiple fault lines stemming from the social and cultural fragmentation of the late 1960s and early 1970s. He discussed pluralism in terms of variations in morals, a growing ethnic diversity, and the general constancy of change.[65] These tectonic shifts coupled with the demands brought about by the communications revolution necessitate, said White, a reconsideration of the dominant forms

---

59. White, "Worship in an Age of Immediacy," 228.
60. White, "Worship in an Age of Immediacy," 228.
61. White, "Worship in an Age of Immediacy," 228.
62. Hardin, "Recommended for Mature and Maturing Preachers Only," 88.
63. White, *Worldliness of Worship*, 81.
64. While not abandoning Casel's emphasis on the mystery of faith, White is clearly influenced by Schillebeeckx's critique of Casel. See White, *Worldliness of Worship*, 54n4.
65. See White, *New Forms of Worship*, 17–20.

of Protestant worship. He did not issue his call for liturgical experimentation without an acknowledgement of norms, however. In his article for *The Christian Century*, White identified three primary norms that needed to be considered for "responsible experimentation." First, experimentation should be historically informed. "The past," wrote White, "is not just a grab bag of ideas; it tells us why some things were accepted, why others were rejected—sometimes for valid, sometimes for mistaken, reasons."[66] Second, experiments in worship must be "theologically reasoned."[67] Finally, worship services must be "pastorally relevant."[68] White argued that experimentation "develops by being immersed in [contemporary] life . . . significant experimentation must have the immediacy of this morning's newspaper that goes out with tonight's garbage. It must relate to people as they are in the here and now."[69] While these three norms would remain for him in the coming years, White would reorder their priority.

White published the culmination of his thoughts on liturgical experimentation in his best-selling book *New Forms of Worship*. Written during the first year after the launch of the 11:00 a.m. service at Cox Chapel, White entitled his first chapter "On Starting with People." He declared early in the book that "The God Whom We Worship" and "The People Who Worship" are "both sides of the [same] coin."[70] The same year his book was published (1971), White explained his shifting liturgical norms in a paper presented to the World Methodist Consultation on Worship in Denver:

> It may be a bit surprising that I have put the pastoral norm first on our list of characteristics of effective Christian worship. I am sure that a few years ago I would not have done so for I was then insisting that we must begin with a theological definition of worship . . . To neglect sociology, as we once did, is just as misleading as overlooking theology, a temptation that sometimes seems to appeal to those experimenting in worship today.[71]

He unpacked this thinking further in *New Forms of Worship* by amplifying his thoughts on the fault line between the "radio" and "television" generations:

---

66. White, "Worship in an Age of Immediacy," 229.
67. White, "Worship in an Age of Immediacy," 229.
68. White, "Worship in an Age of Immediacy," 229.
69. White, "Worship in an Age of Immediacy," 230.
70. White, *New Forms of Worship*, 38.
71. White, "Characteristics of Effective Christian Worship," 199.

> We adults are largely oriented to verbal forms of perception, since we have been watching television for fewer years than we have been reading. The question we still ask when we miss church is, 'What did he say?'—meaning, 'What was the sermon about?' The younger generation is more likely to ask, 'What happened?' For them the problem is that nothing happened, or at least very little and much of that was insignificant. The congregation stood, sang a few hymns, and went home.[72]

Subsequent chapters in *New Forms of Worship* offered prescriptive details for ways congregations might reconsider how space, physical movement, visual art, and music could redress the generational gap.

White's emphasis on "starting with people" was also a recognition that much of mainline Protestant worship of the early 1970s seemed to matter little to the social concerns of the baby boomers.[73] For both Grady Hardin and James White, efforts at liturgical experimentation had to be intimately connected with social justice. White once recalled an epiphany he had while presiding at the Lord's Supper in the Perkins Chapel. He remembered: "'this is my body' also means: 'this is my precinct,' 'this is my district,' 'this is my state' . . .'this is my body' is a very political statement."[74] In *New Forms of Worship*, White applauded how liturgical processions, for example, had been reimagined as a form of protest against suppression of civil rights.[75]

While the thrust of *New Forms of Worship* was to encourage the church in its efforts to bridge the gap between the "radio" and "television" generations, White maintained the essentiality of the theological and historical norms, albeit with a prioritization of "starting with people." For example, he devoted one chapter to exploring the "hard core" of Christian worship in which he identified "the observance of time," "rites of initiation," "the Eucharist," and "the Divine Office," as shared ecumenical "cores" of the church's liturgical practice. While he held firm to these "cores," he did so while emphasizing the need for such elements to be reimagined with an eye to the communications revolution of the day.

## Cox Chapel as a Liturgical Laboratory

When one reads *New Forms of Worship* with an eye to the "contemporary" worship services held in Cox Chapel at the time one sees remarkable

---

72. White, *New Forms of Worship*, 31.
73. White, *New Forms of Worship*, 17–20.
74. White, "Order of Saint Luke Keynote Address."
75. White, *New Forms of Worship*, 116.

parallels. This should come as no surprise, of course, as much of White's thinking during this period of liturgical experimentation was forged out of his experiences in designing worship for Cox Chapel and Perkins Chapel. In effect, Cox Chapel functioned as a liturgical laboratory of sorts. One is afforded, therefore, some key insights when exploring the 11:00 a.m. Cox Chapel service. First, the service emerged out of concerns that Highland Park was not connecting with the "television generation." As evidenced in both Hardin and White's writings, sermons, and interviews from the time, liturgical "gap" thinking was clearly a driving factor in the creation and design of the service.[76] The messaging and publicity surrounding the launch of the 11:00 a.m. service made this blatantly obvious.

Second, there was a central concern to engaging cultural patterns of thought and cultural forms of communication in an effort to bridge this gap. Of course, because of McLuhan's influence on both Hardin and White, those two men placed a premium on experimenting with new forms of media. From drama troupes that presented plays with social-political critique to folk songs popularized in the Civil Rights movement, the 11:00 a.m. service sought to connect with the cultural current of the late 1960s and 1970s.

Third, the service at Cox Chapel evinced an ecumenical cross-pollination sparked by the ferment of the Second Vatican Council. Hardin and White both had the benefit of reading some of the seminal theologians shaping the work of the Second Vatican Council. At the same time, both men understood the significance of experimenting with the ramifications of these ideas in "real" worshiping communities. This influence of the Second Vatican Council is most acutely seen in the way the service was designed with the "full, conscious, and active" participation of the congregants in mind. The Eucharistic focus and experiments with the text of the Great Thanksgiving also stemmed from this influencing factor.

Each of these three dynamics contributed to the focus on liturgical experimentation: 1) liturgical "gap" thinking, 2) attempts at liturgical inculturation to address that gap, and 3) processing the implications of the Second Vatican Council in a university setting. The rejection of the Elizabethan verbs and pronouns of previous rites, the use of the scrim sheet and "multimedia presentations," and the performance of songs from *Godspell* all illustrate these dynamics. Even the semblance of "hard cores" of an ecumenical order emerge out of Hardin's and White's engagement with the broader liturgical renewal.

---

76. To place this way of gap thinking into a broader context, please see the introduction to this book.

This latter point is also important to keep in mind in that the subcongregation of the 11:00 a.m. Cox Chapel in the early 1970s represented a larger movement of liturgical innovation. Alongside their articles on the 11:00 a.m. Cox Chapel services, *The Dallas Morning News* also highlighted similar innovations at Episcopal, Presbyterian, and Baptist congregations in the area.[77] Reflecting on the liturgical milieu of the late 1960s and early 1970s some twenty years later, White would offer this synopsis:

> [it] was a period of euphoria for ministers and priests, who acted like people released from long years of imprisonment. All manner of common assumptions about worship were questioned and found to be purely arbitrary. The organ was challenged by the guitar, stained glass by cloth banners, and the seated congregation by dancers . . . Much of that now seems silly—the balloons and confetti, the wordy banners and placards—was a necessary part of experiencing liberation before the work of reconstruction could begin.[78]

## Conclusion: A Harbinger of Things to Come

Four years after publishing *New Forms of Worship*, James White reassessed the sentiments of his earlier work: "It was a heady time. Experimentation in worship had burst out everywhere; we were in the midst of exciting changes. Today much of that enthusiasm has disappeared, but the accomplishments and mistakes of that period live on."[79] In *Christian Worship in Transition* (1975) White acknowledged five contributions of the period of liturgical experimentation that remained "irrevocable": 1) the essential need to consider the lived experiences of those in a given ecclesial context, 2) the value of imagination in worship design and practice, 3) an acknowledgement that true worship is a "humanizing experience," 4) an ecumenical liturgical awareness, and 5) a deeper commitment to social accountability in the liturgy.[80]

He also enumerated some of the mistakes seen in retrospect. First, he acknowledged that his obsession with electronic media had proven to be a bit of a passing fad. White suggested that much of the focus on "the medium as message" was really a recognition of a changing, pluralistic America.[81] Sec-

---

77. See "Some Dallas Churches 'Tuning In,'" 1.
78. White, "Protestant Public Worship in America," 122.
79. White, *Christian Worship in Transition*, 7.
80. White, *Christian Worship in Transition*, 132–42.
81. White, *Christian Worship in Transition*, 131.

ond, he pointed out that liturgical experimentation turned out to be "more work for everyone" and that too often changes were implemented without serious consideration of how they would be received by congregants.[82] To this point he later lamented that "the 1960s made creativity a high value in worship without basing it on sound theological, historical and pastoral substance necessary to prevent creativity from being destructive."[83] It is worth noting that White's priority of liturgical norms has again been shuffled in this quote. Thirdly and relatedly, White was most critical of efforts at liturgical experimentation that made much of creativity and little of content. As early as 1972, White began raising cautions about emphasizing stylistic qualities over the substance of the liturgy. "There seems to be so little concern for what we celebrate," wrote White, "compared with the deep and genuine concern that we celebrate it (whatever it is) with 'warmth, momentum, expectancy and surprise and astonishment and awe.'"[84] For White, such shallow approaches to Christian worship were the outcome of liturgical experimentation gone awry: "I would propose a moratorium on the word 'celebration' or on 'celebrate' without an object."[85]

This final caution, perhaps, was the most prescient for contemporary congregations as the "fix" to liturgical doldrums in any context begins often by emphasizing aspirational qualities: "we wish our service had more energy, etc." White's assessment of the lessons learned from the liturgical experimentation of the late 1960s or 1970s reminds us that the more difficult task of renewal starts with finding truly substantive ground. Perhaps it is telling that White's work on "Word and Table I" far outlasted the "contemporary" 11:00 a.m. Cox Chapel service. This is due in part to the fact that the rite was authorized and used at a denominational level. But one wonders if a service designed out of liturgical "gap" mentality faces an inevitably truncated life due to its concern with connecting to the broader culture. Cultural patterns, after all, are diverse and can shift quickly in a consumer context. The North American landscape today is replete with new services and churches that are launched in attempts to connect with their local context through new forms of worship. If the study of the 11:00 a.m. Cox Chapel service teaches us anything, it is that such efforts must take seriously White's encouragement to anchor liturgical experimentation in theological and historical norms.

Forty years after launching their first "contemporary" service, Highland Park United Methodist Church now offers five different styles of

---

82. White, *Christian Worship in Transition*, 132–42.
83. White, "Shattering Myths about Worship," 4.
84. White, Review of *Contemporary Celebration*, 41.
85. White, Review of *Contemporary Celebration*, 41.

worship in their congregation.[86] This pluriformity of worship services in a single congregation is not uncommon for North American churches. While the 11:00 a.m. Cox Chapel service itself did not last through the 1970s, its formation created ramifications that continue. In exploring its history one wonders if the creation of the 11:00 a.m. Cox Chapel service was an opening of a liturgical Pandora's Box, namely, the breaking apart of centuries-old expectations that members of a particular congregation would hold to a common way of worship. For good and for ill these changes remain with us today. This is what makes the 11:00 a.m. Cox Chapel case study so fascinating: it not only provides remarkable insight into the liturgical milieu of its day, but it serves as a harbinger of things that were to come for both Highland Park and much of North American Protestant worship.

## Bibliography

"Alpha-Omega Players in Cox Chapel." Highland Park Methodist Church. *The Tower* 17 (Aug 27, 1971) 1.
Atkinson, Marilynn (formerly Marilynn White). Interview by R. Matthew Sigler. June 23, 2014.
Avery, Richard, and Donald Marsh. *Hymns Hot and Carols Cold*. Vinyl. Proclamation Productions, 1972.
Bergler, Thomas E. *The Juvenilization of American Christianity*. Grand Rapids: Eerdmans, 2012.
*Building for Service*. Highland Park Methodist Church, internally published pamphlet. Nov 1945.
"Contemporary Poetry and Music in Cox Chapel Sunday." Highland Park Methodist Church. *The Tower* 18 (Nov 10, 1972) 1.
"Grady Hardin to Lead New 11:00 Worship in Chapel." Highland Park Methodist Church. *The Tower* 16 (Mar 13, 1970) 1.
Hardin, H. Grady. "Recommended for Mature and Maturing Preachers Only." *Perkins Journal* 22 (1969) 87–90.
———. Review of *Leave It to the Spirit: Commitment and Freedom in the New Liturgy*, by John Killinger. *Perkins Journal* 25 (1972) 43.
———. Review of *Let Us Pray: A Book of Prayers for Use in Families, School and Fellowships*, by the Committee on Public Worship and Aids to Devotion of the General Assembly of the Church of Scotland. *Perkins Journal* 14 (1960) 40.
"Highland Park Holds Unusual Chapel Service." *Dallas Morning News*. Aug 21, 1971.
"Methodist Men Enhance Worship." Highland Park Methodist Church. *The Tower* 17 (Dec 31, 1971) 2.
"Millions Avoid Church." *Dallas Morning News*. Jul 17, 1965.
"New Contemporary Worship Begins April 5." Highland Park Methodist Church. *The Tower* 16 (Mar 6, 1970) 2.
"New Worship Service Begins at 11:00 A.M. in Cox Chapel." Highland Park Methodist Church. *The Tower* 16 (Apr 3, 1970) 1.

86. "Worship and Music," http://www.hpumc.org/.

Peiffer, Robert, B. "How Contemporary Liturgies Evolve: The Revision of United Methodist Liturgical Texts (1968–1988)." PhD diss., University of Notre Dame, 1992.

Sigler, R. Matthew. *Methodist Worship: Mediating the Wesleyan Liturgical Heritage.* London: Routledge, 2018.

"Some Dallas Churches 'Tuning In.'" *Dallas Morning News.* Apr 16, 1970.

"Teams Study Changing Attitudes." *Dallas Morning News.* Oct 17 1966.

Van Marter, Jerry L. "Don Marsh Is Dead at 86." https://www.pcusa.org/news/2010/4/27/don-marsh-dead-86/.

Westerfield Tucker, Karen B., ed. *The Sunday Service of the Methodists: Twentieth-Century Worship in Worldwide Methodism.* Nashville: Abingdon, 1996.

White, James F. "Characteristics of Effective Christian Worship." *Studia Liturgica* 8 (1971) 195–206.

———. *Christian Worship in Transition.* Nashville: Abingdon, 1976.

———. "The God Whom We Worship." *Motive* 20 (1960) 29–32.

———. "The New American Methodist Communion Order." *Worship* 41 (1967) 552–60.

———. *New Forms of Worship.* Nashville: Abingdon, 1971.

———. "Order of Saint Luke Convention 2000 Keynote Address." Cleveland: Order of St. Luke, 2000.

———. "Our Apostasy in Worship." *Christian Century* 94 (1977) 842–45.

———. "Protestant Public Worship in America: 1935–1995." In *Christian Worship in North America*, 115–34. Collegeville, MN: Liturgical, 1997.

———. Review of *Contemporary Celebration*, by Ross Snyder. *Perkins Journal* 25 (1972) 41.

———. "The Sacrament of the Lord's Supper: The New Alternate Rite." *Christian Advocate* 16 (1972) 13–14.

———. "Shattering Myths about Worship." *Circuit Rider* 7 (1984) 4–5.

———. *The Worldliness of Worship.* New York: Oxford University Press, 1967.

———. "Worship in an Age of Immediacy." *Christian Century* 85 (1968) 227–30.

# 2

# John Wimber and the Vineyard Influence on Charismatic Catholic Worship

——————————————— Billy Kangas ——

The 1980s marked a turning point in the Pentecostal and Charismatic tradition. The 1970s had seen an explosion in traditions that were using the charismatic gifts. Suddenly thousands of mainline Protestants and Roman Catholics were flocking to gatherings that involved speaking in tongues, prophecy, and other extraordinary manifestations of the Holy Spirit in worship. Church bodies all over the world were forced to face a new reality and a new challenge. Councils and committees met in nearly every significant denomination to wrestle with the challenges theological and doxological of this new form of expression. For many within the movement they believed the growth was evidence that they were involved with the means by which God would use to bring about an eschatological vision for the world. The momentum was tangible and exciting, and then suddenly things changed. The explosive growth stopped being explosive.

By 1980 the Charismatic Renewal movement within the United States had hit a plateau, both in the mainline Protestant denominations and in the Catholic Church.[1] Growth had slowed, or in some cases even begun to decline. What was once a radical subculture within the church was gradually becoming absorbed into the larger corporate bodies. For Catholic Charismatics, in particular, this slowdown in growth had been amplified by scandal between communities.[2] The "covenant communities" that had once formed the central

---

1. For insider looks at this period of decline, see Hocken, *Pentecost and Parousia*, 51, and Ghezzi, "Catholic Charismatic Renewal," 12.

2. Since the earliest days, several covenant communities had been the primary leaders in the movement, organizing conferences, publishing, and coming together to form the core of the National Service Committee. By 1976 this core had become an association unified around the two major communities, the Word of God in Ann Arbor,

organizing model of the community had gone through an ugly and public falling out with one another in the late 1970s.[3] This created a crisis of identity and mission for many of the key communities who had led the charismatic explosion in the decade before. And the distinctiveness of what it meant to be charismatic was shifting, too. Contemporary worship, passionate praise, and openness to the Holy Spirit had become more acceptable to congregations generally.[4] Many leaders had shifted into leadership in less overtly charismatic roles, or within other movements within the church.[5]

Thus there was much less of a draw to become charismatic and people within the movement began to question what had happened. If the communities that had been forged in the fire of renewal were to continue to have a vital core and a prophetic edge, something new would need to emerge. Movement leadership began to look outside of themselves for inspiration and revitalization. For one of the most influential charismatic communities in the United States, a community in Ann Arbor called the Word of God, the major outside stimulus for change and revitalization became a burgeoning movement called the Vineyard under a new leader, John Wimber, who also was the pastor of a growing congregation in Anaheim, California. Although Wimber's and the Vineyard's impact on the Church of England is a familiar story, the narrative of their impact on charismatic Roman Catholics is less so. But this impact was significant, nonetheless. As the new Vineyard model and approach to leadership and worship became more influential it contributed to tensions within the Word of God community. In retrospect both of the central leaders of this community look at the influence of the Vineyard as one of the "eminent reasons for the break-up of the community," an event that would have a ripple effect throughout worldwide charismatic Catholicism.[6]

---

Michigan, and People of Praise in South Bend, Indiana. By the early 1980s, however, continuing tension had brought about yet another realignment into three networks (the third formed around the Community of God's Delight in Dallas, Texas). See Dinolfo, "Growing Unity among Charismatic Covenant Communities."

3. This split was primarily between Paul DeCelles and Steve Clark who were leaders in the People of Praise and Word of God communities, respectively. Martin, Interview.

4. The growth of seeker-sensitive churches and the rise of the Church Growth movement (see chapter 3 in this volume) contributed to this as well as many of the congregations involved with the Jesus People movement.

5. The tension of Charismatics joining other movements would increase within the Catholic Church throughout the 1980s as word spread of an apparent Marian apparition at Medjugorje in Bosnia/Herzegovina region. Many Charismatic groups transformed into Medjugorje groups, particularly in Ireland. See Fichter, *Sociology of Good Works*, 92.

6. This quote is from Ralph Martin. Steve Clark also points to the Vineyard's

## Big Changes in Ann Arbor

It is hard to overestimate the importance of the Word of God community among Charismatics. The community had been the example par excellence for charismatic life and worship in the Catholic Church and had also been a major source of influence for Charismatics from other denominational backgrounds. Their publications had measured the movement's pulse. Their worship had been recorded and distributed around the world. Their way of life had been modeled by dozens of other covenant communities.

The Word of God community had pioneered a particular model of covenant community for Charismatics that had begun to spread across the world. Christians who had an experience of the "baptism of the Holy Spirit" began to come together to form communities of like-minded individuals. These communities had created life together based in a covenant commitment to one another through their commitment to a shared life in the community they were a part of. This movement, called the "covenant communities movement," was one of the foundational models of Catholic Charismatic life throughout the 1970s and 1980s.[7]

Leaders in the Word of God had literally written the book on how to live a community life, and the world seems to have listened.[8] The leaders had helped develop communities both throughout the United States and abroad. Key leaders within the community had been invited to move to Europe by Leo Joseph Cardinal Suenens to help advise how to integrate the charismatic life of the renewal into the broader life of the Catholic Church.[9] Suenens viewed the Charismatic Renewal one answer to the prayer of John XXIII for a "new Pentecost," which had opened the second Vatican council.[10]

With this global perspective came global concerns. The late 1970s and early 1980s were marked attempts to build a network of covenant communities that would act as a kind of leaven within the global church. Many communities wanted to unify the work they were doing, and to create a network for mutual support for the ministry and life of one another.[11] The Word of God community had experienced some difficulties unifying

---

influence as a central reason for the split. Martin, Interview. See also Clark, *Where Has the Prophetic Movement Gone?*

7. Neitz, *Charisma and Community*, 215.
8. Clark, *Building Christian Communities*.
9. Althoff and Thornson, "Catholic Charismatic Renewal," 149.
10. Suenens, "Foreword," 7.
11. The Word of God had been a part of a number of efforts, but had created tensions. Martin, Interview.

the major strands, but by the early 1980s they thought they had finally come up with a solution.[12]

Leaders in the Word of God, most notably Steve Clark, envisioned a new way to be community. They sought to unite communities around the world into a singular way of life. Each community would be governed by an international leadership board. In 1982 they reconstituted themselves as an international community called the Sword of the Spirit.[13] This new community then extended an invitation to other communities to join as individual branches of the community. Individual members would make a covenant with the international body. Each branch would live their own way according to the pattern of life of the community as it was determined by the international leadership body.[14]

The first years of the Sword of the Spirit were marked with invitation and development. Leaders in the community extended invitations to select communities they believed would be a good fit to come alongside them and discern joining the Sword of the Spirit and branches. Those who were interested sent leaders to Ann Arbor to be trained in learning how the Word of God community lived life. This was called the "development year." After the year was over leaders headed back to their own communities and began to explore how they could incorporate the life of the community in Ann Arbor into their own contexts.[15]

An international board was formed from the leaders of all the communities that had become full members of the Sword of the Spirit. Steve Clark and Ralph Martin were still the most visible leaders of this community. Increasingly attention was turned toward the implementation of a shared community life at a national level. Back home in Ann Arbor, however, tension was building. The community had begun to experience crisis on a number of fronts.

---

12. Earlier attempts had been the "Association of Communities" and then after the split with People of Praise the "Federation of Communities."

13. Another significant change that happened in this time period was the shifting of the organizational center of the international office of the Charismatic Renewal of the Catholic Church to Rome in 1982. Since 1972, the Word of God leaders had been essentially in leadership of the international aspect of Catholic Charismatic Renewal. But then Cardinal Suenens had moved the central office to Belgium and then to Rome where it became the International Catholic Charismatic Renewal Office (ICCRO).

14. Martin, Interview.

15. There were many in the community that had long believed that the community was to have a national and even global influence as noted in a 1967 prophecy that indicated a special role that God had given to the community as a training and sending ground. Compare Tiews, "Word of God History."

## Meanwhile in Anaheim

Across the country, in California, the period of decline in the Charismatic Renewal had marked a period of explosive growth for a different community. A new movement had begun to emerge that would come to be known as "The Third Wave" of the pentecostal experience. This movement witnessed the rise of a new breed of Evangelicals who had a heart for seeking after the charismatic gifts and experiences they read about in the Scriptures, but who were not formed primarily out of the pentecostal groups that many other groups had been formed from. This new generation of Charismatics or "neo-Charismatics" as they would come to be called had one man who was firmly in the center of what was happening. His name was John Wimber.

## John Wimber

John Wimber was a pastor, a musician, an evangelist, and a church planter (one who founds or "plants" a church in a location). He was a dynamic leader and a passionate evangelist who was not afraid to cut his own path and try new things to find a deeper intimacy with God and to lead more people into an intimate relationship with their Creator. By the beginning of the 1980s he had already impacted the world of Christianity in California in several ways.

John Wimber had been raised in an unchurched family. He had not gone to church and knew next to nothing about the Bible.[16] What he did know about was music. He loved to play music and he was good at it. His life in the early 1960s had been marked by a somewhat successful career in the music industry.[17] He had played in and managed a number of bands, most notably being the musical director of the group that would become the "Righteous Brothers."[18] All signs were good that he would have a successful career in music, but his home life had begun to unravel. By 1962 Wimber and his wife, Carol, had separated; he was living in another state away from his wife and children. At this point he began to explore spirituality. He began to pray and read the Bible. Through this and the influence of friends who brought him to their Quaker church and Bible study John made the decision to become a Christian. He described his conversion as making the decision to be a "fool" for Jesus for the rest of his life.[19]

---

16. inthelight1776, "John Wimber Signs Wonders."
17. Spinks, *Worship Mall*, 99.
18. Bronson, *Billboard Book of Number One Hits*, 166.
19. inthelight1776, "John Wimber Signs Wonders."

At the time of his conversion, Wimber had had two records that were top ten singles, yet he felt convicted to leave the music industry entirely.[20] He pulled out of all his projects and began to pursue a ministry of leading Bible study and evangelizing, which he did first as a volunteer. His Bible study eventually grew and he began to host new studies on different nights of the week. Soon hundreds were attending his groups. He was ordained a Quaker pastor. His Quaker church continued to grow and became one of the largest in the Friends denomination.

## Wimber and Church Growth

In 1974 Wimber was offered a job at the Fuller Institute of Evangelism and Church Growth. The invitation had come at the request of C. Peter Wagner, who had been impressed with the evangelistic efforts he had made the cornerstone of his ministry. Wimber studied the literature on the burgeoning Church Growth movement and began to travel the country consulting churches and ministries on how they could incorporate the principles of Church Growth into their own ministries. Wimber described this period as a time where he became burnt out. He was spending a lot of time teaching about God but he had lost the experience of the life of his faith. It seems to have come to a head one day on a trip to Detroit to consult at a church. After falling asleep, praying for God to help him, he awoke with a sense that God had responded to his distress.[21] From this point on he had a number of experiences that culminated in him deciding to leave his work doing Church Growth consulting and join a small gathering of other burned out church leaders from the Friends congregation of Yorba Linda. The move marked another dramatic change in Wimber's ministry.

## The Birth of the Anaheim Vineyard

The small group that had begun meeting in 1976 experienced explosive growth. They quickly outgrew the house they met in and soon they had discerned it was time to plant a new church in May, 1977. After quickly outgrowing a number of venues, the church settled into a home in the gym of Canyon High School in Anaheim, California.[22]

In some ways the group had also begun to outgrow the Quaker theology they had been rooted in. The group had asked to be released from

20. inthelight1776, "John Wimber Signs Wonders."
21. Jackson, *Quest for the Radical Middle*, 61.
22. Park et al., *Worshiping with the Anaheim Vineyard*, 10.

the Quaker church they had been a part of and joined a new network of churches that was being birthed out of the Calvary Chapel in Costa Mesa, California.[23] When Wimber's church plant launched in 1977, it was known as the Calvary Chapel of Yorba Linda (California).

In these early years John Wimber and others had begun to explore some of the more supernatural expressions of spiritual gifts they were reading about in the Scripture. Wimber himself read as many books as he could find on the subject of healing. After nearly a year of attempts to begin a healing ministry with little success, suddenly things started happening; people began to report healings. This was only the beginning of more charismatic happenings. On Mother's Day in 1980, an evangelist by the name of Lonnie Frisbee preached to the church and a new chapter in the life of the church was born. This service was marked with substantial public demonstrations of glossolalia, people swooning, and prayers for healing.[24]

Soon word of what was happening in Anaheim spread, and many evangelical pastors became curious about the explosive growth and evangelism that was happening in Wimber's church. They were interested in the miraculous signs they were hearing about. Wagner responded in 1982 by inviting Wimber to teach the first section of a course at Fuller Theological seminary called "Signs, Wonders, and Church Growth (MC510)." It drew a large number of participants and Wimber's theology of signs and wonders was spreading throughout the church world.

Signs and wonders were not the only things that gained attention. The worship had begun to attract attention too. Worship at Wimber's church seemed different. It boasted long, heartfelt worship sessions that were marked by repetitive choruses that could be easily memorized without song sheets and that focused on a deep personal intimacy with God. Wimber himself often helped lead by playing the keyboard, leaning into his previous life as a musician. Visitors to the church reported how impacted they had been and a demand arose to hear what worship sounded like at the church. As a result, 1982 marked the launch of the first album the church would produce.

Another major shift in the church in 1982 was that they broke ties with the Calvary Chapel network. Increased tensions over the overt focus on the Holy Spirit and charismatic gifts had come to a head. Mutual

---

23. The Calvary Chapel network was one of the central bodies in the Jesus People movement that marked the 1970s landscape of American religious movements. As such, it connected prominently with the youth and hippie subcultures. For a study on this movement, see Eskridge, *God's Forever Family*, and Bustraan, *The Jesus People Movement*.

24. Scotland, *Christianity Outside the Box*, 294.

discernment suggested affiliating with another network of churches that likewise had Calvary Chapel origins and connections, i.e., the Vineyard. The Vineyard was a small network that had been started in the Los Angeles area in the mid-1970s by Kenn Gulliksen, a church planter who himself had earlier Calvary Chapel (and charismatic) connections. (After Wimber's congregation joined the Vineyard in 1982, Gulliksen handed leadership of the whole network to Wimber.)

Soon Wimber's involvement with the Vineyard network catapulted him to become the face of the whole movement. His own story and experience with leaning into miraculous gifts began to spread among the evangelical world. Hundreds of leaders in churches with no previous experience of glossolalia, prophetic words, and prayers for healing in their worship were becoming interested, and the charismatic world began to catch wind of a new stream of vitality within the area of pentecostal experience.

## Ann Arbor Goes to Anaheim

John Wimber's journey of faith had grown in parallel to the faith journey of the founders of the Word of God community. Word of God founder, Steve Clark, had come to faith in the early 1960s. He had developed a model for Christian life and a developed curriculum for impacting college campuses with the Cursillo movement.[25] This model had resulted in the conversion of a young student named Ralph Martin and the deepening of the faith of many others at the University of Notre Dame.[26] Clark became a prolific writer and speaker about the model and traveled around the country with Ralph Martin sharing his material and leading communities on retreats.[27] Clark and Martin's work planted the seeds that blossomed into the Catholic Charismatic Renewal in 1967.[28] Soon they became central leaders in the movement. Their writings and teachings became central touchpoints for

---

25. The word Cursillo itself can be translated "minicourse." This is because the course in its origins and in the development of a training course in Christianity that was only three days long, and could be completed over the course of a weekend. The impetus of the movement was the need for lay leaders in Spain to raise up pilgrimage guides with an ability to lead and live out the Christian faith. The content of the retreat was spread across fifteen short talks, led by a mix of priests and lay people. By the 1970s it had become a large movement within the Catholic Church in the United States.

26. Manney, "Before Duquesne," 12–17.

27. The number of resources authored by Clark on the Cursillo is impressive, including *Desarollo*, *The Evolution of the Cursillo Literature*, *The Purpose of the Movement*, and *The Work of the Cursillos and the Work of Renewal*.

28. For an account of how Martin and Clark impacted and inspired the birth of the Charismatic Renewal, see Mansfield, *As by a New Pentecost*, 32–34.

communities in the Charismatic Renewal and John Wimber himself became familiar with their writings and listed them as influences on his own journey exploring charismatic gifts.[29] It was nearly inevitable that Wimber and the Word of God would connect as the Vineyard grew.

As word about what was happening at the Vineyard began to spread, there was within the Word of God community increased interest in seeing what was happening in California. A relationship between the leaders began to emerge. The impact of the Vineyard on the Word of God was significant. Influence from the Vineyard began to show up in the publications of the Word of God community. Their magazine *New Covenant* began to feature Vineyard, as did their periodical for leaders, *Pastoral Renewal*.

Perhaps most notably, Kevin N. Springer, the editor of *Pastoral Renewal* interviewed John Wimber in 1983 for the magazine for the article "A Third Wave?"[30] This began a relationship that deepened later that year when Springer traveled to California to conduct a conference for *Pastoral Renewal* at the Anaheim Vineyard. Wimber was impressed by the work Springer was doing at *Pastoral Renewal*, stating, "[Springer] captured in writing [my] beliefs better than anyone else up to that time."[31] That began a relationship that led to Springer and Wimber signing a four-book contract resulting in the books *Power Evangelism*, *Power Healing*, *Power Points*, and *Riding the Third Wave* that Springer co-authored with Wimber.

In 1986 one of the community coordinators, Peter Williamson, took a trip to Anaheim to learn more. He brought with him John Blattner, a musician and composer from the Ann Arbor community. Peter found the trip and the meetings with John Wimber encouraging.[32] Communication continued and more community members began to visit the Anaheim Vineyard and listen to Vineyard music. Soon there was a cohort within the Word of God that was pushing to adopt more of the methods and culture of the Vineyard and looking to John Wimber as a mentor and guide. This effort was spearheaded by Jim McFadden and Dave Nodar.[33] To understand the nature of that influence I now turn to an examination of the approach toward worship that was taken by John Wimber.

---

29. John Wimber stated that leaders within the Word of God were subjects of his own study on his path of better understanding of his own ministry in light of history. Wimber and Springer, *Power Evangelism*, 127.

30. Wagner, "A Third Wave?"

31. Springer, "Letter to Pastor Delaney."

32. Peter Williamson, personal letter to John Wimber, March 27, 1986.

33. Clark, *Where Has the Prophetic Movement Gone?* 22.

## Worship in the Vineyard

One of the most apparent areas of impact that the Vineyard had was in their worship. Worship in the Vineyard was marked by unique characteristics. Wimber's congregation had a unique approach to the kinds of music it was producing and a unique approach to the pattern of worship it brought to its services.

## The Vineyard Pattern of Worship

By the latter half of the 1980s, the Anaheim Vineyard had developed its own pattern of worship. It was not based on a strict *ordo* or even a formally written out order of service. Instead there was an awareness of one's posture in relationship to the presence of God. As taught by John Wimber and other Vineyard worship leaders, the opening extended time of congregational singing normally progressed according to five phases. For example, in 1987 Eddie Espinosa described worship according to a "relationship approach": from invitation to engagement to exaltation to adoration to intimacy.[34] Wimber himself offered a similar model in the same year:

1. Call to Worship: In this phase Wimber talked about worship leaders "setting the tone" for worship. Leaders should be aware of any concerns that might arise given the context and carefully select particular songs to introduce that will "set the tone for the gathering" and can help members of the congregation become "conscience of [the] concerns."

2. Engagement: At the center of this phase is the "electrifying connection to God and to each other." This is marked by individual expressions of "love, adoration, praise, jubilation, intercession, [and] petition." In this phase the personal relationship to God that is experienced by members is "multiplied" as they express devotion together.

3. Expression: In this phase the participants have become increasingly aware of God. Attention is drawn to what is happening, and how it connects to the eternal worship of God. As Wimber described it, "worship is going on all the time in heaven, and when we worship we are joining that which is already happening." This phase is marked by a response to that heavenly worship of God and to "praise him for the deeds he has done, how he has moved in history, for his character and attributes." In more formally liturgical terminology, this phase might be considered a focus on God anamnetically and a response to that

---

34. Espinosa, "Worship Leading," 82.

perspective. The response in this phase is very individualistic and focused on personal imagery. Wimber compared it to making love. This underscored his desire that the response should include some physicality. People should respond with their "hearts, minds, and bodies." The result should be natural movement, like dance, and expressions of emotion. Wimber did emphasize that physical response should not be the point of this phase, but that everything should flow from "true jubilation."

4. Visitation: In this phase Wimber emphasized that worshipers have "expressed what is in [their] hearts and minds and bodies." It is now time to "wait for God to respond." This theology is rooted in the passage in the Psalms (22:3b) that states God "dwells in the praises of his people." The dwelling of God among the worshipers can take many forms. The manifestations are personal. Wimber listed a few ways this can happen including salvation, deliverance, sanctification, healing, and prophetic gifts. There is a marked emphasis on the charismatic dimension here.

5. Giving of substance: This is a phase in which the worshiper, in awareness of God's generosity, is to respond in generosity, offering one's whole life to God. This offering often takes the form of giving. Wimber listed some possible gifts people may give including hospitality, money, and information.[35]

After the musical service or sermon, Vineyard meetings could include times of ministry where people could receive individual prayer for things in their lives. This dimension in particular was influential in the life of the Word of God. Prayer meetings began to have times of "ministry" following the main meeting where individuals could go to experience prayer and personal prophetic words given by members in the community who were identified as having prophetic gifts.

## The Impact of Vineyard Music on Word of God Music

One of the clearest places to see the impact of the Vineyard on the Word of God is in their music. Since the mid-1970s, the Word of God had begun to publish songbooks and song sheets These publications were originally produced to provide a way for charismatic prayer groups around the country to gain access legally to many of the songs that were used at prayer meetings. The Word of God had been the primary source for many in the Charismatic

---

35. Wimber, "Worship: Intimacy with God," 4–5, 13.

Renewal for both sheet music and recorded music. These sheets included both compositions written by members of the community as well as popular songs from other communities and churches. In the mid-1980s there was a sudden influx of songs from the Vineyard into the community as can be seen by looking at the history of Word of God musical publications:

- In 1975 the Word of God published the first volume of *Songs of Praise*. It included seventy-nine songs. Of those seventy-nine, twenty-one of them were original content created by the Word of God community members.[36]
- In 1977 the second volume was published. This included forty-one songs. Of these songs, only six had been written by community members.[37]
- In 1979 a third volume was published including thirty-nine songs. This volume also included six original compositions from the Word of God members.[38]
- In 1981 Volume 4 with twenty-eight songs was released. It included twelve original songs, the highest percentage of original material to that date.[39]
- In 1985 a volume entitled *Lift Up Your Voice* was published. It was aimed at "continuing the tradition of the popular *Songs of Praise*."[40] It contained thirty songs, only one of which was an original composition from the Word of God.
- In 1987 a short supplement was produced containing twenty-three songs. In this volume there is an explosion of Vineyard material. Ten of the songs originated in the Vineyard while only one of the songs was composed by Word of God members.
- In 1988 another supplement was released. In this volume there was only one Vineyard song of the thirteen songs. The Word of God songwriters were much more represented with ten songs.
- Finally, in 1989 the final supplement before the split of the community was released. This volume contained sixteen songs. Six of the

---

36. *Songs of Praise* (1975).
37. *Songs of Praise* (1977).
38. *Songs of Praise* (1979).
39. *Songs of Praise* (1981).
40. Crossroads, *Lift Up Your Voice*.

songs were Word of God originals and five of the songs were from the Vineyard.

Evaluating the content of Word of God original music and comparing it to the content of Vineyard music that the Word of God included in their song sheets illuminates a number of subtle shifts that occurred as the community began to feel the influence from Anaheim.[41]

## Analysis of the Data: Song Length

The average length of a song published by the Word of God by one of their own members is 127 words. On the other hand, the average length of a song published by the Word of God that was written by a Vineyard composer is seventy words. This underscores the stronger emphasis on repetition that the Vineyard songs had. Fewer of the songs from Vineyard had lengthy theological statements. They focused on a central idea or concept and allowed the participant to encounter that particular idea in relationship with God as both the verses and chorus were repeated. The Word of God music included a number of short and repetitive songs as well, but by in large their songs tended to be longer, often drawing on and occasionally reproducing in their entirety passages from Scripture or from the ancient hymns of the church, most commonly drawing from psalms and canticles.

## Analysis of the Data: Pronoun Usage

Vineyard composers tended to use less diversity in the pronouns they used and to limit the pronoun usage to speaking either about the singular subject singing or to the God they were singing to or about.

Analysis revealed that pronouns used for the subject of sentences within the Word of God were more diverse. They included "I" with 18 percent of usage, "you" with 39 percent of usage, "he" with 20 percent of usage, "it" with 2 percent of usage, "they" with 5 percent of usage and "we" with 16 percent of usage.

The Vineyard songs only used three subject pronouns: "I" at 41 percent, "you" at 46 percent, and "he" at 13 percent. This underscores a level of intimacy in the lyrical content of the songs. These are not songs the gathered community is singing as a corporate body, but instead reflect a gathering of individuals who are addressing God individually. The emphasis is very much on the "I and thou" dynamic. There was no mention of

---

41. Songs were evaluated given lyrical content in the published versions. Analysis includes the chorus or refrain of a song only once.

what the corporate body is together. What God has done, or is doing, was more focused on how God related to the individual. This emphasis is underscored in an analysis of the titles used for God in the published songs.

## Analysis of the Data: Names and Titles of God

There are forty-eight titles for God used in the Word of God and Vineyard material evaluated. There was significant overlap in the ways that both communities addressed God in their compositions.[42] However, there was also divergence. Seeing how the communities spoke about God helps illustrate ways in which the Word of God and the Vineyard were different in their worship.

The unique addresses to God that the Word of God community uses were, generally, related to things that God is recorded as doing in the Scripture (e.g., redeemer, sacrifice, One who died and rose, one who set the stars) or images of materials and objects in the world (e.g., water, rock, treasure, light, fortress).[43] These images of God indicate a strong emphasis on biblical fidelity. They sing the Scripture. They tell of what God has done in the Scripture. They recount the mysteries of the faith. They are focused on the community life they believe they are a part of in Christ. A connection that links their story to the whole testimony of the Scriptures.

In contrast, the unique addresses to God used by the Vineyard were more personal (e.g., my strength, my song) or a description of a kind of individual someone has a personal relationship with (e.g., counselor, potter), a result not surprising in light of the Vineyard five-phase model of worship.[44] These divine names emphasized a more intimate relationship with God as the God who is with us (Emmanuel). The nature of these songs was more of a personal testimony relating to the distinct experiences of the individual singer.

---

42. Titles for God used in both groups as represented in their songs: Almighty, Creator, Father, God, Holy One, Jesus, King, Lamb, Lord, Master, Mighty One, Spirit, and Word.

43. Titles used by Word of God composers but not used in Vineyards songs: Alpha and Omega, Ancient of Days, Beloved, Christ, Eternal light, Fortress, Founder, Galaxy Builder, He who was and is and is to come, Judge, Lover, Offspring of David, One who died and rose, One who raised Jesus, One who raised man, One who saves, One who set the stars, Redeemer, Rock, Sacrifice, Savior, Shepherd, Son, Son of man, Son of the Father, Treasure, Water, and Yahweh.

44. Titles distinctly used by Vineyard composers: Anointed One, Counselor, Emmanuel, My Song, My Strength, Potter, and Wonderful One.

## Changes in Ann Arbor

The Word of God community, although mostly made up of individuals with more of a liturgical background, did not have a rigid structure to their worship in their early days (between 1967 and 1971). In the earliest days of the Catholic Charismatic Renewal worship created a dilemma. There was not clear leadership and prayer meetings would go on without a clear direction or even a way to end. They would often last five hours and could become chaotic. The meeting would start and people would move from praise, to prophecy, to singing "in the Spirit" and back to prophecy, and on and on. As a result they developed leaders who would facilitate what was happening, but this development increasingly meant that the direction of worship was governed by a few people.[45] As a result, as time went on, some members who had experienced the ungoverned spontaneity of the "early days" began to feel worship had become prescriptive and planned.[46]

As the Vineyard was beginning to gain notoriety, the leaders in Ann Arbor had become concerned about the direction of their community. The community had developed patterns of control in the lives of their members that many had begun to feel were harmful. As Ralph Martin put it, "here in the Word of God community which was the laboratory of the whole [Sword of the Spirit] experiment, things weren't working in people's lives. People were leading double lives. The standards were so high, [with the training course], people could not [live up to] them." A former coordinator shared that the key turning point for him was when a community member told him that nearly half of the members of the community were secretly seeking help from counselors, twelve-step programs, and similar programs but the members felt so ashamed and afraid they could not even tell their pastoral leaders.[47]

The Word of God had become increasingly hierarchical, too. As a part of the Sword of the Spirit there was increasing pressure to form their life according to a formalized rule. Before Wimber, prayer meetings had become more "solemn" and hierarchal. The leaders had become more distant in worship. They were placed on a stage far from the people. People were coming dressed in their Sunday best. There was even a special system of "mantels" and "veils" that identified those who had made a public commitment to the community.[48]

---

45 For a detailed look at the development of the Word of God methodology, see Cavnar, *Participating in Prayer Meetings*.

46. Martin, Interview.

47. Tiews, Interview.

48. Csordas, *Language, Charisma, and Creativity*, 111.

Some people within the community began to feel concerned. As a former coordinator shared, "There was a fading of the 'Holy Spirit fire.' Life in the spirit seminars were fewer . . . the Thursday night group was closed. It had become insular . . . the Word of God had been set up to be hungry . . . there was complaining about 'where's the Holy Spirit?' . . . things had closed down." Then along came John Wimber. "He had more Holy Spirit stories then we had ourselves . . . so Wimber had a kind of credibility because of that."[49]

The influence of the Vineyard was seen by many as a breath of fresh air. One of John Wimber's famous sayings was "everyone gets to play." This struck a chord with many. People in the community began to feel they had a role again in the prayer meetings.[50] People began to feel personally and intimately connected. Soon leaders in the Word of God began to borrow elements from the order of worship the Vineyard followed, including special times for "ministry" after prayer meetings.

Ralph Martin says that Wimber had given the Word of God a "new model" for ministry. Martin recounts, "He was so laid back; he was so normal; he was so unpretentious. I remember one day someone asking him how do you prepare for a big healing meeting, he said 'I take a nap and drink a diet Coke.' He would introduce himself saying, 'I'm just a fat guy trying to get to heaven.' It was so clear that he was looking for the power of God, and not anything in himself."[51] This approach caused the leadership to begin to question their own model, which was different. One coordinator at the time said that Wimber embodied, "the only revivalist movement that did not represent heavy handed authority at the time."[52] There had become some tension about how prescriptive the way of life needed to be. This tension was exacerbated by the influence of the Vineyard.

## Concern about the Vineyard Influence

By the late 1980s Vineyard had become the primary musical influence in the Word of God. Wimber's methodology to meetings began to have an influence on the worship as well. The change was noticeable and soon some leaders in the Sword of the Spirit began to have concerns about how the Vineyard was impacting the life of the "flagship" community back in Ann Arbor.

49. Wilson, Interview.
50. Dieterich and Dieterich, Interview.
51. Martin, Interview.
52. Wilson, Interview.

Some of the Sword of the Spirit leaders were concerned about an outside voice speaking into the leadership. The concerns were deepened because of a perceived threat that this group was undermining the foundational Catholic nature of the community as well. This perspective became a significant issue when some members of the community connected to the Vineyard believed God was leading them to leave the Catholic Church.[53]

Conversions were not new in the community, but they had been mostly Protestants becoming Catholics. This reversal caused concern among the leadership, which was primarily Catholic. A fear grew that the culture of the community itself was under attack. Among the leadership, this influence seemed to trouble Steve Clark the most. As Ralph Martin put it, "Steve was very, very against the influence of John Wimber and the Vineyard."[54]

## Music Critiques

One of the sharpest critiques of the Vineyard came from those who simply had a problem with the music the Vineyard was producing. As the analysis of their influence shows there was a significant influence in the mid- to late 1980s on the music of the Word of God, and there were substantial differences in the kind of music that was being produced. There were concerns over the lyrical content of the songs.[55] Steve Clark, for example, had a strong critique of Vineyard music. He thought it was too focused on "me and Jesus." It was neither objective enough nor "focused on worshiping God."[56] There is record of at least one worship leader who would change the lyrics of the songs when they got too "touchy feely."[57] Many of the musicians and composers had serious concerns too, not only over the lyrics but also over the "feel" of the music. One musician described the music as more "feminine" and less assertive.[58]

## Prophetic Voice

Prophecy had always played a role in the community. Many of the pivotal moments of their life throughout the late 1960s and the 1970s had been powerful prophecies about what God was going to do. Over their history

53. Gryniewicz and Gryniewicz, Interview.
54. Martin, Interview.
55. Kennedy, Interview.
56. Martin, Interview.
57. Wilson, Interview.
58. Kennedy, Interview.

that influence had become a formalized part of their life. One man, in particular, was put over the prophetic life of the Word of God, a man named Bruce Yocum.[59] Under his leadership the Word of God had a way to help discern what words should be taken seriously.

In the 1980s there was a developing practice of naming "territorial spirits" sought to identify the names of demons that were active in particular areas. A few key demons had been named over Ann Arbor. Wimber challenged this practice saying that no good would come from focusing on and calling the demons by name.[60] This was felt as an undermining voice against the prophetic practice of the community's prophetic leadership headed up by Bruce Yocum.

Wimber also brought his own prophetic insights and influences, which brought their own controversy. Wimber shared he believed that the members of the Word of God were like the colt in the Palm Sunday narrative.[61] They needed to be untied because the Lord had need of them. This prophetic tension was heightened as Wimber became connected to a man named Paul Cain. Cain was part of a movement of prophets. He spoke prophecies over many of the leaders in the Word of God, which some leaders believed were influential in deepening rifts.[62]

## Unsuccessful Intervention

As leadership in Ann Arbor continued to ask how they could reform their community, leadership in the Sword of the Spirit began to sense a growing unrest in their flagship community. Leaders believed action needed to be taken. Ralph Martin was sent home from Belgium to try to set things right. The main contention was around control. Leaders in Ann Arbor wanted the freedom to change the life of the local community to meet the specific needs they encountered. Sword of the Spirit leaders wanted a unified community life that was reproducible across their global network. As Martin describes it, "Peter Williamson and others were trying to carry on the Wimber ministry in the structure of the [Ann Arbor] ministry . . . while I was part of the 'out of town' group living in Belgium . . . there was unrest in the Word of God. [Leaders] had felt like something was going wrong. I was appointed [by Sword of the Spirit leaders] to take over in Ann Arbor to 'put down the rebellion.' But I wound up joining it because I believed what those guys were

---

59. Csordas, *Language, Charisma, and Creativity*.
60. Wilson, Interview.
61. Williamson, Interview.
62. Clark, *Where Has the Prophetic Movement Gone?* 22–25.

saying. So that became a big, big problem."⁶³ Once Ralph Martin became part of the group seeking to give more local control, the tensions between the two groups of leaders intensified.

During this period of intensification, John Wimber's influence increased with the Ann Arbor leadership. As one of the head coordinators recounted, "[By 1988] the head coordinators were meeting and we functioned as a kind of support group for what was going wrong in the community ... I hosted the meetings at my house ... we all felt acute psychological pressure because Ralph (Martin) and Steve (Clark) were not on the same page ... it was an intense period and Wimber became an outside ear."⁶⁴ Although most admit that Wimber was not really at the center of any of the major disputes between community leaders, his influence was significant. As one coordinator put it, "all the pieces were there [for the split]. They just hadn't all come together." For a group of leaders struggling to reform their own community, Wimber became "an unfortunate intensifier."⁶⁵

## The End of the Unified Community

The tensions within the community only intensified. In 1990 the community finally broke off from the Sword of the Spirit. This decision caused massive repercussions for the community in Ann Arbor as well as the Catholic Charismatic Renewal at large. The community in Ann Arbor shattered. The core group that wanted to split away maintained the name "The Word of God." Another group soon formed with those who had a desire to become a part of the Sword of the Spirit. They named themselves, Washtenaw Covenant Community. All the churches that had been started by the community began to operate independently of community oversite, as did the school that had been founded by the Word of God.

For many leaders in the Word of God, the Vineyard was seen as an influence that helped them return to their roots as a Holy Spirit-led community. They did not see the Vineyard as a cause of the problems they were having but simply a force that brought those problems to a head more quickly. The "free church fellowship" that was the nondenominational church founded by the community eventually became a Vineyard church and their pastor continued to participate in the life of the community throughout much of the next decade. Similarly, Ralph Martin continued to connect with John Wimber. Martin's and Wimber's relationship deepened as the two of them began to minister side-by-side in Poland. Together they hosted both

---

63. Martin, Interview.
64. Wilson, Interview.
65. Wilson, Interview.

leadership summits and a large conference that helped to bolster a charismatic movement in Poland that endures to this day.

For those who remained connected to the Sword of the Spirit, the influence from Wimber was seen as a destructive and seriously misguided alliance. Many saw Wimber as a wedge that had shattered their community. The most notable example of this can be seen in a small book published by Steve Clark in the immediate aftermath. Entitled *Where has the Prophetic Movement Gone?*, it presents a scathing critique of Wimber and his connection to Paul Cain. A central argument of his book is the personal anecdote of what he saw transpire when the Word of God went through the crisis in the late 1980s.[66]

The true impact and legacy of the Vineyard in the Word of God community has become, in the final analysis, that of a catalyst. Their worship, music, and leadership created new paradigms of ministry that widened the cracks in an already crumbling façade. For those who felt trapped within the walls, Vineyard was seen as a liberator. For those who saw the walls as a secure refuge, Vineyard embodied a destructive earthquake. For everyone it was a turning point. The collapse of the Word of God marked the end of an era. Never again would Ann Arbor be seen as the center of the Catholic Charismatic Renewal in the world. A new "wave of the Holy Spirit" had crashed into the world.[67]

## Bibliography

Althoff, Andrea, and Jakob Egeris Thornson. "The Catholic Charismatic Renewal (CCR) in the Americas." In *The Changing Faces of Catholicism*, edited by Solange Lefebvre and Alfonso Pérèz-Agote Poveda, 147–64. Leiden: Brill, 2018.
Bronson, Fred. *The Billboard Book of Number One Hits*. New York: Billboard Books, 2003.
Bustraan, Richard A. *The Jesus People Movement: A Story of Spiritual Revolution among the Hippies*. Eugene, OR: Pickwick, 2014.
Cavnar, Jim. *Participating in Prayer Meetings*. Ann Arbor, MI: Servant, 1974.
Clark, Stephen B. *Building Christian Communities: Strategy for Renewing the Church*. Notre Dame, IN: Ave Maria, 1971.
———. *Where Has the Prophetic Movement Gone?* Christian Concerns Series. Dexter, MI: Tabor, 1993.
Crossroads. *Lift Up Your Voice*. LP. Ann Arbor, MI: Servant Music, 1985.
Csordas, Thomas J. *Language, Charisma, and Creativity: The Ritual Life of a Religious Movement*. Berkeley: University of California Press, 1997.
Dieterich, Henry, and Rosalind Dieterich. Interview by Billy Kangas. Apr 9, 2018.

---

66. Clark, *Where Has the Prophetic Movement Gone?*
67. C. Peter Wagner had coined the term "third wave of the Holy Spirit" to describe what was happening with Wimber, Vineyard, and similar folks. Interestingly one of the first places he spoke of this idea was in one of the Word of God's own publications: Wagner, *Pastoral Renewal*.

Dinolfo, Paul. "Growing Unity among Charismatic Covenant Communities." *Living Bulwark* 92 (2017). http://www.swordofthespirit.net/bulwark/june2017p9.htm.

Eskridge, Larry. *God's Forever Family: The Jesus People Movement in America*. New York: Oxford University Press, 2013.

Espinosa, Eddie. "Worship Leading." In *Worship Leaders Training Manual*, 81–82. Anaheim: Worship Resource Center/Vineyard Ministries International, 1987.

Fichter, Joseph Henry. *The Sociology of Good Works: Research in Catholic America*. Chicago: Loyola University Press, 1993.

Ghezzi, Bert. "The Catholic Charismatic Renewal in the United States, Growth and Decline." Unpublished manuscript, 1991.

Gryniewicz, Ellen, and Thomas Gryniewicz. Interview by Billy Kangas. Jun 4, 2018.

Hocken, Peter. *Pentecost and Parousia: Charismatic Renewal, Christian Unity, and the Coming Glory*. Eugene, OR: Wipf & Stock, 2013.

inthelight1776. "John Wimber Signs Wonders 1985 1/12 (Personal Pilgrimage)." *YouTube*, Jan 30, 2013. https://www.youtube.com/watch?v=wGkobon363A.

Jackson, Bill. *The Quest for the Radical Middle: A History of the Vineyard*. Cape Town: Vineyard International, 2000.

Kennedy, Ted. Interview by Billy Kangas. May 21, 2018.

Manney, James. "Before Duquesne: Sources of the Renewal." *New Covenant* (Feb 1973) 12–17.

Mansfield, Patti Gallagher. *As by a New Pentecost: The Dramatic Beginning of the Catholic Charismatic Renewal*. 1st ed. Phoenix: Amor Deus, 2016.

Martin, Ralph. Interview by Billy Kangas. Apr 26, 2018.

Neitz, Mary Jo. *Charisma and Community: A Study of Religious Commitment within the Charismatic Renewal*. New Brunswick, NJ: Transaction, 1987.

Park, Andy, et al. *Worshiping with the Anaheim Vineyard: The Emergence of Contemporary Worship*. Grand Rapids: Eerdmans, 2017.

Scotland, Nigel. *Christianity Outside the Box: Learning from Those Who Rocked the Boat*. Eugene, OR: Wipf & Stock, 2012.

*Songs of Praise*. Vol. 1. Ann Arbor, MI: Servant Music, 1975.

*Songs of Praise*. Vol. 2. Ann Arbor, MI: Servant Music, 1977.

*Songs of Praise*. Vol. 3. Ann Arbor, MI: Servant Music, 1979.

*Songs of Praise*. Vol. 4. Ann Arbor, MI: Servant Music, 1981.

Spinks, Bryan. *The Worship Mall: Contemporary Responses to Contemporary Culture*. London: SPCK, 2010.

Springer, Kevin. "Letter to Pastor Delaney." Jun 24, 2011. https://kingdomfireministries.org/wp-content/uploads/2015/05/Kevin-Springer-Reference-June-24-2011.pdf.

Suenens, Leon Joseph. "Foreword." In *Charisms and Charismatic Renewal: A Biblical and Theological Study*, by Francis A. Sullivan, 7–8. Ann Arbor, MI: Servant, 1982.

Tiews, Phil. Interview by Billy Kangas. Mar 29, 2019.

———. "The Word of God History." Presentation at the Word of God Sunday prayer meeting, Covenant Presbyterian Church, Ann Arbor, MI, Feb 5, 2017.

Wagner, C. Peter. "A Third Wave?" *Pastoral Renewal* (Jul/Aug 1983) 1–5.

Williamson, Peter. Interview by Billy Kangas. May 27, 2019.

Wilson, Ken. Interview by Billy Kangas. Feb 5, 2019.

Wimber, John. "Worship: Intimacy with God." *Equipping the Saints* 1 (1987) 4–5, 13.

Wimber, John, and Kevin Springer. *Power Evangelism*. Harper & Row, 1986.

# 3

## The Path to a Second Service

*Mainline Decline, Church Growth,
and Apostolic Leadership*

— GLENN STALLSMITH —

It is commonplace now for mainline American churches—ranging in size from large to small—to offer more than one worship option on Sunday morning. This is not about large congregations that, for lack of space, need to offer several iterations of the same service, stretching from Saturday evening to Sunday afternoon. Rather, this chapter is about congregations within the largest American Protestant denominations that have added a second service, one that follows a Contemporary Praise & Worship format. Attentive passersby who read church signs will recognize some version of this phenomenon in many places throughout the United States, whether rural, suburban, or urban:

First Methodist/Presbyterian/Lutheran Church

Sunday Services:

8:30 Contemporary

9:30 Sunday School

11:00 Traditional

The question this chapter aims to answer is: How did this arrangement become so common? In other words, what led so many church leaders, beginning in the early 1990s, to add a contemporary service to their existing Sunday morning worship offerings?

Adding an additional service in an alternative format was certainly not an invention of the 1990s. Indeed, as chapter 1 in this volume shows, mainline churches have been experimenting with new worship forms for decades, e.g., folk masses in Roman Catholic parishes or jazz services in Protestant churches. However, these experiments involved mostly isolated pockets of interest groups within a few congregations. What was different in the last decade of the twentieth century, however, was the confluence of several important factors, all leading to a nearly exclusive emphasis on adding contemporary services. Primary among these was a growing sense of decline among denominational churches that gained traction throughout the 1980s. As a growing number of church leaders looked to the Church Growth movement for answers in reversing this decline, and as its core missiological principles were popularized for North American pastors, pastors saw the Homogeneous Unit Principle (one of the core missiological principles) as the answer for reducing the cultural barriers that blocked potential newcomers from attending. For congregations wanting a concrete example of how to reach potential newcomers, no congregation was as influential in modelling how to tailor a worship service for the unchurched as Willow Creek Community Church in South Barrington, Illinois. Thousands of church leaders, eager to grow their weekly attendance numbers, went to Willow Creek to learn how to create different kinds of worship services. Although many congregations tried to emulate the worship style at Willow Creek, very few were able to accomplish what they saw there. The impact of Willow Creek can be found, therefore, in how it combined popular Church Growth ideas with leadership principles. This chapter argues that pastors who returned from Willow Creek site visits and conferences created second services for a mixture of reasons, primary among them the twin desires to exercise visionary leadership and to create a new worship option for outsiders. These two principles were at the core of Willow Creek's success in bringing in visitors, which was lifted up as a model for those who were anxious about declining numbers in the mainline.

## Fall and Rise: Mainline Decline and Church Growth

Rhetoric about the decline of membership numbers in mainline churches was common by the 1980s, even though most denominations had been losing members for several prior decades. The United Methodist Church, for example, lost over two million members from 1969 to 1993; its membership peak was in 1968, the date of its constitutive merger between The Methodist Church and the Evangelical United Brethren Church.[1] By 1972

---

1. Langford and Willimon, *New Connection*, 20.

the sense of decline among mainline churches was already widely felt, at least enough that Dean Kelley was able to make a splash that year with his book *Why Conservative Churches are Growing*.[2] (His original title was *Why Liberal Churches are Declining*.) This book tapped into and generated a decades-long period of collective hand-wringing about the ongoing drop in membership numbers across the biggest Protestant denominations. For Kelley, a lackadaisical stance toward traditional and orthodox beliefs was the primary factor for this decline, but many other reasons were suggested by others, creating a cottage industry of consultants and authors who tried to diagnose the problems. Proposed remedies were aimed at a host of concerns: progressive, activist pastors of the 1960s and 1970s who alienated their mostly conservative congregations; an urbanizing United States that was breaking apart the kinship-based neighborhood ties that constituted most mainline churches; or older generations who were missing the cultural shifts relevant to Baby Boomers. Denominational publications and conferences throughout the 1980s addressed this perceived crisis, and by the end of that decade even the mainstream media were reporting on shrinking denominational congregations.[3]

As concerns about membership decline became more publicized throughout the 1980s, solutions offered by the Church Growth movement seemed increasingly attractive. Mainline congregations looking for new members were captivated by the application of its Homogeneous Unit Principle, a foundational tenet that goes back to Donald McGavran, the founder of the overall movement. McGavran, who served for decades as an American missionary to India, sought to ignite "people movements" that would bring entire ethnic groups into the church *en masse*. He began to systematically study the reasons why Indians were not converting to Christianity, in the process identifying cultural barriers that could be addressed and removed. This would be his life-long work, yielding missiological theories that focused on cultural impediments to Christian conversion. The removal of these barriers served as the focus of his numerous books, driving his career as dean of the School of World Mission at Fuller Theological Seminary. Writing in his pivotal book *Understanding Church Growth*, McGavran urged missionaries to present the gospel in ways that minimize communication barriers through familiar linguistic and cultural forms:

---

2. Kelley, *Why Conservative Churches Are Growing*.

3. Dudley, "How Churches Grow." On September 15, 1990 the *Los Angeles Times* had reported on the decades-long decline of mainline denominations in "Mainline Protestant Ranks Continue Decline of the '60s."

> When the Christian faith moves from one culture to another, the churches in the second culture would not be expected to look exactly like the churches from the missionaries' culture. Missionaries who do not understand this and who feel that their mode of church government, their requirements for ordination, their sense of punctuality, their liturgical tastes, their musical idioms, their rules for baptism, their ethical taboos, and what have you need to be cloned in the churches in the new culture raise artificial barriers to church growth.[4]

Given McGavran's belief that priority should be given to the local cultural context of would-be converts, it follows that churches ought to worship in ways that are culturally and linguistically distinct. This Homogenous Unit Principle urged church planters to create congregations that attract people of a similar demographic, because, "People like to become Christians without crossing racial, linguistic, or class barriers."[5]

McGavran originally created the Church Growth movement for foreign missionaries, but American church leaders also yearned to apply its principles in their own churches. For several years after the 1965 founding of the School of World Mission, McGavran refused to accept North American pastors, fearing that opening his program to Americans would water down the movement and detract from the work of reaching the yet unconverted elsewhere in the world.[6] In the 1970s, however, C. Peter Wagner, a colleague of McGavran at Fuller, began to offer Church Growth courses to American pastors who were enrolled in the school's Doctor of Ministry program. This pivot to American pastors gave a giant boost to a newly forming wing of the movement, one that Gary McIntosh has named the "popular branch" of Church Growth. This new branch of the movement, oriented toward North American contexts, would come to develop its own set of organizations and institutions, mostly focused on conducting research that addressed mainline decline like, among others, the Alban Institute, Gallup, and the Barna Group.[7] The growth of this popular wing also incorporated students like Rick Warren, Leith Anderson, and Eddie Gibbs, thus establishing a new set of American church leaders who would assert certain principles of McGavran's. Core among these was the commitment to contextualization—that

---

4. McGavran, *Understanding Church Growth*, 94–95.

5. McGavran, *Understanding Church Growth*, 163.

6. Entrance to the program at the School of World Mission at Fuller required an applicant to demonstrate three years of cross-cultural experience and fluency in a second language—a set of competencies specifically designed to keep out pastors of churches in North America. McIntosh, *Evaluating the Church Growth Movement*, 16.

7. McIntosh, *Evaluating the Church Growth Movement*, 19.

is, the lowering of communication barriers—that resulted in an emphasis on forming homogenous congregations.

## Popular Church Growth: Lyle Schaller and the Second Service

A key figure who extended Church Growth principles into the worship life of North American churches was an urban planner turned church consultant named Lyle Schaller. Schaller conducted thousands of consultations with churches throughout his decades-long career, which was at its most productive in the final four decades of the twentieth century. Schaller not only consulted widely, but he also wrote over fifty books between 1964 and the early 2000s and was a featured speaker at conferences and seminars, especially in the 1980s and 1990s. Although Schaller was not a student of McGavran, some of his proposed solutions for increasing worship attendance aligned with the Homogeneous Unit Principle. Schaller, for instance, urged American churches to add a new worship service to their weekly schedule. Not only would a new timeframe accommodate people who could not attend the regularly scheduled worship time, but it would also allow churches to create specific affinity groups within a single congregation:

> Any *long-established* middle-sized congregation seriously interested in numerical growth should consider offering people the choice of worship experiences on Sunday morning. The more pluralistic or diverse the membership, the stronger the case for offering people a choice between two *different* worship experiences on Sunday morning. As a general rule, in long-established and pluralistic congregations, consideration should be given to the possibility of two worship services when the average attendance on Sunday morning passes eighty-five.[8]

Schaller saw the way to church growth was to diversify; to him it was entirely appropriate for a growing church to comprise numerous communities within it. These may break down across cultural or ethnic distinctions, or they may be organized by other differences. A church divided into "closely knit and supportive communities" could be seen as diverse, if the various groups within were all considered part of the whole.[9] Using the Homogenous Unit Principle, church leaders were urged to attract newcomers to a subset of people within a larger congregation, people whom they were

---

8. Schaller, *Growing Plans*, 76.
9. Schaller, *Choices for Churches*, 72.

like in terms of ethnicity, class, social location, education level, or political affiliation. Schaller cited research that healthy (i.e., growing) churches were generally homogeneous, and, like McGavran, taught that newcomers like to attend services with people who are like them: "Prospective new members do display a strong resemblance to the members."[10]

Schaller's original advice for starting second services preceded the debates around Contemporary Praise & Worship; in the 1980s the "worship wars" had not yet begun in mainline congregations. Decisions to begin a second service in this time frame were largely pragmatic, as yet unaffected by commitments to one worship style being right or proper. Instead, decisions about how to program the second service were based on what generated higher attendance numbers. If attendance was growing in the main service, then the new second service should follow the same format. If attendance in the congregation had plateaued or was declining, then the second service should be offered in a different style.[11] Herb Miller, another popular Church Growth consultant of the same era, cited statistics to support this strategy: a second service like the first will increase attendance by 5 to 15 percent; if the new service is different from the first, then the jump will be even higher.[12] Likewise, in 1980, long before the widespread adoption of contemporary services in mainline congregations, George Hunter suggested that new services were mostly important for bringing in groups of people who were left out of the congregation's typical worship services:

> Probably the most significant single worship trend in our denomination is the trend in churches toward alternate worship services that include groups of people that felt excluded before. Sometimes this alternate worship takes place at the same hour as the "regular" worship service, in another part of the building. More often, alternate worship services are held at other times—such as 9:30 Sunday morning.[13]

Indeed, although these new services provided an opportunity for congregations to break into homogeneous affinity groups, Church Growth consultants like Schaller, Miller, and Hunter did not at first imagine them as aligning with contemporary styles. How, then, did we arrive at the scenario imagined in our opening paragraph, wherein almost all newly

---

10. Schaller, *Choices for Churches*, 70.

11. Schaller, *44 Steps up off the Plateau*, 88. For more details on his ideas for Sunday morning programming, see also Schaller, *44 Ways to Expand the Ministry of Your Church*.

12. Miller, *Vital Congregation*, 38.

13. Hunter, *Finding the Way Forward*, 32–33.

created "second" services in mainline congregations were contemporary services? It happened quickly, with significant changes happening in the early 1990s. By the time George Hunter wrote his 1996 book, *Church for the Unchurched*, all ten of the listed exemplary congregations, several of which were a part of mainline denominations, were using contemporary styles in at least some of their weekend services.[14] Church Growth principles may have urged churches to offer more worship options, but it was the influence of one particular congregation in the late 1980s and early 1990s, with its focus on the unchurched, that created the Contemporary service phenomenon. Willow Creek Community Church, by using contemporary styles to attract newcomers, cemented the place of Contemporary Praise & Worship in the mainline second service. In addition to the tens of thousands of visitors who checked out Willow Creek in the 1990s, there were also thousands of pastors and church leaders who traveled there, seeking to imitate this strategy of combining homogeneous church growth with Contemporary Praise & Worship.

## Willow Creek: Homogenous Units Meet Contemporary Praise & Worship

By the early 1990s Willow Creek Community Church (WCCC), under the leadership of pastor Bill Hybels, had become the primary place where mainline church leaders saw Contemporary Praise & Worship used in the application of the Homogenous Unit Principle. Begun in the 1970s as an outgrowth of the youth ministry of a Chicago-area congregation, Willow Creek was founded for middle-class suburbanites who did not attend church, building their congregation around the needs of these prospective attendees. In 1975, prior to the launch of the congregation, leaders conducted a survey of neighborhood residents by asking why they did not already attend church. The number one response given was that churches are always asking for money. Coming closely behind were additional critiques such as "I am unable to relate to the music" and "I am unable to relate to the message." All of the programming of Willow Creek's worship life was a response to these negative results.

Focusing tightly on the desires expressed in these surveys, Willow Creek's leaders created an imaginary profile of the typical person they wanted to be drawn to their new congregation. "Unchurched Harry" was the name given to this composite character, imagined as a college-educated professional between the ages of twenty-five and forty-five, who

---

14. Hunter, *Church for the Unchurched*.

was "the person . . . in his family room—feet upon the footstool, reading the paper, watching TV, a can of beer in hand."[15] Nancy Beach, Willow Creek's Program Director in the 1980s and early 1990s, explained that: "[Harry] is a person who lives out here in the suburbs . . . He probably has some church experience but most likely he left it for various reasons: it became irrelevant, he became too busy and decided it wasn't important to his life."[16] Willow Creek created an entire service for the unchurched pre-Christian Harry. This "seeker service" was meant to lower the cultural barriers to church attendance by making Sunday morning as much as possible like the world that Harry inhabited throughout the week. For example, the sanctuary (called an auditorium) contained no overt Christian symbols, celebrations of sacraments were not offered to seekers, and sermons were introduced with dramas.[17] Bill Hybels described the church as completely focused on those who were not yet believers:

> What does the seeker walk into in 99 out of 100 churches across this land? He walks into a service that has been designed from stem to stern to the already convinced. It's a worship service. It's designed all the way through for someone who has a long background in church involvement, who understands the lingo, who has all the prerequisite knowledge, the whole thing is designed for the already convinced.[18]

Amid all the contextualized aspects of the seeker service, visitors heard music that was not commonly played in mainline churches at that time: a pop-rock style that was close to what Harry listened to on his favorite top-forty radio station. A writer for *The Christian Century*, reporting on a WCCC seeker service in 1991, described how the seeker service began with an easy-listening ensemble resembling "something between a band and an orchestra" that played "lively, upbeat music that gradually, not abruptly, engages the audience."[19]

Throughout the 1980s and 1990s Willow Creek maintained a schedule of two different kinds of services each week: the (multiple) weekend seeker services for Unchurched Harry, in addition to two midweek New Community services (on Wednesday and Thursday evenings) for committed church members. By the year 1991, WCCC hosted more than 15,000 participants

---

15. Bill Hybels, quoted in Pritchard, "Strategy of Willow Creek," 11.

16. Quoted in Pritchard, "Strategy of Willow Creek," 230.

17. For more on Willow Creek and the seeker service as a new form of liturgy, see Ruth, "Lex Agendi, Lex Orandi," 386–405.

18. Pritchard, "Strategy of Willow Creek," 217–18.

19. Robinson, "Learning from Willow Creek Church," 68.

across these services each week, giving it the largest weekly worship attendance in North America. Mainline (and other) pastors flocked to Willow Creek during the 1990s to witness the seeker services firsthand, impressed with the congregation's success in attracting upwardly-mobile unchurched suburbanites. It would be difficult to overestimate the impact that Willow Creek had on churches that were looking to reverse the decline in attendance and membership. Indeed, even *The Christian Century* took note, featuring the church in a 1991 article.[20]

To meet the growing demand of pastors who were coming to the church for in person visits, Pastor Bill Hybels developed a series of conferences and seminars about the Willow Creek approach, designed for inquiring pastors and worship leaders. This teaching ministry became so important that the Willow Creek Association (WCA) was formed in 1991 to focus on producing and delivering leadership content to thousands of church leaders. The WCA provided conferences, books, video and audio tape series, and newsletters to a wide spectrum of churches, regardless of denominational affiliation. WCA grew throughout that decade to become a parachurch umbrella organization, one that *Christianity Today* called a "nondenominational denomination."[21] Its reach was so widespread that roughly six thousand churches worldwide were enrolled as members of the association by 2001.

But if mainline pastors liked what they saw and heard at Willow Creek, they found it difficult to emulate back home. The seeker services used a style of music that few mainline churches could handle. Not only did Willow employ top-level professionals from the Chicago area, but many of the songs were not truly songs for worship. In its commitment to keep seeker services welcoming to the unchurched, Willow Creek refused to use songs that would cause discomfort to a spiritual seeker. Worship leaders at WCCC were therefore tasked with presenting simple songs with innocuous lyrical content that avoided offensive (think sacrificial atonement) or deeply theological language (such as trinitarian formulas). Nancy Beach admitted that locating songs with all these qualities was difficult, resulting in a short repertoire.[22] As a result, most of the music in a seeker service was designed to be listened to, not sung, by the congregation. Visiting pastors, by and large, did not come home from Willow Creek with a catalog of songs that they could use in their own mainline worship services.

20. Robinson, "Learning from Willow Creek Church," 68.
21. Hamilton, "Willow Creek's Place in History," 62–68.
22. Beach stated, "We're putting words in the mouths, in a sense, of people who don't believe whatever those words are. And so our list of songs that we comfortable with is so short." Pritchard, "Strategy of Willow Creek," 297.

Indeed, Willow Creek was not, and truly never has been, a distribution hub for worship materials. In fact, promoting a particular kind of music or worship style was not Willow Creek's primary aim. They were instead more interested in teaching the principles of contextualization, urging church leaders to find ways to reach those who were not coming to church. Visiting mainline pastors did not receive a package of how-to materials on Contemporary Praise & Worship. Rather, they took home lessons and principles about how to find a homogenous group of people in their respective communities; drama, music, and the arts were merely means for drawing them in. Figuring out how to make that all work in a different situation would ultimately be quite difficult, with very few congregations able to imitate Willow Creek. Not only was the production quality out of reach, the entire structure of services focused solely on seekers was unsustainable for mainline congregations.

## Seeker Services: An Unsustainable Model for Mainline Churches

Most other congregations, even large ones located in growing suburban areas, found it impossible to imitate Willow Creek's distinction between seeker services and worship services for believers. In some cases this distinction was counter to a congregation's commitment to worship for worship's sake. For instance, Community Church of Joy (CCJ), an Evangelical Lutheran Church of America (ELCA) congregation in Phoenix, Arizona, decided that a seeker service—that is, one with goals not primarily centered around worship—would not fit as part of its weekly programming. This was not a lack of concern for the unchurched. Indeed, CCJ held many of the same commitments as Willow Creek, echoing the same Church Growth admonishments to lower cultural barriers to the gospel.[23] The church even credited much of its innovative strategies to Willow Creek; Pastor Walt Kallestad had a transformational experience in the late 1980s at a pastor's conference led by Rick Warren and Bill Hybels, crediting that moment with the advent of his vision for "entertainment evangelism."[24] Timothy Wright, an associate pastor at CCJ, similarly urged other congregations to communicate in culturally-appropriate ways: "Attracting and reaching the unchurched means a thorough

---

23. Kallestad asserted, "If secular people do not understand the jargon, relate to the music, know when to stand up or sit down, identify with the people, or feel comfortable in the facility, they infer that Christianity and the Christian God are not for people like them." Kallestad, *Entertainment Evangelism*, 69.

24. Kallestad, "'Showtime!' No More," 39–43.

and sympathetic understanding of their unique values and motivations. It means seeing life and church through their eyes. It means designing worship services that correspond to their needs and values."[25]

Community Church of Joy did not, however, fully adopt the Willow Creek model of seeker services. That is, they did not make a clean distinction between worship services for Christians and other services for the unchurched. Rather, their contemporary services were presented as options for *worship* designed for Christians and seekers alike. Some of these were designed with lower levels of congregational participation, with the realization that unchurched people might not know all the expectations of a Lutheran worship service.[26] However, even these "low barrier" services were still presented as a means for people to meet with God. That is, according to the leaders at CCJ, a contemporary style of worship was not primarily a means for attracting people to a worship service; it was in fact a way for them to truly worship. Although the order of the service might look like a Willow Creek seeker service—intro music followed by an easy-listening pop instrumental, a contemporary chorus, a drama that supported the Scripture reading and a sermon—CCJ was offering a worship service.[27] These sentiments about the power of music—not to attract based on showmanship, but as a signifier of God's presence—resonated with the hopes for divine intimacy that were shared by adopters and early pioneers of the praise and worship movement, where good music was a byproduct of authentic encounter with the divine.[28]

Other churches set aside the seeker service because their members were not committed to maintaining two separate services. Granger Community Church, a United Methodist Church in South Bend, Indiana, attended Willow Creek seminars and training events, and the congregation was at one time a member of the Willow Creek Association. As part of its church growth strategy, Granger sought to lower barriers to the unchurched by appropriating accessible music and using non-churchy language. Following the WCCC model, they set up weekend services for seekers and midweek services for committed believers and church members. Like WCCC, they hoped to convince seekers to become Christian disciples, eventually

---

25. Wright, *Community of Joy*, 17.

26. Kallestad, *Entertainment Evangelism*, 72.

27. "Irreligious people visit churches in the hope of encountering God personally. They not only want to know *about* God; they want to *know* God." Wright, *Community of Joy*, 21.

28. If Wright's words seem more Pentecostal than Lutheran, then we should not be surprised that Community Church of Joy, after leaving the ELCA in 2012, later became a campus of Dream City Church, an Assemblies of God megachurch in Phoenix.

involving them in the midweek services that included worship, sacraments, and leadership training. However, Granger found that this distinction did not work for them like it did for Willow Creek. By the mid-1990s Granger stopped holding two different kinds of services, conceding that their members were coming to church only once a week. They expected to worship on Sunday, and they did not want to come back to church on a different night of the week for a believer's service.[29] While Granger retained some of the visitor-friendly forms, including Contemporary Praise & Worship music, the weekend services were no longer set up to accommodate only a distinct set of unchurched people.

## The Commitment to Apostolic Leadership: The Ongoing Tie to Contemporary Praise & Worship

Mainline pastors who sought to reverse decades of decline were attracted by the seeker-sensitive movement pioneered at Willow Creek. There they found Contemporary Praise & Worship used as a tool to attract a new demographic of people to church. Instead of learning how to reproduce this style of worship, however, they gained a new way to think about how to communicate their own pastoral vision to reach the congregation's mission. When these pastors returned home from a Willow Creek site visit or conference, they wanted to do more than simply tweak a few components of the worship service—they felt compelled to convince their congregations that a new kind of ministry was required. Indeed, the call to find unchurched groups of people required a new kind of leadership, one that had not before been necessary for the typical mainline parish in the mid-twentieth century. Inspired by the visionary leadership modelled and taught by Bill Hybels, a new generation of pastors began to rethink the role of a pastor as the congregation's visionary leader. Adding a new contemporary service on Sunday morning became an important display of that leadership, not just for how it might attract a new group of people, but to signal a bold new style of being the church. A host of mainline Protestant pastors were hungry for this convergence. They wanted the increased numbers that Contemporary Praise & Worship might bring, but they also used the adoption of non-traditional worship styles to show what kind of leader they were becoming.

One of the primary messages that some pastors wanted to communicate was their disdain for denominational leadership structures, particularly the bureaucracy that they saw as an impediment to change. For some mainline pastors, especially those who sought to operate as bold and original

---

29. Ruth, "Lex Agendi, Lex Orandi," 398.

leaders, the very denomination they were ordained into was their primary opponent. For many, boundedness to tradition could only restrain and mute the passion and charisma of a pastor.[30] Along this line Andy Langford and Will Willimon wrote in 1996 *A New Connection: Reforming the United Methodist Church* as a call to widespread change in their own denomination. Many of their recommendations called for strengthening the role of pastor as the primary leader and freeing him or her from restraints that prevent the setting, communicating, and administering of a coherent vision. They even borrowed language from corporate leadership resources to suggest changes to the denomination's Book of Discipline: "the pastor shall be the *chief administrative officer* of the local church."[31]

Pastors who were dissatisfied with congregational decline and frustrated with denominational hindrances found encouragement from leaders in the popular branch of the Church Growth movement. C. Peter Wagner, who we already saw as a pivotal figure in popularizing Church Growth principles, was also a pioneering figure in a movement known as the New Apostolic Reformation. Under the umbrella of this movement, Wagner taught a form of church leadership that encouraged pastors to be visionary leaders and to refuse to be hampered by denominational hierarchies and structures. Wagner urged pastors to set a new course and communicate the need for radical changes in their congregations: "Vital Sign Number One of a healthy, growing church is a pastor who is a possibility thinker and whose dynamic leadership has been used to catalyze the entire church into action for growth."[32] These calls for a new class of entrepreneurial leaders came packaged with rhetoric that described the pastor's work as "apostolic"—that is, as centered in an individual leader. Wagner noted that emerging trends in church leadership in the 1990s, as opposed to earlier eras in the church, were centered in the gifts and skills of an individual pastor:

> Here is the main difference: *The amount of spiritual authority delegated by the Holy Spirit to individuals.* I have attempted to use each word in that statement advisedly. We are seeing a transition from bureaucratic authority to personal authority, from

---

30. Robert H. Schuller, pastor of the Crystal Cathedral, marveled at what his protégé Bill Hybels was able to do at Willow Creek: "He didn't belong to a denomination that says that you have to follow a certain church order on Sunday morning. You have to open with a hymn, you have to have the Scripture reading, you have to have a congregational prayer, you have to serve communion once in a while. The Dutch Reformed in my denomination didn't allow me to just break loose and do anything I wanted to do." Pritchard, "Strategy of Willow Creek," 205.

31. Langford and Willimon, *New Connection*, 42. Emphasis mine.

32. Wagner, *Your Church Can Grow*, 57.

legal structure to relational structure, from control to coordination and from rational leadership to charismatic leadership.[33]

An apostolic leader was necessarily one who would not be slowed down by denominational bureaucrats. The appropriation of the title apostle corresponded with a freedom from organizational strictures, an independence that could be demonstrated by one's freedom to stray from the denomination's prescribed worship resources.

In the late twentieth century new nondenominational ministries were offering a range of resources to congregations—from mission opportunities to theological training—that were superior to what the denominations could provide. Willimon and Langford noted that many United Methodist congregations were finding resources outside of the church's official channels, including worship materials.[34] These outside music options were proliferating, such that ministries like Maranatha! Music were making the United Methodist Hymnal and other denominational music supplements less relevant.[35] By finding worship resources outside of the denomination, pastors were able to differentiate themselves from organizations that many of them viewed as too theologically liberal, too focused on internal hierarchies, and largely ineffective in reaching new groups of people. Contemporary Praise & Worship was increasingly seen as a way for apostolic pastors—that is, those with dynamic, visionary leadership skills—to exercise personal authority over their congregations. They did this by pioneering new services that were in a style unlike what previous generations had experienced.

A key example of this convergence of worship and leadership styles in a mainline congregation was Mike Slaughter, pastor of Ginghamsburg United Methodist Church in Tipp City, Ohio. Ginghamsburg had grown from less than one hundred to 2,100 weekend worshipers between the late 1970s and the early 1990s, and pastors who sought to grow their own small-membership congregations hoped that Slaughter's advice would give them the key for overcoming decline. Slaughter's approach combined leadership principles and worship revitalization as necessary ingredients for a revitalized church so that "the liturgical principle" and "the leadership principle" were two of six components in his "Renewal Theology." Like Hybels and Wagner before

---

33. Wagner, *New Apostolic Churches*, 19–20. Emphasis original.

34. Langford and Willimon, *New Connection*, 29.

35. This is similar to the movement that Robb Redman had seen happening for at least twenty years prior, writing that in the 1970s many Presbyterians were setting aside their own denominational hymnal—*The Worshipbook* from 1972—in favor of an independent commercially produced hymnbook, *Hymns for the Family of God*. Redman, *Great Worship Awakening*, 49.

him, Slaughter located the vitality of an organization on its singular leader's ability to set and cast a clear vision: "Leaders are the people who have seen burning bushes. They have heard God's voice. They have a very clear picture in their minds of what God wants them to accomplish . . . The leader is able to articulate clearly the 'why' and 'where,' and speaks with the authority of God."[36] By his definition, an effective leader is one who leads a congregation to something new, such as a new way of worshiping.

Throughout the 1990s a combination of apostolic and visionary leadership was increasingly promoted in how-to books for those hoping to start new contemporary services. Tim and Kathy Carson's (Disciples of Christ) 1997 book *So You're Thinking about Contemporary Worship* was written for leaders who have already made up their minds about using Contemporary Praise & Worship styles.[37] The audience for the book were not those still considering the pros and cons of adding a new format; there was little in the way of theological or sociological rationale for changing worship styles. Rather, the authors' purpose was to instruct pastors how to lead a congregation to accept a new service that he or she had already decided was necessary. Similarly, *Come Celebrate: A Guide for Planning Contemporary Worship*, by (United Methodists) Cathy Townley and Mike Graham was not a manual for guiding a team in mutual discernment about possibly adding a contemporary option. The practice of "listening" was only recommended as a means for building buy-in, a way to convince the laity that they are being heard, thereby allowing the pastor to do what he or she already envisioned. Townley and Graham instructed leaders that God moves through them and that offering a new service of Contemporary Worship was about confronting parishioners who do not want to change by "dealing with sameness and stagnation"[38] and "keeping the service evolving."[39] According to these books, visionary leaders know that adding a contemporary service is the right move, and they must overcome the barriers—within the congregation and within the wider denomination—that seek to prevent it.

## Conclusion: Stuck between Multiple Worlds?

We have seen that mainline churches that launched contemporary services since the 1990s have done so for a variety of reasons. Unfortunately, the convergence of factors covered here has led to confusion in many

36. Slaughter, *Spiritual Entrepreneurs*, 104.
37. Carson and Carson, *Thinking about Contemporary Worship*.
38. Townley and Graham, *Come Celebrate*, 33.
39. Townley and Graham, *Come Celebrate*, 161.

congregations where new services were started. For instance, the desire to add a second service may have provided opportunities for new people to attend, but there was often a lack of clarity about who should be invited. Should it be non-religious seekers or Christians who are looking for a different style of music? Should these new attendees be a different set of people than the wider congregation, segregated out from the primary service according to the Homogeneous Unit Principle, or should all the services offered by the congregation seek to draw from the same demographic? Some congregations formed concise answers to these questions, but many did not. As a result, the original purpose for the second service has often been forgotten, leaving a blend of traditional and contemporary styles that hopes to cater to as many people as possible. During this same time, many non-denominational congregations have streamlined their weekend options, offering multiple services all in the same contemporary style. These (usually) bigger churches—frequently independent and conservative—have committed to a consistent format that boasts high production values, making it difficult for mainline churches to compete for worshipers who desire Contemporary Praise & Worship.

Meanwhile, the issue of leadership still dogs mainline pastors who lead multiple services. Many of the exemplary leaders who combined visionary leadership with new worship styles—e.g., Bill Hybels, Rick Warren, Mike Slaughter—have enjoyed decades-long tenures in their respective congregations. This longevity is not the norm for most mainline churches, where seven years is still considered a long stay. Many congregations are on their fourth or fifth pastor since implementing a secondary contemporary service in the 1990s or 2000s, and current successors are left maintaining a service whose origins they do not fully understand.

In addition, there is an ongoing fundamental theological misunderstanding by which mainline churches miss the point of the Contemporary Praise & Worship movement. In the formative decades of the 1970s and 1980s, contemporary services initially grew in charismatic and pentecostal congregations, where popular music forms accompanied a freedom that was manifested in the charismata of the Holy Spirit. The music, like the spiritual phenomena it supplemented, was meant to flow in a way that mimicked and facilitated the breath of the Holy Spirit on and among the people. Matt Sigler has written that most mainline congregations have failed to fully implement Contemporary Praise & Worship for a simple reason: they are not charismatic.[40] The underlying assumptions of what a worship service should do—that is, bring the worshipers into a heightened sense of

---

40. Sigler, "Misplacing Charisma."

God's presence—is lost on most mainliners. This means that the idea of a flow in which songs move seamlessly from one to another without breaks is rarely implemented in a mainline contemporary service. Although these services use Contemporary Praise & Worship songs, they are often not sung or played continuously and are instead interrupted by prayers, offerings, Scripture readings, and announcements. These secondary services might have the window dressing of Contemporary Praise & Worship, but they are still captive to a traditional model in which a worship service is understood to accomplish a certain set of activities.

Mainline churches also struggle with implementing pure contemporary styles for another, very practical reason: the vast majority of them meet in buildings that were constructed long before the 1990s. Accommodating Contemporary Praise & Worship requires alteration to most traditional worship spaces, either by inserting a band into a sanctuary, modifying an existing room, or, more commonly, finding a "blurry midpoint" between those two options.[41] Many churches that launched a new service have ended up with a "blended" model due to the accommodated space that they are given. Mainline congregations who adopted contemporary styles are now competing in a saturated cultural space where newer churches now dominate, ones with buildings designed for a Contemporary Praise & Worship format. As a result, mainline secondary contemporary services, like the buildings that host them, tend to be a hybrid—neither fully contemporary nor fully rooted in a Methodist, Presbyterian, or Lutheran tradition.

We have seen that, although mainline churches did not use Contemporary Praise & Worship as their native language, they nonetheless found several reasons to incorporate this style into new services in the 1990s. For one, adding additional services was part of the strategy recommended by Church Growth consultants for at least a decade prior. Furthermore, Willow Creek Community Church provided a tangible application of the Homogenous Unit Principle to worship services, eager to show pastors around the country how to reach the unchurched in innovative ways. Underlying these developments was the ongoing anxiety about the decline of church attendance and membership, which many pastors increasingly blamed on the denominations themselves. New forms of apostolic leadership presented Contemporary Praise & Worship as a means for overcoming bureaucratic barriers that stunted visionary pastors, thus allowing the second service to be a way of signaling one's visionary and antiauthoritarian credentials. What has been largely lost in this convergence is a coherent understanding

---

41. Lim and Ruth, *Lovin' on Jesus*, 42.

of the purpose of this new form of worship, particularly when it comes to answering the question: "Who is this service for?"

## Bibliography

Carson, Timothy, and Kathy Carson. *So You're Thinking about Contemporary Worship*. St. Louis: Chalice, 1997.
Dudley, Roger. "How Churches Grow." *Ministry: International Journal for Pastors* (Jul 1981). https://www.ministrymagazine.org/archive/1981/07/how-churches-grow.
Hamilton, Michael S. "Willow Creek's Place in History." *Christianity Today* 44 (2000) 62–68.
Hunter, George G. *Church for the Unchurched*. Nashville: Abingdon, 1996.
———. *Finding the Way Forward*. Nashville: Discipleship Resources, 1980.
Kallestad, Walt. *Entertainment Evangelism: Taking the Church Public*. Nashville: Abingdon, 1996.
———. "'Showtime!' No More: Could Our Church Shift from Performance to Mission?" *Leadership* 29 (2008) 39–43.
Kelley, Dean M. *Why Conservative Churches Are Growing: A Study in Sociology of Religion*. New York: Harper & Row, 1972.
Langford, Andy, and William H. Willimon. *A New Connection: Reforming the United Methodist Church*. Nashville: Abingdon, 1996.
Lim, Swee Hong, and Lester Ruth. *Lovin' on Jesus: A Concise History of Contemporary Worship*. Nashville: Abingdon, 2017.
"Mainline Protestant Ranks Continue Decline of the '60s." *Los Angeles Times*. Sept 15, 1990. https://www.latimes.com/archives/la-xpm-1990-09-15-ca-286-story.html.
McGavran, Donald. *Understanding Church Growth*. Edited by C. Peter Wagner. 3rd ed. Grand Rapids: Eerdmans, 1990.
McIntosh, Gary, ed. *Evaluating the Church Growth Movement: 5 Views*. Grand Rapids: Zondervan, 2004.
Miller, Herb. *The Vital Congregation*. Nashville: Abingdon, 1990.
Pritchard, Gregory Allen. "The Strategy of Willow Creek Community Church: A Study in the Sociology of Religion." PhD diss., Northwestern University, 1994.
Redman, Robb. *The Great Worship Awakening: Singing a New Song in the Postmodern Church*. San Francisco: Jossey-Bass, 2002.
Robinson, Anthony B. "Learning from Willow Creek Church." *Christian Century* 108 (1991) 68–70.
Ruth, Lester. "Lex Agendi, Lex Orandi: Toward an Understanding of Seeker Services as a New Kind of Liturgy." *Worship* 70 (1996) 386–405.
———. "A Theological Critique of Church Growth Worship." In *The Ministries of Christian Worship*, edited by Robert E. Webber, 440–46. Complete Library of Christian Worship 7. Nashville: Star Song, 1994.
Schaller, Lyle E. *44 Steps up off the Plateau*. Nashville: Abingdon, 1993.
———. *44 Ways to Expand the Teaching Ministry of Your Church*. Nashville: Abingdon, 1992.
———. *Choices for Churches*. Nashville: Abingdon, 1990.
———. *Growing Plans: Strategies to Increase Your Church's Membership*. Nashville: Abingdon, 1984.

Sigler, Matthew. "Misplacing Charisma: Where Contemporary Worship Lost Its Way." https://www.seedbed.com/misplacing-charisma-contemporary-worship-lost-way/.

Slaughter, Michael. *Spiritual Entrepreneurs: Six Principles for Risking Renewal.* Nashville: Abingdon, 1995.

Townley, Cathy, and Mike Graham. *Come Celebrate! A Guide for Planning Contemporary Worship.* Nashville: Abingdon, 1995.

Wagner, C. Peter, ed. *The New Apostolic Churches.* Ventura, CA: Regal, 1998.

———. *Your Church Can Grow: Seven Vital Signs of a Healthy Church.* Reprint. Eugene, OR: Wipf & Stock, 1998.

Wright, Timothy. *A Community of Joy: How to Create Contemporary Worship.* Edited by Herb Miller. Nashville: Abingdon, 1994.

# 4

## Sounding God's Enthronement in Worship

*The Early History and Theology of Integrity's Hosanna! Music*

— Adam Perez —

On July 10, 1985, *New Wine* magazine announced to its sixty thousand-member mailing list that they were launching a new tape ministry for praise and worship music. By their third release—just six months after their initial advertisement—thirty-six thousand subscribers had signed up for the bi-monthly praise worship tape subscription program. By year three, using only direct-to-consumer marketing, each album was selling one hundred fifty thousand units. This tape series that would become known as Integrity's Hosanna! Music (hereafter IHM) eventually peaked in sales between two hundred twenty-five thousand to two hundred fifty thousand units of everything produced[1]—and all of this outside of the traditional marketing and distributing networks of the US Christian music industry. By the time Integrity released Hillsong worship leader Darlene Zschech's *Shout to the Lord* album in 1996 (the label's first worship album with a female worship leader), it was more than clear that IHM had become a major player in the Christian music industry.

Yet despite their meteoric rise and the important role that IHM has played in the spread of praise and worship music, academic scholarship has largely overlooked its history. Up to this point, the history of IHM has either been treated as incidental to the development of the worship music industry in general, subsumed into the 1960s Jesus People narrative, or overlooked entirely. Scholars have explored Calvary Chapel's Maranatha! Music, the worship theology of the Vineyard movement, and some of its music.

1. Gustafson, Interview.

However, IHM's contribution to the transformation of worship practices over the last half century has not yet been treated at length in musicological, liturgical, or theological scholarship. As a result of this oversight, the history of Contemporary Praise & Worship (hereafter CPW) has suffered from a number of deficiencies. First, the history has not adequately accounted for the way in which pentecostal and neo-charismatic theological streams have influenced CPW. Second, because the history of CPW has been filtered through the 1960s, the mid-1980s have not been treated as a development worth consideration but rather as a decline that was overcome in the return to the rock-inflected "modern worship" of the late 1990s. Finally, insofar as the history of the Christian music industry is integral to the spread of praise and worship music, the particular contributions of IHM must be explored in order to tell a more coherent and complete history of CPW as a phenomenon. In this paper, I largely take for granted *that* IHM is significant in the history of CPW and focus on *what* exactly their contribution to the history entails. I begin by reviewing the way the secondary literature has previously told the history of Christian music (esp. "Praise and Worship")[2] in the second half of the twentieth century, with special attention to IHM's near absence in the historical record. Next, I use interviews with early IHM leaders alongside articles from *New Wine* magazine to reconstruct the theological, ecclesial, and interpersonal contexts that birthed IHM, paying special attention to the impact of evangelist Terry Law as well as the International Worship Symposium on IHM. Third, with this history and context established, I turn to an analysis of the first IHM album, *Behold His Majesty*. I argue that within the field of CPW, this album is an archetype for how the worship theology prevalent in its originating context—praise and worship understood as a process of enthroning God upon musical praise—has been imprinted sonically on this musical artifact and, by extension, the body of recordings produced by IHM. Furthermore, I suggest that within the Christian worship music industry, this theology of worship is particular to the albums produced and distributed by IHM.

---

2. Here I am using the term "Praise and Worship" in a technical sense to circumscribe the repertory coming from pentecostal contexts and used in the liturgical practice of Praise and Worship. I am intentionally trying to distinguish this repertory from the more generic terms "contemporary worship music" or "contemporary Christian music" which are used in other musicological and sociological scholarship.

## IHM in the History of Contemporary Praise & Worship: Overshadowed and Understated

A variety of scholarly fields have made contributions to the emerging study of CPW in the last forty years, with a significant concentration in the last decade.[3] For a number of reasons, IHM has not garnered much scholarly attention: IHM's ecclesial context is somewhat veiled as a private company,[4] the label did not publish music easily categorized under the genre of "rock"[5] nor did IHM directly develop out of the Jesus People movement,[6] most current scholarship employs ethnographic rather than historical methods,[7] and most current scholarship has simply focused on other kinds or periods of development.[8]

Of the possible reasons why current scholarship has not focused on IHM, two stand out especially. First, in historical research on CPW, scholars have paid special attention to the Jesus People and their role in mainstreaming Christian folk and rock music in worship contexts since the 1960s. This avenue of research has, therefore, appropriately attended to the history of another important Christian music company: Maranatha! Music and its background in the Calvary Chapel network of churches. Nevertheless, scholars in this vein each do their own work to outline and defend the Jesus People movement as central to the development of "Praise and Worship" or "Contemporary Worship." The narrative common to these sources is a focus on the development of Maranatha!, a largely linear, historical development from the late 1960s to today, and a geographic dissemination of resources from Southern California

---

3. For a fuller—though less recent—account of the state of the question on the writing of the history of Contemporary Praise & Worship in general, see Ruth, "Divine, Human, Devilish?" 303–7.

4. Consider, for example, Miller, *Reinventing American Protestantism*, a sociological study focusing on Calvary Chapel, Vineyard, and Hope Chapel as ecclesial institutions. See also the focus on the emergence of para-church organizations in Bergler, *Juvenilization of American Christianity*.

5. See Howard and Streck, *Apostles of Rock*; Reagan, "A Beautiful Noise"; Nekola, "Between This World and the Next"; and Mall, "'The Stars Are Underground.'"

6. See, especially, Fromm, "Textual Communities and New Song in the Multimedia Age," a very popular citation utilized by many of the above-mentioned ethno/musicological dissertations. See also Peacock, *At the Crossroads*, and Thompson, *Raised by Wolves*.

7. Justice, "Sonic Change, Social Change, Sacred Change," which focused on one Presbyterian congregation, and Busman, "(Re)sounding Passion," which studied Passion conferences.

8. Cusic, *Encyclopedia of Contemporary Christian Music* (focused on the popular recording industry and radio) and Evans, *Open Up the Doors* (mainly interested in IHM only for its distribution of Hillsong albums in the mid-1990s).

(and later, Nashville) to the rest of the United States and abroad. The second, more recent reason is that scholars have used ethnographic studies to explore the important impact of worship conferences and concerts on contemporary worshipers and concertgoers. Given that methodological boundary, these sources do not tend to pay extended attention to the history of the musical practices of CPW where we might expect to find an account of the origins of IHM and how it has shaped later worship practices.

## IHM in Recent Scholarship

There have, however, been some important (though understated) contributions to understanding the origins and influence of IHM on CPW. In the field of ethnomusicology, Monique Ingalls's dissertation provides the most theologically sensitive description of Contemporary Praise & Worship and does so by utilizing an interview with Gerrit Gustafson (an early leader at IHM) and a volume by Judson Cornwall.[9]

The two most helpful contributions for understanding the history and significance of IHM come from volumes more ostensibly related to recent changes in worship including, but not limited to, music. Lester Ruth and Lim Swee Hong's *Lovin' on Jesus*[10] pays special attention to musical style while Robb Redman's *The Great Worship Awakening* provides a general history of Christian music and industry development. In *Lovin' on Jesus*, Lim and Ruth also analyze the overall organizational structure of music on IHM's first release, *Behold His Majesty*.[11] Similar to (and following from) the musicologists mentioned above, Lim and Ruth summarize that they "have situated the contemporary worship song genre in the context of the 1960s."[12]

In his book *The Great Worship Awakening*, insider Robb Redman—teacher and worship leader himself—situates the history of IHM within the history of the "big four" music companies: Maranatha!, Mercy (affiliated with the Vineyard association of churches), IHM, and EMI Christian Music Group/WorshipTogether. For Redman, the "big four" emerge out of the context of earlier commercial music recording and publishing, and Redman

---

9. Ingalls, "Awesome in This Place," especially 84–100. Ingalls's goal was primarily to distinguish between the stylistic characteristics that separate the genres of CCM and CWM. In doing so, she gestures toward a theology of worship—the manifest presence of God and Psalm 22:3—that she briefly compares to Wimber's concept of divine visitation at the end of a worship set.

10. Lim and Ruth, *Lovin' on Jesus*.

11. Lim and Ruth, *Lovin' on Jesus*, 59–71, especially 68. Lim used the generic term "album" to denote the recording. The format of the release was actually cassette tape.

12. Lim and Ruth, *Lovin' on Jesus*, 59–60, 71.

describes each in relation to rock music sounds—save for IHM which lacks any musical description.[13] What Redman does say about IHM is filtered through the CCM industry lens, saying that songwriters active among independent pentecostal churches had difficulty getting their songs published and recorded at Maranatha! or Mercy. "To address this problem," says Redman, "a group of pastors met to form a new company, called Integrity Music, in 1987. Collecting songs from around the country and connecting with leading independent songwriters and worship leaders, the company began releasing a steady stream of projects in a variety of musical styles."[14] Redman's summary of this initial process suggests that IHM was a strategic collaboration in response to the Christian music market, a response lacking a theological or ecclesial dimension.

In an attempt to overcome these concerns, I temporarily sideline the above-mentioned, dominant narratives that fold IHM into the history of the Jesus People movement and I also set aside the ethnomusicological and sociological discourse around the mainstreaming of rock music into American Evangelicalism. In their stead, I turn to a number of interviews with key persons involved in the founding of IHM alongside other primary sources. A very different picture emerges from these conversations, especially regarding the central role of previously unidentified influences on the theology of worship that guided the crafting of IHM's early sound and, consequently, what IHM has contributed to the development of CPW at the end of the twentieth century.

## Commercial and Ecclesial Origins

The heart of IHM as an organization sits at the intersection of two important and overlapping contexts: *New Wine* magazine and Covenant Church of Mobile (Alabama).[15] What these two entities share is the large pentecostal base or network that is just one stream within and alongside the broad Charismatic Renewal movement of the second half of the twentieth century. Both pentecostal and ecumenical, these networks—or "fellowships" as they were often called—facilitated the sharing of ideas and practices across the United States, Canada, and around the world. Understanding both that these overlapping and interlaced contexts exist in the backdrop of IHM and the nature

---

13. Redman, *Great Worship Awakening*, 57.

14. Redman, *Great Worship Awakening*, 56–57.

15. This section has been crafted largely from my personal interviews with Michael Coleman, Don Moen, Tom Brooks, Marty Nystrom; an interview by Gerrit Gustafson by Lester Ruth and Lim Swee Hong; and primary materials from *New Wine* magazine (unless otherwise noted).

of their connection are the first steps to understanding the music that would later be produced by IHM. This context—the church, magazine, and broader pentecostal connection—was directly responsible for shaping the persons in leadership at IHM, their emerging theology of worship, and the musical worship practices that would later be imprinted on IHM tapes.

*New Wine* magazine was founded in 1969 as "The Official Publication of the Holy Spirit Teaching Mission" out of Ft. Lauderdale, Florida. *New Wine* magazine described its work as to "promote the unity and maturity of the Church and individual Christians by presenting sound biblical teachings and testimonies from a variety of Christian authors."[16] Among the authors who contributed to the magazine were a variety of preachers and teachers from within the Charismatic Renewal movement alongside the pentecostal ones who would come to dominate the list of contributors by the early 1980s. In the 1978 to 1979 time period, the offices of *New Wine* relocated from Ft. Lauderdale to Mobile—possibly as a result of the controversy surrounding the "Shepherding Movement"[17]—and began a deeper coordination with the administration of the Gulf Coast Fellowship[18] church, both in its pastoral leadership and in its administration.

Gulf Coast Fellowship was a church community that Charles Simpson founded in August 1973. Simpson fostered a connection to the "Shepherding Movement" and its pastors in Ft. Lauderdale through shared pentecostal networks and circuits for teaching, preaching, and publishing. During the 1970s, the church became an important node in a robust network of pentecostal churches. Music was important for the church during this period as it hosted musicians like Pete Sanchez (for whom IHM CEO Michael Coleman produced an album in 1977), who would later feature as worship leader on IHM's sixth album, "I Exalt Thee" (1986). Dave and Dale Garrett, the influential duo from New Zealand who authored the landmark "Scripture in Song" volumes,[19] also came through the church in 1976.[20] As Gulf Coast Fellowship church grew into the early 1980s, it was renamed as Covenant Church of Mobile, purchased a new property, and moved (along with the *New Wine*/

---

16. This purpose statement is found in *New Wine* (July 1985), 2.

17. For more on the Shepherding Movement, including the leadership of the pastors at Covenant Church of Mobile, see Moore, *The Shepherding Movement*.

18. Elsewhere I have published the name of this church as "Gulf Coast Covenant Church," following my interviewees, but have since learned that this attribution was a collapsing of two names—one earlier, one later—from Gulf Coast Fellowship to Covenant Church of Mobile.

19. Cf. Lim and Ruth, *Lovin' on Jesus*, 109–10.

20. Coleman, Interview.

Integrity Communications offices) to a new location in west Mobile.[21] It was during this time that church administrator Michael Coleman, who had a background in music and in finance, shifted in his role from administrating church matters to the administration of the *New Wine* magazine as president and publisher around 1981.

*New Wine* had a pivotal year in 1984, especially for what would become the core leadership staff of IHM. In October of that year, Coleman hired Edward Lindquist full time as marketing director for the magazine. Coleman had met Lindquist the previous year at a church conference hosted by Covenant Church of Mobile. After their initial connection, Coleman hired Lindquist as a consultant to assist with market research on the magazine's readership into the kind of teaching readers desired. What Lindquist and *New Wine* learned was that readers desired more teaching on praise and worship. In response, the magazine provided a three-part series of articles on the topic that ran from August through October 1984. The articles were based on a series of teachings initially offered as a three-day seminar at Covenant Church in the summer of 1984.[22] The leader of that seminar was evangelist Terry Law, who toured with Living Sound, a music group led by Don Moen and deeply connected to Victory Christian Center and to Oral Roberts University in Tulsa, Oklahoma. Through the connection with Law and Moen, Coleman also gained a connection to Tom Brooks, a music producer at Grace World Outreach—a church with a prominent music ministry in St. Louis, Missouri. Law and Moen had encountered Brooks and Grace World Outreach while touring with Living Sound. IHM later developed a standing relationship with Brooks by contracting him for an exclusive recording and production agreement; Brooks arranged, produced, recorded, and regularly played keyboard for the entirety of the Hosanna! Music series (the series ran consistently into the mid-1990s).[23]

By 1985, the year IHM was launched, Coleman—who would later purchase and become CEO of IHM—was serving as publisher of *New Wine* and president of the magazine's parent company, Integrity Communications. Support for the magazine came from a board of directors that was anchored by Charles Simpson (board chairman), Don Basham, Bob Mumford, Derek Prince, and Ern Baxter, all pentecostal teachers whose writing formed a significant bulk of contributions to the magazine. These teachers also had their own syndicated cassette tape ministries that

21. Simpson, "Charles Simpson."
22. "Seeing the Power of Praise and Worship," 8.
23. Brooks, Interview.

functioned through the umbrella organization of the magazine as tape-of-the-month subscription clubs. Beyond the editorial board, the list of *New Wine* contributing editors also include notable pentecostal leaders such as the above-mentioned evangelist Terry Law as well as Pastor Dick Iverson of Bible Temple in Portland, Oregon, among others.[24]

With the new demand stirred up by Law's articles, alongside Lindquist's market research, Coleman sought to provide the *New Wine* audience with recordings of actual worship music. The goal of providing musical materials was not simply so that they could demonstrate or reference the kind of musical worship that was discussed in Law's articles but rather so that people could, through the music, have an experience of the presence of God. Coleman and Lindquist knew that the market for Christian music at the time was already being met by other music companies like Benson, Word, Maranatha! and Sparrow. But Coleman summarized the distinctive mission and contribution of the Hosanna! Music ministry saying, "I don't want to do music unless it brings people into the presence of God," which was a strategic positioning Coleman felt was *not* being met by those other companies. To fulfill this sense of mission, IHM began to seek out albums that could be (re-)released as part of a subscription based direct-to-consumer club (modeled after the other teaching tapes already offered by *New Wine*). With Coleman's background and experience producing albums from Pete Sanchez and Gerrit Gustafson, he knew that music copyright permissions were difficult to obtain. Rather than license songs to be recorded, Coleman's original goal was to lease the master copy of the original worship tapes that were already recorded and send them out to the Hosanna! music club.[25] The first advertisement for IHM appeared in the July 1985 issue of *New Wine* with a two-page spread describing the personal benefits the tapes promised to yield.[26]

Searching for albums that would fit the bill for the subscription club, Coleman came up with only two. In my interview with Don Moen, he remembers being tapped by Coleman and Lindquist for albums that they might be able to use for IHM but Moen did not have any of his own at the

---

24. *New Wine* (July 1985), 2. Dick Iverson and his church Bible Temple in Portland, Oregon are an important node in the praise and worship network, training many music leaders at the church and Bible College. It is out of this church that Howard Rachinski would eventually establish Christian Copyright Licensing International (CCLI) in 1989. CCLI would become the most important copyright licensing group for praise and worship music and would quickly wield significant influence on the worship music industry. CCLI's top song lists also act to codify the core repertory of praise and worship music since the early 1990s.

25. Coleman, Interview.

26. "*New Wine* Introduces Hosanna!" 6–7.

time. Instead, Moen connected Coleman and Lindquist with Tom Brooks, whose tapes Moen described as fitting the unique niche of being both "very anointed and very professional."[27] One of Brooks's albums would become the first IHM release entitled *Behold His Majesty*. The album featured Ron Tucker (pastor at Grace World Outreach) as worship leader and was recorded and produced by Brooks at Grace World Outreach in St. Louis two years prior (in 1983). What would become the second IHM release was an album titled *Let Praise Arise*. The album featured John Sellers as worship leader, was produced by Don Collins, and was previously released on the Birdwing label of Sparrow Records. Of course, two albums were not enough to support an every-eight-weeks subscription service and so IHM faced a dilemma: they did not have a third album and yet one was slated for release in just a few short months.

To meet the need, Coleman, Lindquist, Brooks, and Gustafson began to solicit songs for new recordings that Tom Brooks would orchestrate, record, and engineer in his St. Louis studio. Early on there were various sources from which the IHM team sourced their songs. Many of the earliest songs recorded on the IHM albums were already circulating in the popular repertory of pentecostal churches, disseminated through church networks and annual conferences like the International Worship Symposium (locations varied year to year) and the Northwest Music Minister's Conference held at Dick Iverson's church, Bible Temple in Portland, Oregon.[28] In my interview with Marty Nystrom, he described IHM's work in this period as "harvesting" songs that were already popular; the church at large had already sorted the proverbial wheat from the chaff and so IHM's work was simply to gather them up and put them onto albums to share back to the church. Other songs were submitted by lay people from all across the country and were considered by the review team regardless of their provenance. Many songs were also sourced from the annual worship albums put out by *Christ for the Nations Institute* (CFNI)—a Bible college in Dallas, Texas through which Marty Nystrom would become connected to IHM as a writer, worship leader, and eventually full-time song development director from 1988 to 1992. Though the worship albums recorded by CFNI were also popular and utilized the format of an uninterrupted musical set, they were not rereleased under the Hosanna! Music label because they lacked the production quality desired by IHM.[29] One example of a song that came through CFNI is Marty Nystrom's song "As the Deer." The song, which had become popular

---

27. Moen, Interview.
28. See above for additional information on Bible Temple and Dick Iverson.
29. Gustafson, Interview; Nystrom, Interview.

in the CFNI community, was recorded on one of their yearly albums, and eventually included on IHM's 1987 *Praise and Honor* tape, with Daniel Gardner as worship leader. In these early years under *New Wine* magazine, many interpersonal connections were made through the church and its broader pentecostal networks that were integral to IHM as it transitioned into becoming an independent company.

## Emerging from under *New Wine*'s Shadow

Around 1986, the primary teachers associated with *New Wine* began to pursue different avenues of ministry and decided to dissolve their formal ties at Covenant Church, along with dissolving their shared leadership of *New Wine* magazine.[30] Initially, the profit from the subscription revenue of these praise tapes, along with the sale of other tape subscription programs, was directed back into supporting the work of the magazine.[31] But, facing financial pressures involving both the magazine and a fractured leadership circle, the magazine eventually published its last issue in December 1986—seventeen issues after the first IHM advertisement—and was liquidated. At the beginning of 1987, Integrity Communications was rebranded under the leadership of board chairman Charles Simpson as Charles Simpson Ministries, and Integrity Music was sold to Coleman as primary owner, with Lindquist as a partner. The opportunity for Coleman to buy the music division was possible because it was the only tape ministry not directly tied to the teaching ministry of one of the leading pastors.[32]

As IHM's recordings had quickly harvested the best and most popular songs already in circulation, Nystrom was brought on to help meet the need for newly composed or commissioned songs. On the same day in 1988, both Don Moen and Marty Nystrom joined the IHM team full-time, Moen as Creative Director and Nystrom in song development. These two new additions thus established the core leadership team at

30. Simpson, "Charles Simpson."

31. Cf. *New Wine* from October 1986. The announcement of the magazine's closure includes a note about the way that the profit of the peripheral ministries of *New Wine* (including IHM) contributed significantly to the financial costs of the magazine but were ultimately unable to continue to make the magazine fiscally viable.

32. Coleman, Interview. Cf. Simpson, "Charles Simpson." The date of IHM's founding has been recorded in other sources as both 1985 and 1987. This confusion is due to the sale to Coleman and incorporation as a private, independent company apart from *New Wine* in January 1987 while, as mentioned above, date of its initial music release in July 1985. The confusion is compounded further because, as I show below, the first two albums released by IHM were previously recorded and published under other labels dating back to 1983.

IHM—alongside Coleman, Lindquist, and Gustafson—with support from approximately sixty staff, many of whom were initially affiliated through Covenant Church of Mobile.[33]

IHM continued as primarily a direct-marketing subscription program that by 1989 also found its way onto the shelves of Christian bookstores with the help of a distribution deal with Sparrow Records.[34] IHM (later Integrity Media) ultimately became one of the two most profitable Christian music companies[35] and introduced many popular songs and worship leaders to audiences around the world (an important history that unfortunately extends beyond the scope of this essay).

## Terry Law's Teaching on Praise and Worship

To this point, I have focused on the history of *New Wine* magazine and of Covenant Church of Mobile as a setting for the interpersonal connections and musical sources at the heart of IHM. Thus I have said little of the content of the theological influences on early IHM aside from generic notes about their connection to networks of pentecostal preachers, teachers, and evangelists. It is impossible to trace every line of theological, spiritual, and practical influence on the founders of IHM because each one exists in overlapping but distinct contexts within de-centralized pentecostal and neo-charismatic movements of the mid-twentieth century. However, two important influences are significant in their connections to the theology and musical worship that nurtured the spiritual lives of the IHM leaders in the early- to mid-1980s: Terry Law and the *International Worship Symposium*.

As mentioned above, Law contributed regularly to *New Wine* magazine and began appearing on the list of its contributing editors a few months before the IHM tapes were announced.[36] More than just a coincidental connection to Law through the context of the magazine, Law's teaching had a direct theological influence on *New Wine*'s readership as well as its leadership. In my interview with Moen, for example, he emphasized that Terry Law's teaching

---

33. Nystrom, Interview.

34. Coleman, Interview; Gustafson, Interview.

35. Coleman, Interview.

36. Terry Law first appears as a contributing editor in the March 1985 issue, the first issue that includes the names of any contributing editors. It is unclear whether this new listing reflected the establishment of a new set of roles within the organizational leadership of the magazine or simply the first time this information was published publically in the magazine. So to say, Law may have served in this capacity prior to March. Law's bibliography is lengthy, including works on biblical theology and worship, including an important 1985 volume, *The Power of Praise and Worship*.

was not only influential on him personally but also critical in the origins and formation of IHM, while Gerrit Gustafson identified Law as one of the persons he initially heard teaching on Psalm 22:3, that God is "enthroned upon the praises of His people," the telltale sign of the influence of a Latter Rain theology of praise and worship.[37] More so, this particular translation of "enthroned"—rather than "dwell" or "inhabitest," as it appears in other contemporaneous translations—already indicates a stream of biblical interpretation that is integral to IHM's music. Thus the influence is direct both on the individuals and, because Gustafson was the worship leader at Covenant Church of Mobile, the worship of that community. For these reasons, it is helpful to summarily explore the content and effects of this particular series of teachings, their theological content, and their connection to broader neo-charismatic and pentecostal worship practices (e.g., the Latter Rain).

After Law's three-day seminar that became a three-part series from August to October 1984, the staff of *New Wine* published a "staff report" in the September issue that described the power and impact of the event:

> It's one thing to read about how praise and worship can put Christians in touch with the supernatural realm. It's quite another to actually see it happen . . . [Law's] message was a prelude to a healing service that followed it. But in that healing service, *instead of laying hands on each person individually*, Law led in a time of praise and worship, during which he asked the Lord to send healing to those in need. Many of the people involved later said that this time of worship was more joyful and more charged with supernatural power than anything they had ever been a part of . . . The entire seminar was a reminder that our praise and worship touch something in the supernatural realm far beyond our understanding—a fact that should encourage us to commit ourselves to praise and worship on a much deeper level than our present involvement. A prophecy during the last session of the seminar challenged the audience not to be afraid to enter this deeper form of worship because *it is actually the gate into the King's throne room*. [emphasis mine]

The article also includes testimonies to the presence of angels that were encountered both visually and aurally as one woman "said that during the singing of praises she had heard angelic voices joining ours as we worshiped together."[38] In this quote we can see at least two very important aspects that

---

37. Gustafson, Interview. For more information on the role of Psalm 22:3 and its connection to Latter Rain pentecostal theology, please see the introduction in this volume.

38. "Seeing the Power of Praise and Worship," 9.

are related to the characteristically pentecostal worship practices. First, the author(s) thought it noteworthy to clarify that spiritual healing was *not* accompanied by the laying on of hands. This is important because the practice of the laying on of hands to accompany healing was, within pentecostal settings, a practice understood to have been "restored" to the church through the Latter Rain Revival (though it had resonances and parallel developments in some other charismatic renewals).[39] The staff report author's note, then, suggests that the community was already influenced in some way by Latter Rain teachings alongside praise and worship and Law was combining them in ways that were new to this particular community. Secondly, the report notes the connection between the practice of praise and worship with the "King's throne room." As we will see, this particular spatial setting for praise and worship is a distinctive aspect in the minds of this community of worshipers and in the music that is produced out of it.

In the same issue first advertising IHM, Terry Law also contributed an article on worship, "Call to Worship: God is Looking for a People to Offer Up the Incense of Praise to His Throne." The title fused together language from a popular worship-related verse in the Gospels regarding worship (John 4:23) with an image of priestly praise as incense, a description adapted from tabernacle worship as described in the Old Testament.[40] The article suggested that the pentecostal and charismatic renewal movement within the Christian church was ushering in a new historical period of revival. Law went on to describe all of Church history as a series of revivals that restored specific truths and practices of Christian worship to the Church. Starting with the Protestant Reformation, Law allegorically mapped these restorations onto the three areas of the Mosaic Tabernacle—outer court, inner court, and holy of holies—and the various pieces of furniture within the tabernacle. Law suggested that the church today was a priestly people standing at the veil of the holy of holies but who "cannot enter His presence without the shed blood of Jesus or the incense of praise."[41] The church, of course, already had the former but required the latter to enter into this final revival. Behind this idea also stood the unspoken presumption that once the Church enters into the holy of holies and experiences God's presence, there they will worship in response to that presence. For Law and other Latter Rain teachers, this final restoration of praise and worship ushers in

39. Faupel, "New Order of the Latter Rain," 247.

40. Law, "Call to Worship," 22–23. Law also concludes the article with a note of acknowledgement to LaMar Boschman's book *The Rebirth of Music*. Notably, Boschman was also involved early on in teaching at the International Worship Symposium and developed his own worship conferences in the mid-1980s.

41. Law, "Call to Worship," 23.

the special period of presence and power of God as King over all the nations and stands as the culmination of all previous restorations. Thus a certain apocalypticism, or end-times imaginary, was tied deeply into the restoration of praise and worship in this community at the time. As we will see, this imaginary was mapped directly onto IHM's musical products.[42]

## The International Worship Symposium

While the theological formation for IHM leaders came from teachers and writings on praise and worship, much of the formation of the musical practices on the albums came from elsewhere. When Don Moen, who was training as classical violinist, dropped out of the music education program at Oral Roberts University in 1971, he was tapped by Terry Law to join the Living Sound music group that accompanied Law's evangelistic tours. For about the next fifteen years, Don toured with Law, eventually becoming the primary music leader in January 1983. In that role Moen would hold one thousand concert/evangelism events per year. During those years, Moen was leading a repertory of music based on *Maranatha!*'s evangelistic songs and music common at youth crusade events like those of Billy Graham (with the music of Ralph Carmichael), along with a later incorporation of the music of Andraé Crouch.

But a radical change occurred in Terry Law's ministry—and consequently in Don Moen's leadership—after the sudden death of Law's wife in 1982. Moen says that Law began looking into praise and worship as a source of his own spiritual and emotional healing—and he found it. After experiencing the power of praise and worship to accomplish the healing Law had been preaching and enacting for decades, he decided to utilize praise and worship in his own evangelistic and healing events. Law instructed Moen to switch all of their music over from a focus on evangelism to a focus on praise and worship. There was one primary challenge: Moen had not himself experienced or encountered the power of praise and worship and the musical practices associated with it. So, in order to learn praise and worship, Law sent Moen to

---

42. While Law was not the only teacher on praise and worship, this exploration has shown some of the particular contours of the theology of praise and worship circulating in this community, both in person and through the magazine. Other teachers who influenced the praise and worship theology of IHM at the time are worth mentioning: Merlin Carothers and Judson Cornwall. In interviews, Coleman described Merlin R. Carother's book *Prison to Praise* as influential on him in the early 1980s while Nystrom described Judson Cornwall's book *Let Us Praise* as influential on him. Cornwall's writings on worship also appeared in *New Wine* magazine as early as 1976 (Cornwall, "Worship," 6–10). Coleman, Interview; Nystrom, Interview.

the 1983 Latter Rain–associated International Worship Symposium[43] gathering in Pasadena, California where both theological and musical teaching on praise and worship were being taught. But because the "weird stuff" associated with music-making at the Symposium "scared" Moen and Law, Law took a didactic approach to explaining the power of praise and worship, eschewed some of the specific embodiment present at the IWS, and transformed his evangelistic ministry into a more "vertical" worship service with healing ministry that followed the message.[44]

By the time Law and Moen visited Tom Brooks at Grace World Outreach Center in St. Louis and Covenant Church of Mobile, Law was preaching that you could be healed when you offer a sacrifice of praise and built a throne for God in your worship.[45] This however, was not where Tom Brooks was introduced initially to a Psalm 22:3 theology of worship and the power of praise and worship. That credit is due to Brooks's own visit to the International Worship Symposium in Pasadena, California (1983) where Jack Hayford was teaching and leading worship, including Hayford's own song "Majesty," which would anchor *Behold His Majesty* as the opening track of the very first IHM tape. Though unbeknownst to one another, all five of the early IHM leaders, Gustafson, Coleman, Brooks, Moen, and Nystrom attended International Worship Symposium regional or national conferences in the early 1980s where they learned a similar style of praise and worship.[46] This theology of praise and worship that was learned at the International Worship Symposium is, I argue, encoded in the music of IHM's first album, *Behold His Majesty*.

Knowing Tom Brooks's centrality in the production of IHM music, it is important to further examine Brooks's work on the first IHM tape. Though the tape was produced before Brooks's formal association with IHM, given the depth of interconnections described above—and the mere fact that it is the *first*—the tape can be understood as an archetype for encoding Latter Rain theology of praise and worship in music and also as a template for later IHM tapes. I turn now to describe the musical and theological content of the

---

43. The International Worship Symposium was a popular worship conference founded by Steve and Barry Griffing and inspired out of the Northwest Ministers Conference at Bible Temple in Portland, Oregon. Originally called the National Music Leadership Conference, the conference was aimed at teaching a Latter Rain pentecostal theology of praise and worship to music ministers. The conference was first held in 1978 and grew in attendance into the late 1980s, drawing thousands of attendees at their national conference annually along with smaller numbers at regional conferences throughout the United States. Cf. Griffing, "Seeing Regional Music Conferences," 1.

44. Moen, Interview.

45. Moen, Interview.

46. Gustafson, Interview.

tape and the practical and theological influences of the International Worship Symposium on the sounds Brooks used to communicate that theology.

## Theology of Worship, Sounded

In order to understand the theological significance of the tape and its theological vision, a brief exposition of its musical content is required. For the sake of brevity in illustrating my point, I will examine just side A of the tape.[47] A timpani roll sets off the (roughly) half a minute orchestral introduction, executed in the manner of a symphonic overture as it unfolds through a variety of moods and colors, marked by moments featuring the brass, string, and woodwind sections. Ron Tucker, senior pastor at Grace World Outreach, leads the singing on *Behold His Majesty*, which opens with an orchestral arrangement of Jack Hayford's "Majesty," replete with brass fanfares, string swells, and full drum kit. The song sets off both the thematic content of the tape as well as making the bold command to the listener to "worship [God's] majesty." "Majesty" gives way to an up-tempo, five-song medley led off by Kirk Dearman's song "[We Bring the] Sacrifice of Praise" which emphasizes the acts of thanksgiving and praise to God. Tracks 7 to 9 comprise a song set that emphasizes love and adoration of God while tracks 10 to 11 exalt and glorify the name of God and continue to transition the tempo down. Finally, tracks 12 to 14 used language from the book of Revelation, including an orchestrated version of the Western classic traditional hymn "Holy, Holy, Holy" to invoke the setting of heavenly worship around the throne of God. The style of orchestral accompaniment of the prelude returns prominently to conclude the setting of "Worthy is the Lamb" before fading into rapturous applause and shouting, marking the end of side A of the cassette. Side B fades into a more up-tempo track and through the end of the album, is generally marked by second person address to God in praise, organized in shorter sets of medleys along similar lyrical themes to Side A. Diverse arrangements and orchestrations provide variety in the musical sound across the tape, including solo wind instruments, keyboard synthesizers, and auxiliary percussion.

Brooks has described his inspiration for the orchestral sound that marked the opening of the tape as how he envisioned the throne room of God. Beyond arrangement and orchestration, Brooks wanted to maintain

---

47. The physical form of a cassette tape is important when interpreting the content of an IHM tape. Specifically, the music sets on these tapes are constrained by the capacity of a single side. The tape's form is important for seeing the larger narrative structure of progression into the throne room of God as each side of the tape is a kind of independent worship set.

a production value that was able to capture the live worship experience of "leading the [congregation] into the throne room of God, because if we do that, [God] is going to 'inhabit it'" (referencing another translation of Psalm 22:3). Brooks wanted to make the tapes as high tech as possible to preserve the "live excitement [and] live flavor" without losing the 'anointing,' unlike the Maranatha! *Praise* albums of the time, which he described as a "tight, clean, studio thing." At once, Brooks attempted to capture a sense of the experience of live congregational worship as a participation in the choir of heavenly worship along with the kingly character of God that Brooks saw as best expressed musically through the orchestral texture.

This album is an archetypal example for understanding the theology of worship at work in musical sound. As mentioned above, this album was originally produced by Tom Brooks at Grace World Outreach Center in St. Louis, Missouri, and was released as the first in the IHM "Praise/Worship" subscription tape series that ran consistently until about 1995. While little has been written about IHM in general, even less has been written about landmark albums such as this one—save for one treatment in Lim and Ruth's *Lovin' on Jesus* that largely overlooks the theological content of the tape and rather focuses on how it structures musical and textual material into "thematic," interchangeable connections during a praise set.[48] Though smaller sets of songs can and do act like interchangeable building blocks for a "praise set"—and this tape is no exception as no song stands alone apart from a larger medley—I suggest here that a larger narrative structure is also at work. Re-centering the theology of worship as the hermeneutic for assessing the narrative arc of *Behold His Majesty* reveals that structure and the significance of its musical and textual themes.

Beyond Brooks's important personal associations with Hayford's song "Majesty"—having had a powerful experience of it under Hayford's own leadership at the International Worship Symposium—the orchestral setting and placement of the song at the opening of the tape indicates the theological vision of the tape. Hayford once described the meaning of the song, saying,

> "Majesty" describes the kingly, lordly, gloriously regal nature
> of our Savior—but not simply as an objective statement in

---

48. Lim and Ruth, *Lovin' on Jesus*, 69. This information is also confirmed by Gustafson, Interview. An offhanded remark at the end of the album's analysis—regarding the final song "Praise the Name of Jesus"—summarizes and redirects their analysis of the album's central textual and theological theme, saying "Like so much of contemporary worship, the liturgical focus sought to love on Jesus" (Lim and Ruth, *Lovin' on Jesus*, 68). However, the song's text does not make direct address to Jesus and, in general, the language of enthronement is central to both the textual themes of the album, and as I argue here, to the prevailing theology of worship.

worship of which He is fully worthy. "Majesty" is also a statement of the fact that our worship, when begotten in spirit and in truth, can align us with His Throne in such a way that His Kingdom authority flows to us—to overflow us, free us, and channel through us.[49]

The description resounds of Brooks's own imagination of grandeur that accompanies worship as the process and practice of the enthronement of God in worship, and is likely directly influenced by Hayford's song and imagination. Further, the process of enthronement is also one that imbues power in and on the worshiper to—taking Terry Law's teaching as an example—manifest powerful words and acts of healing. The musical flow from Hayford's "Majesty" to "Worthy Is The Lamb," which concludes side A of the tape, is thus a structured movement in thanksgiving, praise, and worship[50] into the throne room of God. Each time the worshiper listens, they aurally participate in a musically-mediated experience into heavenly worship around the throne of God modeled in Revelation 5:12, where the Lamb is exalted on the throne.

This structural progression is integral to the structure of *Behold His Majesty* and a template for later tapes. The pattern of progression in praise and worship into the throne room of God modeled in *Behold His Majesty* would come to mark at least the first four to five years of IHM projects, before the stricter adherence to album projects as patterns for worship was diversified.[51] Beyond those first few years of bi-monthly releases, the textual themes associated with the enthronement of God remain very evident in the lyrical content and album titles of later IHM albums. Ultimately, this specific theological vision is a unique contribution of IHM among the "big four" music companies and to the North American Christian music industry in general.

## Conclusion

In exploring the origins of IHM, I have tried to show how the backdrop of pentecostal networks of interpersonal and theological influence have shaped the worship music published and popularized by IHM. Each

49. Hayford, "The 'Birth' of 'Majesty.'"

50. This structure of worship is derived from the progression of the text of Psalm 100 and is a widely circulated pattern for organizing praise and worship in this context at the time.

51. Marty Nystrom, Interview, and Gustafson, Interview. Later album projects included thematic collections, instrumentals, and other progressions less closely tied to the typological or allegorical temple and tabernacle models of praise and worship.

source of influence—*New Wine* magazine and Terry Law, Covenant Church of Mobile, and the International Worship Symposium—had an impact on the theology of worship captured on the IHM albums, namely that of musical praise and worship as a process of enthroning God. In turn, that theological content encoded on the incredibly popular and influential IHM tapes has had an indelible influence on pentecostal and evangelical Christian worship in the US and abroad. Focusing on the development of IHM, I hope to have shown how the whole musical artifact carries with it a very specific, pentecostal, theological vision into the marketplace of worship music in the mid-1980s.

Admittedly, an examination of IHM's origins cannot alone account for their influence on worship music and theology over time, but this work contributes to a growing body of scholarship that seeks to examine more closely the mechanisms and agents of change that have been involved in the radical reshaping of worship in American Christianity in the latter half of the twentieth century. In detailing the particular influences on IHM, it becomes clear that IHM's origins in the 1980s stand apart from the common narratives in musicology and liturgical studies of the development of the worship music industry. Likewise, the relationship between IHM's theological influences and the musicological understandings of CPW as a performance of authenticity must be clarified—especially regarding the link between present practices in CPW and Jesus People musics.

Much work is yet to be done and a number of further avenues emerge from this initial assessment. Potential avenues for further research on IHM that build upon this initial historical and theological account are varied. How has worshiping along with the tapes shaped a social and theological imaginary of God's enthronement in worshipers and in their communities? How have musical styles and associated *theological* visions changed over time? Or alternatively, how has the theology of praise and worship present at the origins of IHM endured (or not) over time as Integrity Music diversified their product offerings beyond the IHM series? How has this enthronement theology of worship been transmitted into non-pentecostal or charismatic contexts (i.e., mainstreaming)? What has the broader influence of the International Worship Symposium been on worship and worship leaders of the period? These are just a few questions that could be addressed. In theological scholarship on CPW music, scholars need to be more intentional about accounting for the pentecostal theological concerns for assessing meaning in worship beyond the gifts of the spirit. Pentecostal theological scholarship must also deepen its assessment of the emphasis on the enthronement of God through musical worship and the manifested presence of God experienced through thanksgiving, praise, and worship (along with other models for organizing worship that have been derived from biblical sources). Musically, broader assessments must be done on how the particularities of musical orchestration and instrumentation have played a key role in expressing and forming the theology of musical worship. The music of worship-as-enthronement must be assessed alongside the role and development of embodied practices of praise and worship such as bowing, raising hands, and dancing. Through explorations in these areas scholarship can continue to understand with greater clarity the tangible impact of pentecostal theologies of worship—and IHM's contribution to them—in making the enthronement of God sung and heard throughout the US and around the world.

## Bibliography

Bergler, Thomas E. *The Juvenilization of American Christianity*. Grand Rapids: Eerdmans, 2012.

Brooks, Tom. Interview by Adam Perez. Sept 8, 2017.

Busman, Joshua. "(Re)sounding Passion: Listening to American Evangelical Worship Music, 1997–2015." PhD diss., University of North Carolina, 2015.

Coleman Michael. Interview by Adam Perez, May 3, 2019.

Cornwall, Judson. "Worship." *New Wine* (Nov 1976) 6–10.

Cusic, Don, ed. *Encyclopedia of Contemporary Christian Music: Pop, Rock, and Worship*. Santa Barbara, CA: Greenwood, 2010.

Evans, Mark. *Open Up the Doors: Music in the Modern Church*. London: Equinox, 2006.

Faupel, D. William. "The New Order of the Latter Rain: Restoration or Renewal?" In *Winds from the North: Canadian Contributions to the Pentecostal Movement*, edited by Michael Wilkinson and Peter Althouse, 239–63. Leiden: Brill, 2010.

Fromm, Charles E. "Textual Communities and New Song in the Multimedia Age: The Routinization of Charisma in the Jesus Movement." PhD diss., Fuller Theological Seminary, 2006.

Griffing, Steve. "Seeing Regional Worship Conferences as Part of Your Music Ministry." *Music Notes* 3 (1981) 1–2.

Gustafson, Gerrit. Interview by Lester Ruth and Lim Swee Hong. July 6, 2015.

Hayford, Jack. "The 'Birth' of 'Majesty.'" http://www.jackhayford.org/teaching/articles/the-birth-of-majesty/.

Howard, Jay R., and John M. Streck. *Apostles of Rock: The Splintered World of Contemporary Christian Music*. Lexington: University Press of Kentucky, 1999.

Ingalls, Monique Marie. "Awesome in This Place: Sound, Space, and Identity in Contemporary North American Evangelical Worship." PhD diss., University of Pennsylvania, 2008.

Justice, Deborah R. "Sonic Change, Social Change, Sacred Change: Music and the Reconfiguration of American Christianity." PhD diss., Indiana University, 2012.

Law, Terry. "Call to Worship: God Is Looking for a People to Offer Up the Incense of Praise to His Throne." *New Wine* (July 1985) 22–23.

Lim, Swee Hong, and Lester Ruth. *Lovin' on Jesus: A Concise History of Contemporary Worship*. Nashville: Abingdon, 2017.

Mall, Andrew. "'The Stars Are Underground': Undergrounds, Mainstreams, and Christian Popular Music." PhD diss., University of Chicago, 2012.

Miller, Donald E. *Reinventing American Protestantism: Christianity in the New Millennium*. Berkeley: University of California Press, 1997.

Moen, Don. Interview by Adam Perez. Sept 7, 2017.

Moore, S. David. *The Shepherding Movement: Controversy and Charismatic Ecclesiology*. London: T. & T. Clark, 2003.

Nekola, Anna E. "Between This World and the Next: The Musical 'Worship Wars' and Evangelical Ideology in the United States, 1960–2005." PhD diss., University of Wisconsin—Madison, 2009.

"*New Wine* Introduces Hosanna!" *New Wine* (July 1985) 6–7.

Nystrom, Martin J. Interview by Adam Perez. May 22, 2019.

Peacock, Charlie. *At the Crossroads: An Insider's Look at the Past, Present, and Future of Contemporary Christian Music*. Nashville: Broadman & Holman, 1999.

Reagan, Wen. "A Beautiful Noise: A History of Contemporary Worship Music in Modern America." PhD diss., Duke University, 2015.

Redman, Robb. *The Great Worship Awakening: Singing a New Song in the Postmodern Church*. San Francisco: Jossey-Bass, 2002.

Ruth, Lester. "Divine, Human, Devilish? The State of the Question on the Writing of the History of Contemporary Worship." *Worship* 88 (2014) 290–310.

"Seeing the Power of Praise and Worship: A Staff Report." *New Wine* (Sept 1984) 8–9.

Simpson, Stephen. "Charles Simpson: Celebrating 60 Years of Ministry." https://csmpublishing.org/charles-simpson-celebrating-60-years-of-ministry/.

Thompson, John J. *Raised by Wolves: The Story of Christian Rock & Roll*. Toronto: ECW, 2000.

# 5

## Robert Webber

*Preserving Traditional Worship through Contemporary Styles*

———————————— Jonathan A. Powers ————

"The road to the future runs through the past." Perhaps this statement is a strange way to open an essay on the history of Contemporary Praise & Worship, but such was the constant refrain of the evangelical thought-leader and worship theologian Robert Eugene Webber.[1] The dictum was his battle cry for reform, one that continues to be echoed today by many who identify with Webber's "ancient-future" approach to worship renewal. Reliance upon the orienting nature of the past for contemporary improvement was Webber's position in all things related to the Christian faith. He treated tradition as a compass and faithful guide, allowing it to direct his work for four decades as he labored as an agent of church reform particularly in the field of worship.[2] To proceed into the future heedless of history was to risk embarking on a foolish and fruitless endeavor, he believed. Thus Webber continually urged the church to retrieve its past, elevating the ancient Christian tradition as the indispensable vehicle of renewal. If the church desired future prosperity, he contended, contemporary recovery of the ancient tradition was essential.[3]

---

1. For example, the phrase can be seen in the following books by Webber: *Ancient-Future Faith*, 7; *Ancient-Future Evangelism*, 10; *Ancient-Future Time*, 11; *Divine Embrace*, 23; *Ancient-Future Worship*, 20. Likewise, see Webber's *Evangelicals on the Canterbury Trail* for autobiographical material detailing his draw to church tradition.

2. Webber published his call to "ancient-future" reform in every decade of his career as an author. See *Common Roots* (1978), *The Majestic Tapestry* (1986), *Ancient-Future Faith* (1999), and *Ancient-Future Worship* (2008).

3. Webber, *Common Roots*, 14.

The significance of Webber's work in worship at the turn of the twenty-first century cannot be overstated, though arguably it has been underappreciated. Located specifically within the American evangelical church, Webber sought reform through the fashioning of a worship theology that allowed the church's past to appraise its present state and influence its future.[4] He believed such a theology was necessary because the American evangelical church stood at a critical crossroad at the end of the twentieth century as it faced unprecedented changes that had taken place in worship over the previous century.[5] Disputes had erupted in congregations over stylistic preferences resulting in an ecclesial phenomenon called the "worship wars," which involved two dominant factions.[6] On one side stood "traditionalists," namely church leaders and laity who desired to hold on to familiar forms of worship handed down by their denomination or ecclesial fellowship.[7] On the other side stood those who desired a more "contemporary" approach to worship. These church leaders and laity set their sights on rejuvenating worship through new, charismatic, and experiential means in place of former conventional practices.[8] Disagreements ran rampant between traditionalists and those seeking contemporary expressions and by the end of the twentieth century, many churches were left in a volatile state.[9]

---

4. Webber was an American Evangelical who spoke primarily to an American evangelical audience throughout his career. As the son of Baptist missionaries, a graduate of Bob Jones University, and a longtime professor at Wheaton College, one of the academic pillars of American Evangelicalism, Webber was familiar with the evangelical tradition and felt his constructive critique came from an insider's perspective. See Webber, *Common Roots*, 13.

5. For example, in his book *Worship Old and New*, Webber identifies six predominant renewal movements that occurred in the twentieth century: the Holiness-Pentecostal movement; the liturgical reform in the Roman Catholic Church; worship renewal among mainline Protestants; the Charismatic Renewal movement; the Praise and Worship movement; and the convergence of worship traditions. See Webber, *Worship Old and New*, 121–33. In addition to these six movements, in the second volume of his Complete Library of Christian Worship Webber includes entries on renewal in Eastern Rite Catholic Churches, the Antiochean Evangelical Orthodox Mission, and the Seekers' Service/Believers' Worship movement. See Webber, *Twenty Centuries of Christian Worship*, 105–41.

6. See Lim and Ruth, *Lovin' on Jesus*, 11–12, and Long, *Beyond the Worship Wars*, 1–5.

7. Webber, *Younger Evangelicals*, 187.

8. See Webber, "Praise-and-Worship Renewal," 131–34.

9. For example, David Di Sabatino states in a response to a survey conducted by Webber regarding the debate of traditional versus contemporary forms of worship, "My head is swirling. There is a sense in which I find myself in agreement with whatever I heard last [in the debate]." See Webber, *Younger Evangelicals*, 187.

The dichotomy in the church between traditionalist and contemporary sympathizers troubled Webber and demonstrated to him the church had become fixated on *atheological* matters founded in personal preference.[10] Likewise, he identified a suppressed historical consciousness extant among Evangelicals on both sides of the divide, resulting in an estrangement from the rich treasury of resources from the collective spirituality of God's people as well as a diminished vision of God.[11] Attention needed to be redirected to critical theological concepts more normative to worship, he insisted, specifically the content of worship rooted in the story of God's mighty acts of redemption.[12]

It was Webber's circumvention of style and primary focus on content that made him such an important figure in discussions on worship at the end of the twentieth century.[13] He was determined the church not lose its focus on theological substance in the midst of rapid change and believed the invariable content of worship was protected within the church's historic liturgy. The contemporary church simply needed to rediscover it. To be sure, Webber viewed style as an important contextual factor in the communication of worship, yet he did not advocate dismissing old forms in favor of new advancements. Rather, he challenged churches to approach worship with a healthy respect for the ancient liturgical tradition while being fully committed to contemporary relevance.[14] He thus advanced a theology of worship in the contemporary church that remained in tune with the dynamic, historic faith as well as ever-evolving cultural patterns.[15] While the label Webber used for his method shifted over his career (i.e., first "blended," then "convergent," and finally "ancient-future"), the underlying spirit of his

10. See Webber, *Ancient-Future Worship*, 84, and *Signs of Wonder*, 5–11.
11. Webber, *Signs of Wonder*, 9–10.
12. Webber, *Ancient-Future Worship*, 84.
13. It should be noted that Webber was not alone in the latter decades of the twentieth century in his advocacy for reclaiming tradition in the contemporary church. Similar evangelical figures would include Donald Bloesch, Thomas Oden, Francis Schaeffer, and Howard Thomas. Several factors set Webber apart, however. The first is how prolific he was as a writer (over fifty books plus regular articles for popular magazines like *Reformed Worship* and *Worship Leader*). The second is the accessibility of Webber's published works for a breadth of readers. The third was his extensive travels to lead workshops at conferences and local churches. People were also drawn to his gracious demeanor, charismatic personality, and profound thought. In addition, Webber created worship programs at several schools and eventually created his own, the Institute for Worship Studies, which was renamed after him posthumously. For more on the impact of Webber's career, see Huyser-Honig and Harris, "Robert E. Webber's Legacy: Ancient Future Faith and Worship."
14. Webber, *Worship Old and New*, 13.
15. Webber, *Worship Old and New*, 15.

paradigm remained consistent: worship should maintain a healthy respect for tradition while staying fully committed to present-day significance and applicability.[16] By drawing spiritual insights and experiences from a variety of liturgical traditions, not only would worship be enriched but churches would also see their own tradition in light of a greater whole.[17] He believed the practice of combining the old with the new held power to nourish, sustain, and bring healing to the church today.

## The Historic Content of Worship

Throughout his career as an educator, speaker, and author, Webber addressed a variety of subjects regarding recovery of the ancient Christian tradition in present-day churches. Topics ranged from ecclesiology and theology to discipleship and mission, but his most notable contributions concerned the practice of worship.[18] Webber considered worship to be the central activity of the church and thus the key to church renewal. "[Worship] stands as the center of the church's life and mission," he claimed in his book *Signs of Wonder*; "It is the summit toward which the entire life of the church moves and the source from which all of its ministries flow . . . In brief, the single most important thing the church can do is worship."[19] Webber believed worship is the primary context where the presence of God is mediated to his people and the true fellowship of Christ's body is realized. Therefore he professed it

---

16. For the sake of the current essay, the term "convergent" is primarily used to describe Webber's method.

17. Webber, *Signs of Wonder*, 56.

18. Notably, of the fifty-two books Webber published over his career (not including eight contributing chapters as well as the seven-volume Complete Library of Christian Worship he compiled), twenty-five deal exclusively with worship while another nine include sections on worship. Webber also wrote a seven-volume worship curriculum for churches, which he entitled *The Alleluia! Series*, and published three prayer books for use in churches and homes: *The Book of Daily Prayer* (1993), *The Book of Family Prayer* (1996), and *The Prymer: The Prayer Book of the Medieval Era Adapted for Contemporary Use* (2000).

19. Webber, *Signs of Wonder*, 16. The impact of the Second Vatican Council is evident here on Webber's thought as he appropriates the twofold importance of worship found in the council's foundational document on the liturgy, the *Sacrosanctum Concilium*. In sum, the *Sacrosanctum Concilium* views worship as the central activity of the church and notes that through the celebration of the liturgy, Christ's work is made real. For Webber, the *Sacrosanctum Concilium* proposed a model where "worship is primarily an action from above and secondarily a response below." He reflected, "When the church worships, God becomes present to give to the church the salvation that comes from Jesus Christ. As the church responds in faith, the church is built into the holy temple of the Lord." See Webber, *Worship Old and New*, 124.

is also the activity where those who participate find meaning, healing, encouragement, and motivation for Christian living. When worship cultivates a conscious awareness of God the natural benefit is the nourishment needed for spiritual life and growth.[20]

Webber was not alone in his view of worship as the key to church renewal. As previously mentioned, by the end of the twentieth century a number of movements and figures emerged seeking revitalization through reexamination of worship practices. The result was the development of several new worship styles and forms.[21] In the thick of these modifications of worship, Webber continually advocated the greatest potential for spiritual growth lay in contemporary dialogue with the biblical and early church tradition.[22] Because he viewed worship as such an invigorating force, Webber felt it imperative the contemporary church not lose sight of essential theological principles of worship. In particular, he argued, worship needed to remain grounded in its historic theological substance in order to foster dynamic Christian spirituality. Webber's desire in maintaining a strong focus on the theological substance of worship was to save the contemporary church from falling into hazardous pitfalls he noticed within his own evangelical upbringing. In particular, Webber believed evangelical worship was exceedingly narcissistic as its focus had become human-oriented instead of God-oriented.[23] Practices and rituals of worship ceased to foster an awareness of God's real and abiding presence and instead relied on human effort to manufacture an encounter with God based on personal stimulation.[24] Two prominent behaviors in worship revealed the pervasive human-oriented attitude in the evangelical church: one, the overemphasis on reaching the mind of the worshiper; and two, the overemphasis on triggering an emotional response in the worshiper.[25] Such reductionism of worship to its intellectual and emotional components nurtured the attitude in worshipers that worship was meant for them rather than something they themselves do.[26] Additionally, it established value for worship based on what an individual

---

20. Webber, *Worship Is a Verb*, 18.

21. Take, for example, the essays included in this volume. Also, see *Exploring the Worship Spectrum*, edited by Paul Basden, which includes conversations between figures such as Joe Horness, Sally Morgenthaler, and Robert Webber on various approaches to worship at the turn of the turn of the twenty-first century.

22. Webber, *Signs of Wonder*, 10.

23. Webber, *Ancient-Future Faith*, 99.

24. Webber, *Ancient-Future Worship*, 84.

25. Webber, *Majestic Tapestry*, 72.

26. Webber, *Planning Blended Worship*, 22–23.

finds meaningful, stimulating, or compelling.[27] To put it crudely, evangelical worship had become merchandise produced for a consumer and focused more on an individual's self-gratification than God's glorification. The music, the testimonies, and the sermon were all designed either to provide information or to facilitate an emotional reaction within the congregation. Moreover, wars over the style of worship proved to him many evangelical churches were more concerned with good marketing rather than the biblical purpose of worship.[28] Noting these problems, Webber concluded that when the entire service of worship is geared toward the congregation, worship is reduced to human indulgence rather than the exaltation of the triune God.

The other significant problem Webber identified in evangelical approaches to worship was the lack of theological substance in worship. Although he claimed them as two separate concerns, Webber perceived the lack of theological substance to be the natural result of the human-centered focus of evangelical worship. He observed, "A [human]-centered approach to worship often occurs as a result of the failure to understand *why* content is necessary in worship, *what* the content should include, and *how* the content should be put together."[29] In Webber's assessment, content is the foremost component of worship, affecting all other aspects of the communal gathering. Worship is to be a faithful rehearsal of who God is and what God has done, giving expression to the relationship between God and his people. When churches seek primarily to educate or to foster human stimulation in worship, they end up missing the point of worship and fail to glorify God in his entirety.[30] At best, he asserted, churches address individual aspects of God's character and actions in the content of their worship, leaving congregations with a limited view of God. At worst, the content is fixed upon the benefits of the creatures rather than the wonder, mystery, and majesty of the Creator, establishing within the congregation a culture of consumerism and self-absorption. Webber believed that by the end of the twentieth century much of the church's worship had become an overly passive, consumeristic, and narcissistic gathering. Furthermore, worship focused more on the worshiper rather than God and needed to be redirected toward a more dynamic, God-oriented, and communal participatory expression.[31] There was thus great need for the church to rethink the content of its worship.

---

27. Webber, *Worship Is a Verb*, 31.
28. Webber, *Ancient-Future Worship*, 85.
29. Webber, *Common Roots*, 78.
30. Webber, *Common Roots*, 78.
31. Webber, *Worship Is a Verb*, 13–14; Webber, *Ancient-Future Worship*, 82–83.

In his quest to offer a corrective to the deficiencies he noted in evangelical worship, Webber established a framework for the theological substance of worship by studying descriptions of Christian worship from the first five centuries of the church. Although he consulted a number of sources, he primarily leaned on the writings of Justin Martyr, Irenaeus of Lyons, and Hippolytus of Rome.[32] The model of early Christian worship was an excellent example for Webber of an approach that combined what he considered to be the best of the "evangelical spirit" (i.e., the experience of Christ being made real within the worshiper) with the theological substance of worship (i.e., the God-oriented narrative quality of worship).[33] Webber thus proposed to the contemporary church a narrative-based theology of worship established in the liturgical principles he discovered through the ancient tradition. The result of Webber's work was a framework for his worship theology based in four essential principles: one, the return to historic Christianity rooted in the first five centuries of the church (historic rootedness);[34] two, the recovery of God's narrative in the worship of the church (narrative quality);[35] three, the active participation of the congregation in worship (participatory engagement);[36] and four, the recalibration of the experiential dynamic of evangelical worship (evangelical experience).[37] By focusing on history, narrative, participation, and experience, Webber aimed to root worship in the story and character of God based on God's covenantal and redemptive acts as well as the witness of the church throughout the ages.[38] Because Webber so strongly believed his ancient-future model held great potential for renewal in the contemporary church, it is worth taking a moment to elucidate his theological framework in further detail.

As previously mentioned, Webber considered the first five centuries of Christianity to be of vital importance for the contemporary church. While he admitted there was warrant for some criticism of the era, he maintained the era endures as the most important historical period in regard to the church's thoughtful working out of the rituals that have characterized it throughout the centuries.[39] Ultimately, Webber's study and

---

32. See Webber, *Worship Old and New*, 51–63.
33. See Webber, *Common Roots*, 17–23.
34. Webber, *Common Roots*, 22.
35. See Webber, *Common Roots*, 99–103; *Worship Is a Verb*, 34–46; *Signs of Wonder*, 31–34; *Ancient-Future Faith*, 102–6; *Ancient-Future Worship*, 93–101.
36. See Webber, *Worship Is a Verb*, 17–20.
37. Webber, *Worship Is a Verb*, 9–15.
38. See Webber, *Common Roots*, 91.
39. Webber, *Worship Old and New*, 98.

examination of the ancient church's worship resulted in his identification of three dominant features:

1. The *content* of Christian worship was Jesus Christ in his fulfillment of the Old Testament, his birth, his life, his death, his resurrection, his ascension, and his return.

2. The *structure* of Christian worship was word and sacrament, including prayers, hymns, doxologies, benedictions, and responses.

3. The *context* in which worship took place was the Christian church, called by God to worship, where each member played his or her part and where God spoke and the worshiper responded. This worship was highlighted by sign-acts (baptism and Eucharist).[40]

The above descriptions (i.e., content, structure, and context) both identify Webber's primary takeaways from early Christian worship and also pinpoint the taxonomy he used to study the ancient church's worship, i.e., content, structure, and context. Webber believed his taxonomy was a helpful evaluative tool and could be employed to examine worship in any era of the church. Considering particularly his examination of the content, structure, and context of worship in the ancient church, Webber concluded the theological substance of worship was the proclamation and reenactment of the Christ-event through Word and Table experienced in the congregated church. The context of the ancient church modeled for him a dual liturgical action where God first initiates worship and God's people then respond in faith through remembrance, anticipation, and celebration.[41] These qualities showcased for Webber a purity of focus and motive in the ancient church's worship. Rather than trying to accomplish something through worship, such as evangelism, education, or appeal, Webber believed the ancient church was concerned with what worship represented, namely Jesus Christ.[42] "This kind of worship is not goal driven, but Christ-driven," he wrote. "And when

---

40. It is notable that Webber uses the terms "style" and "context" interchangeably in his work. For Webber, the issue of style was a contextual concern rather than a marketable one. He believed cultural factors should influence the style of worship in order to foster greater participation and engagement in the congregation. No one style of worship is suitable for all people always and everywhere but instead differs according to time and place relative to the changing patterns of culture. He maintained each congregation must carefully discern a style that is not only comfortable for its congregants but also expresses the character and personality of the worshiping community. Webber, *Worship Old and New*, 62. See Webber, *Worship Old and New*, 151, and *Planning Blended Worship*, 21.

41. Webber, *Worship Old and New*, 62.

42. Webber, *Signs of Wonder*, 33.

Christ is the center of worship, all of the goals for worship are achieved: Christ-centered worship educates, evangelizes, heals, develops spirituality—and is most enjoyable."[43]

There were numerous ways Webber believed the principles he discovered in the ancient model of worship should influence the contemporary church. First and foremost, Webber insisted worship should be grounded in the character and actions of God. The church's worship is to God, for God, and because of God. God is to be worshiped simply for the fact that he is God and therefore worthy of praise and adoration. Likewise, God is to be worshiped for his great and mighty acts of redemption and because of his steadfast, covenantal love.[44]

Secondly, Webber identified a striking narrative quality in the worship of the ancient church. In worship, he contended, the church comes together to celebrate God and to remember God's mighty acts of salvation through Jesus Christ. In its celebration, worship proclaims and reenacts the story of God. Moreover, through the words and actions of worship the church participates in retelling and dramatizing the gospel. "The church is all about the continuation of God's narrative in this world," Webber wrote in *Ancient-Future Worship*.[45] "Worship gathers to sing, tell, and enact God's story of the world from its beginning to its end."[46] Because he saw an explicit and indispensable narrative quality in the worship of the ancient church, Webber argued this narrative quality was the central feature, or the content, that should define worship in any era. As the people of God gather to both remember God's mighty acts of salvation and anticipate God's ultimate restoration of the cosmos in their worship, the entire spectrum of the Christian faith is celebrated. When the content is altered, the story becomes fragmented and worship is corrupted. Webber thus contended the unchanging theological substance of worship should be rooted in God's narrative. He reflected:

> Worship is all about how God, with his own two hands—the incarnate Word and the Holy Spirit—has rescued the world. The biblical God is an active God—he creates, becomes active in the world to rescue his creation from sin and death, and restores the world to paradise and beyond in the new heavens and new earth. The centerpiece of his saving action is the incarnation, death, and resurrection, where sin and death have been defeated

---

43. Webber, *Signs of Wonder*, 33.
44. Webber, *Common Roots*, 84–85.
45. Webber, *Ancient-Future Worship*, 39.
46. Webber, *Ancient-Future Worship*, 40.

and where the deliverance of creatures and creation, which will be consummated at the end of history, will begin. In the meantime, worship is the witness to this vision. In worship we *remember* God's redemptive work in history . . . We also *anticipate* the future. Worship connects the past with the future, for it is here in worship where God recasts his original vision.[47]

Remembrance and anticipation were key features of Webber's narrative concept of worship. Through a convergence of past and future, the church in the present discovers its place in the narrative of God's covenantal love and redemption of the world. Worship tells a polemical narrative that claims the world, its history, and its future belong to God. Webber affirmed that, when worship remembers the past, it praises God by proclaiming God's work in history whereby he has already begun to restore the world.[48] Likewise, when worship anticipates the future, it witnesses to the victory of Christ over all powers and principalities and proclaims his rule over creation as Lord of the universe.[49] The proclamations and actions done in worship are thus the means by which a congregation is able to participate in God's story. Again, Webber emphasized the story of God's creation and redemption as the critical content throughout a service:

> The story is *remembered* through Scripture reading and preaching; the story is *anticipated* through the Table. The story is also the very substance of our singing, praying, and testimonies. It shapes our environment, determines how the arts are employed, and informs everything else we do. And, though God is the subject of worship, acting among the people, it is the *people* of God who remember God's story, not as an audience, but as true participants in the very story that tells the truth about the world and all of human existence. The two sides of this substance in worship are the content, which is God's story, and the energy with which God's story is remembered and anticipated by the people.[50]

Webber's emphasis on the participatory nature of worship in the above passage is notable inasmuch as it pointed out another key principle of the ancient church's worship he believed to be relevant for the contemporary church. Webber insisted participation in God's story through proclamation and action, especially in word and sacrament, makes the Christ-event real

---

47. Webber, *Ancient Future Worship*, 66.
48. Webber, *Ancient-Future Worship*, 61.
49. Webber, *Ancient-Future Worship*, 61.
50. Webber, *Ancient-Future Worship*, 107.

in the here and now for the worshiper.[51] To put it another way, for Webber, congregational participation adds a crucial and appropriate experiential dynamic to worship.[52] When worship focuses on celebrating God's mighty acts, Webber reasoned, the gathered congregation becomes so in tune with God and with God's reconciliation through Christ that Christ's death and resurrection become a lived experience within the worshiper.[53] "In Christian worship," he wrote, "we are not merely asked to believe in Jesus Christ, but to live, die, and be resurrected again with him . . . When our life story is brought up into the story of Christ's life, death, and resurrection, it then gains meaning and purpose."[54] For Webber, personal experience in worship was rooted in the worshiper's participation in the story of God. He did not dismiss the value of personal experience in worship but, as alluded to earlier, saw experience as a valued byproduct rather than the goal of worship.[55] Likewise, Webber saw the experiential nature of worship as more than emotional or intellectual stimulation, i.e., two of the problems he detected in late twentieth-century evangelical approaches to worship.[56] Instead, Webber insisted that from beginning to end worship must be rooted in the formidable experience of dwelling in the presence of God. God is active in worship by the power of the Holy Spirit speaking through his word and acting through his sacraments. Human acts of worship such as singing, prayer, verbal expression, and personal commitment, among others, are thus responses that arise from the heart of the worshiper due to God's merciful and loving presence. As Webber concluded in *Worship is a Verb*: "Since God is speaking

---

51. Webber, *Worship Is a Verb*, 31. Elsewhere, Webber articulates, "Although worship dramatizes an event which happened long ago, it brings that event into the present by the power of the Holy Spirit. In each worship experience, I am present in the actual event. Each worship experience contains the fullness of the birth, life, teachings, ministry, death, resurrection, and promised return of Christ. The rites evoke the historical event and bring it into the present." See Webber, *Worship Is a Verb*, 120.

52. Webber's focus on the experiential dynamic of worship is significant inasmuch as it fought against what he maintained was the predominant narcissistic emphasis on experience in the Contemporary Praise & Worship movement. He saw too often the focus of Contemporary Praise & Worship services to be on the individual and the individual's worship of God. He asserted, "The focus seems to be on self-generated worship. God is made the object of *my* affection, and worship is measured by how strongly I am able to feel this gratitude and express it to God" (Webber, *Ancient-Future Worship*, 84). What Webber desired instead was for worship to focus on God's mighty work of redemption, bringing the whole church into an experience of God's saving grace as it participated together in the proclamation and reenactment of God's story.

53. Webber, *Worship Is a Verb*, 31.
54. Webber, *Worship Is a Verb*, 31.
55. See the quote referenced in footnote 19.
56. These two problems are further examined later in the chapter.

and acting in worship, response to God who speaks and acts is of great importance. In my response, I am once again saying yes to God. As with that initial response when I first heard the Word of God's love and grace, I again respond to him [in worship] in faith and love."[57]

## The Liturgical Structure of Worship

The second component of Webber's worship taxonomy, and another notable component of his theological framework, is the liturgical structure of worship. Although Webber held structure in secondary importance to the content of worship, he nevertheless endorsed structure as a significant area of concern. The structure of worship needs careful attention, Webber argued, since structure gives form to worship's theological substance.[58] As previously noted, Webber believed worship is the primary way the church experiences God's saving work in history, which is why he advocated worship should be oriented around the proclamation and reenactment of God's saving work from creation to final consummation. The reason for Webber's concentration on structure, therefore, was to identify a model that organized patterns and practices of worship intentionally through proclamation and action so the congregation could more fully participate in worship. In his view, the structure of worship outlined a drama in which each person in the congregation was invited to play a part.[59] Participation in the drama is cultivated as structure brings together the many acts of worship into a coherent whole providing direction, facilitating action, and ordering the meeting between God and his people. When each act of worship is treated with intention and care, the structure guides the experience of the worshiping congregation and orients it in God's cosmic narrative.

Webber believed participation in worship was best fostered and guided through a fourfold structure centered in Word and Table. The model of Word and Table was the basic form he saw exemplified in the ancient church's regular worship gathering; however, he also acknowledged that over time the church added to it acts of gathering and sending, establishing a narrative framework that directed congregated worship from beginning to end.[60]

57. Webber, *Worship Is a Verb*, 125.
58. Webber, *Worship Is a Verb*, 61–65.
59. Webber, *Worship Old and New*, 263.
60. While he admitted there was no direct biblical teaching on the structure of worship, i.e., a specific rubric handed down by Jesus or his disciples, Webber noted certain New Testament passages along with early descriptions of worship strongly pointed to Word and Table as the standard practice of the church since the church's inception. For example, Webber notes: "The description in Acts 2:42 of the earliest Christian worship

Adherence to the fourfold model was the stance of the church for the majority of its history, Webber maintained, and thus should continue to be the standard practice of the contemporary church, not simply because of its historic precedent, but chiefly because of the way gathering, Word, Table, and sending represent God's story and facilitate remembrance and anticipation. He observes, "Churches aware of their historical roots celebrate the life-changing Christ-event in four movements: worshipers enter God's presence, hear God speak, celebrate God's work of restoration at the Table, and are sent forth into the world to love and serve the Lord."[61]

Notable in Webber's description above of the fourfold structure is his attention to the posture of the congregation in various stages of the worship service. Because he maintained worship is a dialogue between God and the congregation, Webber acknowledged in the structure both human activity as well as the activity of God. For example, Webber stated that in the gathering God calls his church to worship, assembling the congregation in his presence. The congregation then responds with singing and prayer, preparing their hearts to hear God's word proclaimed. In the Word fold God speaks to the congregation in the reading of Scripture and through the sermon. The congregation then responds at the Table with thanksgiving, receiving God's grace and committing to Christ-like transformation. Finally, in the sending God sends the congregation out to continue Christ's ministry in the world. The congregation responds through service and holy living.[62] The fourfold structure thus invites the congregation into a dual liturgical action where God first initiates and then God's people respond.[63]

Webber believed the fourfold structure was a useful resource for any worshiping community, regardless of tradition or background. In *Signs of Wonder*, he observed many renewing churches aware of their historic roots

---

recounts how early Christians gathered around the apostles' teaching and the breaking of bread in the context of prayer and fellowship. This passage provides evidence that from its inception, Christian worship had two primary focuses: Word and Table." See Webber, *Planning Blended Worship*, 20.

61. Webber, *Signs of Wonder*, 41.

62. For a further exploration of each the four folds of worship, see Webber, *Worship Old and New*, 153–94, and Webber, *Planning Blended Worship*, 50–189.

63. Taking up Webber's mantle, Constance Cherry, a former student of Webber's, wrote and published a book entitled *The Worship Architect*, which is a theological and practical guide to a convergent approach to worship. In the book, Cherry examines the fourfold structure of worship and provides helpful practical tools for planning worship that remains biblically faithful, historically grounded, and contextually sensitive. Since its publication in 2010, the book has been used in numerous colleges, seminaries, and churches around the world. The book has been translated and published in Korean, Chinese, and Spanish. See Cherry, *The Worship Architect*.

were reclaiming the ancient form, bringing the content of worship in line with the order of worship.[64] Within the fourfold order, Webber insisted the two acts of Word and Table were among the most significant actions of renewing worshiping communities since they are the focal points of proclamation of the gospel in worship.[65] Preaching the word proclaims God's story and remembers his mighty deeds of salvation, Webber said, and the Eucharist dramatizes God's story and its anticipated future, ushering the congregation into God's kingdom.[66] As both preaching and the Eucharist celebrate and proclaim Christ, Christ is given to the gathered congregation through them.[67] In the practice of Word and Table, the church hears a declaration of God's almighty grace and then receives from God the grace it needs to go forth as the imitation of Christ to the world. The congregation thus not only hears God's story in the preaching, but through the Table it also sees God's story as God is disclosed through revelation and incarnation.[68] Moreover, Webber suggested, through Word and Table the story of God's saving work is ordered so it is clearly experienced by the gathered congregation.[69] The two acts foster within the church a vision of the whole story of God, including creation, fall, incarnation, death, resurrection, ascension, church, the kingdom, and the promise of the new heavens and new earth accomplished through Jesus Christ.[70] The covenantal relationship of God and his people is expressed through the whole of worship, displaying the character of the God who first loved so that his people may respond in love.

## The Varied Style of Worship

The final category in Webber's worship taxonomy is the context of worship, which he sometimes refers to as "style." To be sure, style was important to Webber, which is why he included it in his worship taxonomy. Because evangelical and mainline churches were so engrossed in debates over style at the end of the twentieth century, Webber could not and did not ignore its significance. His goal, however, was to keep style in its rightful place, namely as a contextual concern tertiary to the content and structure of worship. Moreover, Webber sought to suppress arguments over style in

64. Webber, *Signs of Wonder*, 41.
65. Webber, *Worship Old and New*, 98.
66. Webber, *Ancient-Future Worship*, 177.
67. Webber, *Worship Is a Verb*, 19.
68. Webber, *Ancient-Future Worship*, 106.
69. Webber, *Worship Old and New*, 150.
70. Webber, *Ancient-Future Worship*, 141.

the church by shifting the conversation away from preferential matters and toward cultural concerns.

Webber viewed the context of worship as the atmosphere in which the content and structure of worship are implemented.[71] Because worship is rooted in participatory proclamation and reenactment of the story of God, Webber advocated the contextualization of worship should be open and flexible based on cultural dynamics within the local congregation such as ethnicity, generation, background, and preference in order to ensure the gospel was communicated clearly in any worship setting and to safeguard participatory engagement in worship.[72] He insisted the content and structure of worship should not be altered; however, Webber believed context is subject to considerable variety since it is relative to the ever-shifting patterns of culture, differing according to time and place.[73] For the historic faith to be accessible to the contemporary church, contextualization was necessary.

## Webber's Contribution: A Blended Approach to Renewal

In the above examination of Webber's theological framework of worship, four principles were identified as central to his work: one, the return to historic Christianity rooted in the first five centuries of the church (historic rootedness); two, the recovery of God's narrative in the worship of the church (narrative quality); three, the active participation of the congregation in worship (participatory engagement); and four, the recalibration of the experiential dynamic of evangelical worship (evangelical experience). These principles undergirded Webber's understanding of the theological substance of worship, which he articulates as the proclamation and reenactment of the Christ-event experienced in the congregated church through gathering, Word, Table, and sending. When contextualized in contemporaneous ways in a local congregation, Webber supposed the historic theological substance of worship held potential for considerable church renewal. He thus reasoned renewal was not to be found in new styles and forms but rather through the reclamation of the historic theological substance of worship in contemporary ways.

By the end of the twentieth century, nearly every branch of the church had been impacted by changes in worship. A growing desire in many churches for revitalization of the Christian faith, as well as a mounting dissatisfaction

---

71. Webber, *Worship Old and New*, 151.
72. Webber, *Worship Old and New*, 263.
73. Webber, *Planning Blended Worship*, 21.

among laity with practices of worship brought about an unprecedented revolution in the church giving rise to a myriad of renewal movements. While many churches followed a singular trend, Webber instead sought a way to mediate between the various movements. He insisted worship communities should learn from traditions other than their own, namely because he saw something missing in both traditional and contemporary approaches to renewal. The traditional church was missing the sense of a real and vital experience with God. The contemporary movement was missing substance. Webber therefore believed a blended approach that brought together the content of liturgy and the experience of the contemporary movement would foster a dynamic and genuine experience with God.[74] Such cross-fertilization held potential to stimulate worship in new directions and engage the congregation in fresh expressions of historic practices.[75]

Webber found two movements to be particularly significant in his modeling of a convergent approach to worship renewal: the Liturgical Renewal movement and the Pentecostal-based Praise and Worship movement.[76] The Liturgical Renewal movement began as a nineteenth-century scholastic effort to reform worship. Particularly, in the Church of England a faction known as the Tractarians arose in Oxford that desired to incorporate High-Church principles in Anglican worship. Their goal was to bring liturgical renewal to the Anglican Church, binding it more closely to Roman Catholic practices through a resurgence of interest in the essence, spirit, and shape of ancient Christian worship as practiced and understood by the church of the first four centuries. Similarly, in the nineteenth century the Roman Catholic Church began seeking to rediscover practices of the ancient church in its liturgical forms. After many unsuccessful attempts in the first half of the twentieth century to make liturgical alterations, in 1963 the Second Vatican Council released the pronouncement of the *Sacrosanctum Concilium*, also known as the *Constitution on the Sacred Liturgy*. As a culmination of many years of study, the main outcome of the *Sacrosanctum Concilium* was the achievement of greater lay participation in the Catholic Church's liturgical practices as well as changes to its Eucharistic prayer forms, which were influenced by the so-called *Apostolic Tradition* of Hippolytus. Moreover, the *Sacrosanctum Concilium* established guidelines in the Catholic Church to include, allow,

---

74. Webber, "Blended Worship," 178–79.
75. Webber, *Signs of Wonder*, 145.
76. See Webber, *Worship Old and New*, 121–34; *Signs of Wonder*, 43–56; and *Twenty Centuries of Christian Worship*, 105–41. Notably, this last book, the second volume of Webber's Complete Library of Christian Worship, provides an extensive examination of renewal movements that took place in the twentieth century. The scope of content in the volume has gone unmatched in any worship resource to date.

and encourage greater use of the vernacular in mass services, particularly for biblical readings and prayers. The constitution ended up being one of the most revolutionary developments in twentieth-century Christian worship causing the Catholic Church to go through a liturgical reform that altered practices in place since the sixteenth century.

Ultimately, the impact of these two nineteenth century Liturgical Renewal movements spread to Protestant mainline churches. Over the next thirty years every traditional mainline denomination imitated the reforms particularly of Vatican II by producing their own new worship books, collections of liturgical resources, and hymnbooks.[77] To be sure, the Liturgical Renewal movement was not a denomination-specific or monolithic movement. While certain denominational distinctives were maintained in each tradition's produced liturgical resources, Webber noticed an emerging consensus regarding worship among the mainline churches as they sought to bring reform based on the spirit and practice of worship in the early centuries. In the various newly produced worship resources, Webber observed denominations followed the ancient pattern of the fourfold structure of worship, paying careful attention to the sequential acts of worship and what each act expresses in the overall narrative of worship. Additionally, the Eucharist became more prominent in the weekly service, as did the significance of the liturgical calendar throughout the whole of the year.[78] The reform taking place through the Liturgical Renewal movement was thus one based in historic precedent and practice. Its impact on the evangelical church was minimal, however, partly due to the ingrained prejudice against Catholic forms of worship amongst Evangelicals. Bridging the gap between the Liturgical Renewal movement and Evangelicalism, Webber based his reform on fundamental notions of the Liturgical Renewal movement, which he offered to Evangelicals in a simple, popular, and compelling way. By highlighting elements such as the prominence of the Eucharist in worship, the emphasis on participation, and the liturgical rhythm of the church year, Webber desired to show evangelical churches how dialoging with other traditions held potential for more mature expressions of Christian faith and spirituality.[79]

---

77. Webber, *Planning Blended Worship*, 15. For example, the Lutheran Church produced a new combined hymn and service book called *The Lutheran Book of Worship* in 1978, the Episcopal Church produced a new *Book of Common Prayer* in 1979, the United Methodist Church produced the *United Methodist Book of Worship* in 1992, and the Presbyterians produced a book of liturgical resources called *The Book of Services* in 1993.

78. Webber, *Worship Old and New*, 126.

79. Webber, *Signs of Wonder*, 6–9.

The second of the two movements significant to Webber's convergent model was the pentecostal-based Praise and Worship movement. As the label suggests, the Praise and Worship movement originated in the Latter Rain revival of the late 1940s but began to gain wider prominence in pentecostal circles in the late 1970s and early 1980s.[80] By the last decade of the twentieth century the movement spread and was picked up by a number of non-pentecostal churches exploring a more contemporary style of worship.[81] Considering the movement's origins in Pentecostalism, Weber noted the Praise and Worship movement developed from several trends in the sixties and early seventies among churchgoers who "felt a concern for the immediacy of the Spirit, a desire for intimacy, and a persuasion that music and informality must connect with people of a post-Christian culture."[82] In Webber's examination, a major feature of the Praise and Worship movement was the intentional distinguishing of praise from worship. The movement identified praise as a ministry offered to God for God's mighty deeds in history, while worship was simply adoring and extoling God for who he is.[83] The pattern of the Praise and Worship movement was thus the gradual shift from praise to worship, seeking greater degrees of intimacy with God usually through the singing of contemporary choruses. Typology from the Old Testament tabernacle or temple was often employed to convey the experiential movement from the "outer courts" to the "inner courts" and ultimately to the "holy of holies."[84]

One clear contribution Webber believed the Praise and Worship tradition offered to the church was its emphasis on the participatory and experiential dynamic of worship, which was particularly evident in the musical component of the movement. Additionally, Webber valued the movement's openness to the spontaneous work of the Spirit through the freedom of physical acts such as the raising of hands, dancing, the laying on of hands for prayer, and the restoration of healing in the context of worship.[85] Webber recognized these aspects of pentecostal worship were not simply stylistic preferences but had roots in practices of the early church. Vestiges of the actions appear in liturgical books of worship throughout history, he noted.

---

80. Lim and Ruth, *Lovin' on Jesus*, 14. For more information, please see the introduction to this book. While Lim and Ruth's research details the origins of the Praise and Worship movement in the 1940s, Webber himself seems to have become aware of it in its explosion in the 1980s. See Webber, *Worship Old and New*, 128–32.

81. Lim and Ruth, *Lovin' on Jesus*, 14.

82. Webber, *Worship Old and New*, 128.

83. Webber, *Worship Old and New*, 129.

84. Webber, *Worship Old and New*, 130–31.

85. Webber, *Signs of Wonder*, 54.

Thus, much of what the pentecostal-based Praise and Worship movement contributed to worship renewal had historic precedent, reintroducing practices forgotten in later manifestations of the church.[86]

In his longing to see all churches experience the fullness of Christian worship and spirituality, Webber blended essential and distinctive elements of the Liturgical Renewal and Praise and Worship movements together. While each of the movements reflected a particular tradition of worship, Webber believed God desired to use a "borrowing" between the traditions to bring about renewal in the church.[87] He identified several features that characterized a convergent model of worship, which he advocated as the proper pathway to renewal: first, there was restored commitment to the sacraments, especially the Eucharist; second, there was continued commitment to the personal experience of Jesus Christ's work through the proclamation of the word and ministry of the Holy Spirit; third, there was increased commitment to the church's historic structure and form, namely the fourfold pattern of worship; fourth, there was interest in integrating bodily action in worship; fifth, there was exposure to styles and practices from various traditions while ecclesial distinctives were maintained; and sixth, there was an emphasis on God's healing power. For Webber, a convergent approach to worship did not mean the abandonment of a particular tradition but rather a convergence of streams. He saw the work of God as inclusive, not exclusive, producing from each tradition gifts God had already authenticated.[88] Important matters such as sacrament, liturgy, healing, and the work of ministry remain intact as the church stays grounded in its historic content and moves forward with fresh expression, allowing the Spirit's power to be released in every facet of the church's life.

Undoubtedly, the significance of Webber's work as a worship theologian at the turn of the twenty-first century was his insistence that biblically and theologically sound worship represents the story of the triune God while standing in continuity with the historic church and remaining pertinent to the contemporary culture. It was an insistence he pressed upon countless workshop participants, readers, and students. His method of convergent worship moved beyond trivial arguments over traditional and contemporary preferences and encouraged thoughtful theological, historical, and cultural reflection on worship. It also set the pervasive issue of style in its proper place—as a matter of fostering participatory engagement. Any movement toward convergence would take a great amount of time and

---

86. Webber, *Signs of Wonder*, 54.
87. Webber, *Signs of Wonder*, 55.
88. Compare Sly and Boosahda, "Convergence Movement," 134–35.

intentional conversation, he acknowledged. Nevertheless, Webber persistently advocated his convergent model with confidence and grace as the church at war faced an uncertain future.

## Bibliography

Basden, Paul A., ed. *Exploring the Worship Spectrum: 6 Views*. Grand Rapids: Zondervan, 2004.

Cherry, Constance M. *The Worship Architect: A Blueprint for Designing Culturally Relevant and Biblically Faithful Services*. Grand Rapids: Baker Academic, 2010.

Huyser-Honig, Joan, and Darrell Harris. "Robert E. Webber's Legacy: Ancient Future Faith and Worship." http://worship.calvin.edu/resources/resource-library/robert-e-webber-s-legacy-ancient-future-faith-and-worship/.

Lim, Swee Hong, and Lester Ruth. *Lovin' on Jesus: A Concise History of Contemporary Worship*. Nashville: Abingdon, 2017.

Long, Thomas G. *Beyond the Worship Wars: Building Vital and Faithful Worship*. Bethesda, MD: Alban Institute, 2001.

Sly, Randy, and Wayne Boosahda. "The Convergence Movement." In *Twenty Centuries of Christian Worship*, edited by Robert E. Webber, 134–40. Complete Library of Christian Worship 2. Nashville: Star Song, 1994.

Webber, Robert E. *Ancient-Future Evangelism: Making Your Church a Faith-Forming Community*. Grand Rapids: Baker, 2003.

———. *Ancient-Future Faith: Rethinking Evangelicalism for a Postmodern World*. Grand Rapids: Baker, 1999.

———. *Ancient-Future Time: Forming Spirituality through the Christian Year*. Grand Rapids: Baker, 2004.

———. *Ancient-Future Worship: Proclaiming and Enacting Gods Narrative*. Grand Rapids: Baker, 2008.

———. "Blended Worship." In *Exploring the Worship Spectrum: 6 Views*, edited by Paul A. Basden, 175–91. Grand Rapids: Zondervan, 2004.

———. *The Book of Daily Prayer*. Grand Rapids: Eerdmans, 1993.

———. *The Book of Family Prayer*. Nashville: Thomas Nelson, 1986.

———. *Common Roots: A Call to Evangelical Maturity*. Grand Rapids: Zondervan, 1978.

———. *The Divine Embrace: Recovering the Passionate Spiritual Life*. Grand Rapids: Baker, 2006.

———. *Evangelicals on the Canterbury Trail: Why Evangelicals Are Attracted to the Liturgical Church*. Waco, TX: Word, 1985.

———. *The Majestic Tapestry: How the Power of Early Christian Tradition Can Enrich Contemporary Faith*. Nashville: Thomas Nelson, 1986.

———. *Planning Blended Worship: The Creative Mixture of Old and New*. Nashville: Abingdon, 1998.

———. "The Praise-and-Worship Renewal." In *Twenty Centuries of Christian Worship*, edited by Robert E. Webber, 131–34. Complete Library of Christian Worship 2. Nashville: Star Song, 1994.

———. *The Prymer: The Prayer Book of the Medieval Era Adapted for Contemporary Use*. Orleans, MA: Paraclete, 2000.

———. *Signs of Wonder: The Phenomenon of Convergence in Modern Liturgical and Charismatic Churches*. Nashville: Abbott Martyn, 1992.

———, ed. *Twenty Centuries of Christian Worship*. Complete Library of Christian Worship 2. Nashville: Star Song, 1994.

———. *Worship Is a Verb*. Waco, TX: Word, 1985.

———. *Worship Old and New: A Biblical, Historical, and Practical Introduction*. Grand Rapids: Zondervan, 1982.

———. *The Younger Evangelicals: Facing the Challenges of the New World*. Grand Rapids: Baker, 2002.

## 6

## Forerunning Contemporary Worship Music

*The Afro-Pentecostal Roots of Black Gospel*

— Wen Reagan —

What does Contemporary Worship Music (CWM), formed mostly in white evangelical churches in the late twentieth century, have to do with the formation of black gospel, a development of a different musical genre separated by time, culture, and often race? Black gospel music is not a direct or major historical tributary leading to CWM. CWM emerged in the rock era, while black gospel music developed and blossomed well before rock music—in its formal sense—even existed. Certainly, if we dug deep enough, we could find a musical lineage connecting black gospel to CWM, whether we looked at the pentecostal influence on early rock and roll pioneers (who then influenced the rock music that made its way into evangelical churches) or toward the emergence of artists who straddled the line between CWM and black gospel, like Andraé Crouch or Israel Houghton. Yet that historical digging is not the purpose of this chapter. Nor is this chapter in any sense a thorough historical treatment of black gospel music or even music in the Afro-Pentecostal tradition.[1] Plenty of fine studies on both subjects already exist, and their complete histories lie outside the scope of this study. Instead, this consideration of the Afro-Pentecostal roots of black gospel will focus on

---

1. In this chapter I primarily focus on the third style of black gospel that emerged from the Holiness-Pentecostal tradition and through the music of pentecostal artists like Arizona Dranes and eventually Baptist songwriters like Thomas Dorsey. For a broader history see Mashego and Price, "Black Church Music—History." In addition, my historical vignette in this chapter primarily focuses on the black experience of Pentecostalism, often referred to as Afro-Pentecostalism or Black Holiness-Pentecostalism, and especially on black subjects who emerged from the Wesleyan-Holiness Trinitarian Pentecostal tradition. For more on Afro-Pentecostalism, see Yong and Alexander, *Afro-Pentecostalism*.

the inherent "American evangelical logic" (evangelical in the broadest sense) that guided the incorporation of external, "secular" musical forms into the black church sanctuary. The emergence of black gospel music provides us with a historical example of how American Christians transformed what many considered a "noxious noise" into something sacred, a transformation that has several parallels with the development of CWM in the late twentieth century. Many of the themes and concerns that dominated black gospel's growth into an American cultural institution were revisited by white Evangelicals pioneering CWM some fifty years later. The historical progression of black gospel in the early twentieth century—from marginalized, folk culture beginnings to widespread adoption (through discourses of appropriateness and authenticity), and then to industrial development—replayed itself in the late twentieth century among white Evangelicals with the rise of CWM. By considering the rise of black gospel music, then, we acquire a deeper historical grounding of the logic that has dominated the incorporation of contemporary musical cultures into the church sanctuary.

## A Short History of Black Gospel Music Origins

As early Afro-Pentecostalism, steeped in the musical accents and rhythms of earlier slave songs, developed its own "sanctified music," it gave birth to black gospel music. Though this musical culture was first maligned by established black denominations, it made inroads into black churches in the 1920s and 1930s, particularly through the work of Thomas Dorsey and the National Convention of Gospel Choirs and Choruses. By the late 1930s black gospel had become a major musical expression of black churches and even began to look beyond the sanctuary walls as it grew into a commercial enterprise and eventually a secular musical genre. With this evolution of gospel music, Afro-Pentecostals and black Baptists focused much attention over which sounds, lyrics, and gestures belonged in the church and which were of "the world." Yet in spite of this cultural war over the music that inhabited black churches, in just a few decades black gospel transformed from a marginalized musical curiosity into a thriving cultural industry.

The "amalgamated sounds"[2] of sanctified music—the blending of slave spirituals and white Protestant hymnody, combined with the emotional angst of the blues and the syncopated rhythms of jazz—first emerged in the storefront Afro-Pentecostal churches that dotted the urban landscape

---

2. Levine, *Black Culture and Black Consciousness*, 179. This new music grew from several influences. For more information see Williams-Jones, "Afro-American Gospel Music," 376; Sanders, *Saints in Exile*, 74.

of early twentieth-century America. Historian Eileen Southern called these "folk churches,"³ congregations that inherited "the musical practices of the slave invisible church" and embraced "the hand clapping, foot stomping, call-and-response performance, rhythmic complexities, persistent beat, melodic improvisation, heterophonic textures, percussive accompaniments, and ring shouts" that marked such music.⁴

Folk churches were mostly attended by lower and lower-middle-class folk who were primarily interested in transcendent encounters with the Holy Spirit, experiences of movement, volume, and emotional expression that pulled them out of the difficulties of daily life and into the communion of the saints, allowing them to worship a God of power. For many poor blacks, surviving in post-bellum segregated America and the mass migration to the urban north required reaching back to the musical survival mechanisms they had employed in the antebellum south, while also embracing the blues and jazz those mechanisms had evolved into.⁵

As Afro-Pentecostals brought the sounds of ragtime, blues, and jazz into the church, they also often brought the accompanying instruments: drums, tambourine, triangle, guitar, upright bass, saxophone, trumpet, trombones, and anything else that felt right in the Spirit. Organs and pianos—commonly used in the "dignified," wealthier churches—were not shunned in the folk churches, though their expense often exceeded the budgets of small storefront congregations. When money was an issue, folk churches simply sang *a cappella*, channeling the dynamic power of congregational voice.⁶

For black pentecostal and Holiness churches, the Holy Spirit did not discriminate against these musical mediums, as long as their use was directed to the worship of the Lord. They looked to Psalm 150, which called for praise with the trumpet, the harp, the timbrel and dance, stringed instruments and organs, and loud cymbals.⁷ As far as they were concerned, any instrument and sound could be captured for the purpose of worship. This guiding ethos, Levine argued, was articulated later by a church

---

3. For Southern, folk churches included Primitive Baptists (Old Baptist or "Hard Shell" Baptist), Free Will Baptists, individual congregations of the Missionary Baptist church, Pentecostal, Holiness and Sanctified churches (what became Church of the Living God, the Church of God in Christ, and the Church of Christ [Holiness] USA), and a few African Methodist Episcopal and Christian Methodist Episcopal congregations. Although she does not mention them, surely the designation would apply to a few African Methodist Episcopal Zion congregations, too.

4. Southern, *Music of Black Americans*, 453.

5. Jackson, "Changing Nature of Gospel Music," 189.

6. Jackson, "Changing Nature of Gospel Music," 189.

7. Darden, *People Get Ready!* 140.

patriarch who riffed on Martin Luther's supposed quip: "The devil should not be allowed to keep all this good rhythm."[8]

But most middle-class, established black denominations were happy to let the devil keep all of it. They scorned early gospel music because it reeked of the blue notes and jazz beats of the late-night saloon.[9] But they also rejected it because its expressiveness hailed to slavery times and its instrumentation signaled the "primitive" behavior of uneducated, poor blacks.[10] Middle-class African Americans were fighting for upward mobility in a socioeconomic world controlled by whites, so for many the best course of action was to gain respectability in the dominant culture by dressing, acting, and worshiping like whites.[11] In her research, Johari Jabir found the same situation, contending that in Chicago the black church was nothing short of an institution of respectability. "In this role," Jabir argued, "the church functioned as a black Protestant project, one that witnessed black church choirs, under the direction of classically trained musicians, performing a mastery of European classical choral music and arranged spirituals,"[12] music that would register as "white" and thus provide a good name for the black community and its aspirations for upward mobility.

While "sanctified music" was originally confined to Afro-Pentecostal worship services, regular attendees were not only Pentecostals. Black folk across the socio-economic spectrum slipped into sanctified services to enjoy the sounds.[13] Yet by the 1920s, they had other avenues to get their gospel music fix. Black pentecostal recording artists—like Sallie Sanders, Ford McGee, and Arizona Dranes—expanded the reach of early black gospel on the radio and in concert, introducing their music to the larger black religious community.[14]

Early black gospel music first made inroads into mainstream black denominations with the publication of *Gospel Pearls*, the first collection of songs to use the term "gospel." Published by the National Baptist Convention in 1921, *Gospel Pearls* revealed that Baptists were beginning to soften their rejection of pentecostal music, though this was no wholesale embrace.

8. Levine, *Black Culture and Black Consciousness*, 180.
9. Burnim, "Black Gospel Music Tradition," 150.
10. Boyer, "Traditional and Contemporary Gospel Music," 144.
11. Scholars like Ashon T. Crawley and Kelly Brown Douglas have argued that the "politics of respectability," often found in black middle-class churches, only served to reinforce whiteness onto black bodies and into black culture. See Crawley, *Blackpentecostal Breath* or Douglas, *Black Bodies*.
12. Jabir, "On Conjuring Mahalia," 652.
13. Southern, *Music of Black Americans*, 459.
14. Daniels, "Navigating the Territory," 49.

*Gospel Pearls* did not endorse the raucous rhythm and wailing styles of Arizona Dranes and Sallie Sanders, but instead promoted a new musical style that sought to bottle pentecostal ecstasy while winnowing out the chaff of emotional "excess." Excess here meant the vocal distortion of wailing, interjecting phrases into the text ("Yes, Lord!," "Hallelujah!," "Thank you, Jesus!"), hand clapping, and spurts of shouting. Instead, *Gospel Pearls* promoted the slow tempo of the Baptist lining hymn tradition. With *Gospel Pearls*, the National Baptist Convention brought some respectability to the newly termed "gospel music," helping it cross denominational music boundaries and land in the pews of black Baptist, Methodist, and pentecostal churches by the 1930s. But the adoption of *Gospel Pearls* in mainstream churches also meant that black Baptists no longer had to attend pentecostal churches to hear the sanctified sound. For those who wanted just a *little* sway and swing, they could now find it in their own churches.[15]

By the 1930s, the Spirit had carried the sanctified sound beyond the walls of the storefront chapel. This was in part the result of the widespread adoption of *Gospel Pearls* and the radio exposure of several pentecostal musicians, like Sallie Sanders and Arizona Dranes. But these developments paled in comparison to the dual impact of the "father of gospel," Thomas Dorsey, and his partner in crime, the "queen of gospel," Mahalia Jackson.

A native Georgian and son of a Baptist minister, Thomas Dorsey started his musical career in Chicago as "Georgia Tom" after World War I, where he served as the blues pianist for famed blues singer Ma Rainey. Yet after a series of nervous breakdowns in the mid-1920s, Dorsey decided to dedicate his songwriting to the Lord and set out to introduce "gospel blues" to black church audiences. At first, the going was slow. As Jabir explained, Dorsey was "initially penalized for [his] bluesy sensibilities and [his] determination to bring a sense of swing to black church music," because it threatened "the black Protestant project of citizenship and respectability."[16]

Before they teamed up to promote gospel music in the late 1930s, Dorsey's fellow Southern transplant Mahalia Jackson shared his struggles in the windy city. Jackson was subjected to rejection and attempts to change her singing style in order to accommodate a more "respectable" approach. At one singing lesson, the teacher stopped her mid-singing and told her to stop hollering: "the way you sing is not a credit to the Negro race. You've got to learn to sing songs so that white people can understand them." At a

---

15. Boyer, *How Sweet the Sound*, 42–43.
16. Jabir, "On Conjuring Mahalia," 652.

church event, a minister denounced her "undignified" swaying, shouting, use of hands, feet, and hips.[17] But her response was just as heated:

> How can you sing of Amazing Grace? How can you sing prayerfully of heaven and earth and all God's wonders without using your hands? I want my hands . . . my feet . . . my whole body to say all that is in me. I say, "Don't let the devil steal the beat from the Lord! The Lord doesn't like us to act dead. If you feel it, tap your feet a little—dance to the glory of the Lord."[18]

And though she encountered resistance from established congregations, Jackson cut her teeth in the small Afro-Pentecostal churches that had no qualms with her soulful style:

> In those days the big colored churches didn't want me and they didn't let me in. I had to make it my business to pack the little basement-hall congregations and storefront churches and get their respect that way. When they began to see the crowds I drew, the big churches began to sit up and take notice.[19]

These gospel crowds crescendoed for Jackson and Dorsey after Dorsey's 1932 gospel breakthrough hit, "Precious Lord, Take My Hand," and building off of its momentum, Dorsey joined forces with pentecostal singer Sallie Martin in founding the National Convention of Gospel Choirs and Choruses in 1933, giving their gospel music a wider audience and an institutional advocate that promoted gospel choirs in black churches. Dorsey's gospel songs were then carried further afield by several pentecostal radio hosts, including Bishop Eva Lambert in New York City and Elder Lucy Smith and Bishop William Roberts in Chicago, who brought Dorsey's gospel music into thousands of homes.[20]

By the late 1930s, gospel music, in some form, had seeped into most black churches, while Afro-Pentecostalism "had become entrenched" in the black community.[21] The sanctified music of the Afro-Pentecostal tradition had evolved into black gospel, and from there "crossed over" into the established black denominations, yet that had come through a series

---

17. Levine, *Black Culture and Black Consciousness*, 184.

18. Jackson and Wylie, *Movin' on Up*, 66. Quoted in Levine, *Black Culture and Black Consciousness*, 184.

19. Jackson and Wylie, *Movin' on Up*, 66. Quoted in Levine, *Black Culture and Black Consciousness*, 183.

20. Daniels, "Navigating the Territory," 49.

21. Boyer, *How Sweet the Sound*, 18.

of developments.[22] Black pentecostal recording artists like Arizona Dranes had spread the sanctified sound over the radio waves, helping prepare the wider black religious community for Dorsey's later compositions that fused blues and jazz musical structures with religious lyrics.[23] *Gospel Pearls* then introduced early gospel music to mainstream black congregations by downplaying the "excesses" of the pentecostal style of singing. And, finally, pioneers like Dorsey, Jackson, and Martin moved black gospel music—and the pentecostal musical sensibilities and dispositions that accompanied it—beyond the class barrier and eventually into a respected position within the "mainline" black denominations.

Dorsey and Jackson were not Pentecostals, but Baptists. *Gospel Pearls* had been published by the National Baptist Convention and embraced by black Baptists and Methodists alike. In short, while black gospel music had emerged from the Afro-Pentecostal church, by the 1930s, it was popularized by non-Pentecostals, particularly Baptists. Moving beyond its source, gospel music evolved and took on the cultural trappings of its new environs. Yet even though it lost its rough edges, black gospel maintained a deep connection to a pentecostal sensibility that championed the union between rhythm and the body, the utilitarian embrace of instrumentation that could facilitate worship, and the singer's ability to leverage the affective power of song to move an audience to emotional participation.

## Developmental Parallels between Black Gospel and Contemporary Worship Music

### Genre Development

Black gospel music emerged and developed in the early twentieth century in two specific ways that paralleled the later emergence and development of CWM in the late twentieth century: through genre development and tensions over the sacred/secular divide.

Black gospel and CWM shared a similar "genre trajectory," moving from marginalized, local music scenes toward industrialization and eventual commercialization. Here we can use sociologists Richard Peterson and Jennifer Lena's typology of music genre development to compare the development of black gospel and CWM. Peterson and Lena found that most popular music genres could be classified into four different types: avant-garde, scene-based, industry-based, and traditionalist. If they survived and thrived, most music

---

22. Levine, *Black Culture and Black Consciousness*, 181.
23. Daniels, "Navigating the Territory," 49.

genres developed over time from the avant-garde type to the industrial type or even beyond, to the traditionalist type.[24]

Avant-garde genres began small with a dozen participants, were leaderless, often fractious, and usually coalesced around a shared effort to create music that was different from what was currently offered. Avant-gardists claimed that "prevailing genres [were] predictable and emotionless and, flaunting the fact that they [could not] play instruments in conventional ways, [made] what others [considered] loud and harsh sounds." In this sense, avant-garde genres often melded different genres in order to create something new.[25]

Like most popular music genres, both black gospel and CWM began as avant-garde genres. Black gospel music emerged as a fusion of blues, jazz, ragtime, Protestant hymnody, and the slave spirituals among a small cadre of storefront Afro-Pentecostal churches. Black Pentecostals embraced the music because it offered something that other church music could not. Gospel singer Willie Mae Ford Smith explained that sanctified music included the use of sanctified bodies: "I'll sing with my hands, with my feet . . . when I got saved, my feet got saved too—I believe we should use everything we got."[26] And Thomas Dorsey warned against gospel music losing its distinctive movement and emotion: "Don't let the movement go out of the music . . . Black music calls for movement! It calls for feeling. Don't let it get away."[27] These testimonies defined and established black gospel as an answer to the problem of "lifeless, respectable" church music. Finally, early gospel music was both "loud and harsh sounds" to many ears, particularly middle-class African Americans invested in cultivating respectability via "quietistic" worship and whites that had racial or socioeconomic disdain for black Pentecostals.

CWM shared a similar beginning as an avant-garde genre, though at first glance this was not obvious. In fact, Lena and Peterson contended that contemporary Christian music (CCM) (of which CWM is often considered

---

24. The sociological concept of "innovation diffusion" might also be helpful in considering the parallels between black gospel and CWM. Innovation diffusion, perhaps best articulated by Everett Rogers, is the process by which an innovation is communicated through certain channels over time among members of a social system. Both black gospel and CWM, in their unique genre innovations and through their specific communication channels, diffused into larger and larger social systems after a period of incubation among first adopters. For more on innovation diffusion, see chapter 1 of Rogers, *Diffusion of Innovations*.

25. Lena and Peterson, "Classification as Culture," 701–3.

26. Heilbut, *Gospel Sound*, 224–25.

27. Dorsey, "Gospel Music," 190–91. Quoted in Levine, *Black Culture and Black Consciousness*, 184.

a sub-genre) skipped the avant-garde type and began as a scene-based type.[28] This was because they approached their study with a bias toward musical sounds. When approached from a secular musical perspective, CWM was not avant-garde, as it provided no new fusion of sounds into a unique musical form. But it was an avant-garde genre in terms of its lyrical content, providing new themes and phrasings for rock and folk music that focused on praising God. More important, from a liturgical music perspective, it emerged as avant-garde because it introduced a host of new sounds and instrumentation into the sanctuary and fused previous "genres" (in this case liturgical genres of hymn texts, psalms, and biblical doxologies) into new hybrids. It began among a small cadre of individuals who saw the church music around them as "predictable and emotionless," who could not play instruments in conventional ways ("rock piano" versus "hymnal piano"), and who produced music that many considered a loud and harsh noise, whether it was fellow believers in the sanctuary or believers in other liturgical traditions.

Both black gospel and CWM moved from avant-garde to scene-based genres, which were predominantly local in their orientation, but large enough to support independent record labels, scene-based fanzines, and local radio stations. Scene-based genres also often took advantage of nascent technologies that allowed for further distribution and popularizing of the genre.[29]

Black gospel developed from an avant-garde genre into a scene-based genre in Chicago in the late 1920s and 1930s with the rising popularity of Arizona Dranes, Thomas Dorsey, Mahalia Jackson, and Sallie Martin. During this scene-based era, black gospel was recorded and distributed on "race records" marketed to African Americans by Victor, Decca, Okeh, Vocalion and others. In 1926, Arizona Dranes recorded for Okeh Records, becoming the first gospel recording artist. In 1932, Dorsey completed his first gospel recording with Vocalion Records, while in 1937, Mahalia Jackson cut her first record for Decca. Gospel during this era also made its way onto several local radio stations. In 1929, Jack Cooper, the first black DJ, began broadcasting early gospel recordings during his "All Negro Hour" on Chicago's WSBC, while in 1934, Chicago's First Church of Deliverance began its weekly church broadcast, which regularly featured gospel tunes, over WIND. Advocate organizations like the National Convention of Gospel Choirs and Choruses, though it had "national" in its name, served as a local activist group in Chicago for the promotion of gospel music, while a

28. For Lena and Peterson, "music scenes" are often localized, whether geographically or virtually, to a small number of artists, fans, and business intermediaries, yet carry a more coherent, cultural "critical mass" than the avant-garde type.

29. Lena and Peterson, "Classification as Culture," 703–4.

dedicated fan base grew among black Baptists, Methodists, and Pentecostals. The technological combination of phonographs, electrical recording equipment, and broadcast radio provided various avenues of distribution and promotion for early gospel music.

Like black gospel, CWM moved from an avant-garde genre to a scene-based one with the rise of records and a fan base in the 1970s and 1980s, primarily located in California. In the early 1970s, Chuck Smith, the pastor at Calvary Chapel in Costa Mesa launched Maranatha! Music as an outreach program to promote Calvary Chapel's in-house bands and record and distribute their records and song sheets. Maranatha! Music eventually grew into a major record label and music publisher for the CWM industry. Like black gospel, early CWM had its artists, like the Maranatha! Singers at Calvary Chapel or John Wimber, Carl Tuttle, and Eddie Espinosa in the Vineyard fellowship. Individuals like Chuck Smith and institutions like Maranatha! Music and Mercy Records (which eventually became Vineyard Music) served as advocates for the scene, while dedicated fan bases developed in Calvary Chapel and Vineyard churches. Also like black gospel, early CWM took advantage of cutting edge technology—in this case cassette tape duplicators.[30]

Finally, both black gospel and CWM developed into industrial-based genres, which formed around the industrial corporation. Industrial firms now shaped the genre, contracting singers and musicians for their services, marketing them to genre-targeted audiences, and distributing their records via national retail outlets. Record companies utilized charting metrics to advertise and promote the genre, while also pressuring artists to conform to the established conventions of the genre in order to appeal to a mass audience.

Black gospel industrialized in the 1950s and 1960s with the rise of gospel stars like Aretha Franklin and James Cleveland. Franklin signed with Columbia Records in the 1960s and found herself regularly featured at the top of the charts. Artists like Aretha Franklin and Sam Cooke, who signed with RCA records, also helped record labels design a more secular, smoothed-over version of gospel music that was marketed as "Soul." Soul music lacked the religiosity of gospel lyrics, but maintained a similar musical style, and thus had a wider appeal for mass audiences than gospel music did. As major labels like Columbia Records and RCA Records got involved in the genre, gospel music made its way into retail stores and spawned several sub genres that could be further marketed to more targeted audiences, like soul, contemporary gospel, and other forms of R&B.

30. Fromm, "Textual Communities," 247.

CWM industrialized in the 1990s and 2000s as part of a larger industrialization of CCM. Major media companies, like EMI, bought out Christian record labels, like Sparrow Records. In 1995, marketing research firm Nielsen began using its Soundscan service to track CCM sales, which *Billboard* utilized in order to chart Christian music. A similar development came for CWM in churches with Christian Copyright Licensing International (CCLI), a licensing firm that developed a royalties infrastructure for CWM songwriters. CCLI industrialized Sunday morning Contemporary Praise & Worship services by providing new revenue streams for worship songwriters, collected from churches that used CWM songs in their services. During this same period, CWM labels, like Maranatha! Music and Integrity Media, began distributing their music with major labels, like Warner Music Group and Sony BMG respectively. Like black gospel, CWM spawned its own world of sub genres in the 2000s, including "modern worship," "folk worship," "emerging worship," and others.

Lena and Peterson argued that as genres became industrial-based, the music, the musicians, and even the signs of group affiliation often became battlegrounds for authenticity. Black gospel and CWM were no different. Fans and artists alike defended the "purity" of black gospel or CWM's sound or social outlook against the homogenizing hand of the corporate record label, which attempted to "smooth over" the genre's music for wider appeal in the pop market.[31]

For black gospel, this discourse focused on lost authenticity, the nostalgia for a previous era when gospel singers lived by the words they sang and performed their craft for ministry, not for money. This critique attracted enough followers to create a traditionalist genre out of industrialized black gospel, where the energy focused on maintaining the musical, performative, and social conventions that had marked gospel earlier in the twentieth century, as a ministry-based music scene that preached the good news.[32]

Because CWM did not begin until the 1970s, the tensions over authenticity have not seen enough of a past to give birth to a new traditionalist genre. But plenty of heated commentary developed alongside the industrialization of CWM in the late 1990s and 2000s. Both worshipers and worship leaders became concerned with the focus of the music they were singing in their churches. Worship artist Israel Houghton, in his book *A Deeper Level*, worried about the authentic intentions of a growing worship music industry:

---

31. Lena and Peterson, "Classification as Culture," 705–6.
32. Lena, *Banding Together*, 73.

> The Christian music industry is now experiencing a tremendous influx of musicians flocking to worship. Why? Because it sells. Worship CDs used to be relegated to a little shelf in the back of the music display. But today, they are big business... Because of that, I'm afraid it is attracting some musicians who are primarily into their music and simply see worship as "the next hot thing."[33]

Both black gospel and CWM shared similarities in their development because they were both genres that attempted to connect the world of secular music to the liturgical space of the church. For black gospel, it baptized the secular sounds and rhythms of blues and jazz into the worship life of the Afro-Pentecostal church and eventually the black church at large. But while the music and instrumentation had been borrowed from the secular world, the intention of the music remained focused on praising the Lord. When industrialization threatened that purpose in the 1960s, gospel purists called for a return to the authentic origins of gospel that were intentionally steeped in praise. Likewise, CWM began by fusing rock and folk instruments and musical conventions with lyrics focused on worshiping God and loving Jesus. When industrialization in the 1990s and 2000s threatened that focus by shifting it to an industrial concern for profitable homogeneity or emotional spectacle, critics responded with a call to return to "the heart of worship," which was a focus on Jesus.

## Suitability: The Sacred/Secular Divide

As established music genres, black gospel and CWM shared a contestation of authenticity, "border skirmishes" that defined the purity of the genres. And while most discourses on authenticity in popular music genres focused on musical or social conventions (styles of dress, cultural postures), the wars of authenticity in both black gospel and CWM primarily focused on intentionality: the intentions of song lyrics in focusing on worshiping God and the intentions of an industry that should primarily serve as a support ministry for the worship of the church, not a money-making scheme for record labels.

But black gospel and CWM also shared a deeper contentious discourse, one over the suitability of incorporating secular music and all of its conventions and trappings into the worship life of the church. Before the "sanctified sound" developed in Afro-Pentecostal churches, African Americans had already drawn rigid lines. Lawrence Levine told the story of young William Handy, who told his teacher that he wanted to be a musician. But

---

33. Houghton, *Deeper Level*, 103.

the teacher informed him that musicians "were idlers, dissipated characters, whisky drinkers, rounders, social pariahs." When his father got wind of young William's vocational preference, he did not mince words: "I'd rather see you in a hearse. I'd rather follow you to the graveyard than to hear that you had become a musician."[34]

Even while black Pentecostals celebrated creative ways to incorporate blues and jazz music into their worship life, black culture often held secular music at arm's length, suspicious of its negative moral associations and influence.

As the "secularization" of black church music reached new heights with gospel music's surge in popularity in the 1930s, reactions surfaced. Several ministers in the city of Chicago denounced Dorsey's "rocking" kind of music and said that it did not belong in their churches. Sister Rosetta Tharpe moved her shows from churches to ballparks because of objections to her "jazz licks and riffs."[35] But even Dorsey had his own limits. In a 1941 letter published in *The Chicago Defender*, Dorsey defended the necessity of using gospel music in its proper context:

> Spirituals should be used only in the church. It not only cheapens the songs for the bands to jazz them, but desecrates and invalidates a thing that is true to our heritage and authentic of our Race . . . I have written more than three hundred gospel songs and spirituals. I do not object to them being used on the air, but they must not be desecrated or used for dance purposes.[36]

As Cheryl Sanders saw it, at issue was not the "sacred or secular origin of the particular style or technique being used," but the intentionality of the performers and their results—would the music "encourage emotional release, spirit possession, shouting, conversion experiences?" If the answer was yes, then play on. But if the answer was no, then the performers were not putting the music to its proper use, not using it in its God-given role of "spiritual formation."[37]

By the late 1950s, black gospel began moving beyond the walls of the church. Black gospel's increasing popularity came via radio, recordings, television and theater, and black Christians reconceptualized gospel as an evangelistic tool. The problem, as Clarence Boyer put it, was "how to get the word to the unsaved [when] the unsaved would not come where the word [was]

---

34. Levine, *Black Culture and Black Consciousness*, 177–78.

35. Boyer, "Traditional and Contemporary Gospel Music," 127.

36. Dorsey, "Gospel Songwriter Attacks All Hot Bands' Swinging Spirituals." Quoted in Sanders, *Saints in Exile*, 72.

37. Sanders, *Saints in Exile*, 72.

preached and sung." The answer was by taking gospel music to the once-off-limits secular venues, and gospel singers responded in kind, as Mahalia Jackson did when she sang at Carnegie Hall in 1950.[38]

If Cheryl Sanders argued that intentionality and results were what separated the sacred from the secular, then Clarence Boyer extended her argument to mood: "it is not the medium in itself that carries the message but how that medium is used and the response it receives . . . the mood of the performer and the listener determines the effect that the music produces."[39] By highlighting "mood," Boyer acknowledged the affective dimension of gospel music, showing that the communication of meaning and the discourse of suitability extended well beyond lyrical topics or spiritual results. In between the holy intentions of the performer and the spiritual fruit of the audience lay a broadband of two-way communication that utilized instrumentation, venue, lyrics, body language, vocal timbre, dynamics, and performative conventions to narrate meaning. Black gospel, like any other musical genre, was its own cultural world with a host of channels available for communication. For gospel and blues, they shared the same musical forms. But the lyrics, the presentation, the delivery and reception were the channels that presented different meanings. In their complete package, gospel and the blues created two different outlooks that were grounded in unique affective dispositions, even though they shared twelve bar progressions and flattened notes.

A similar phenomenon happened with CWM. The musical forms of CWM were indistinguishable from rock, pop, folk and adult contemporary, yet the other channels of meaning—lyrics, presentation, delivery, and reception—were all critically different. Though the same guitar riffs, drum beats, and vocal timbres could be heard at the club down the street, it only took a few minutes to recognize that for the worship leaders and the enthralled congregants, the rock music in the church communicated something wholly different.

Yet as it was with black gospel, there were also congregants in CWM services who were not enthralled but appalled. In the 1950s and 1960s, evangelical leaders condemned rock and roll for its "jungle rhythm," rebellious lyrics, and implicit sensuality.[40] Youth for Christ leader Marlin "Butch" Hardman declared that rock music exerted a physical effect on listeners that was not "in line with the Word of God."[41] And Hardman was just one of

---

38. Boyer, *How Sweet the Sound*, 187–88.
39. Boyer, *How Sweet the Sound*, 193–94.
40. See Ayer, "Jungle Madness," 19–21.
41. Hardman, "Real Scoop on Rock n' Roll," 10.

many evangelical leaders who saw rock music as a gateway for licentiousness, whether dancing, drinking, or sexual impurity. As CWM grew in popularity, critics from all different sides spilled plenty of ink denouncing it as, at best, a terrible art form and at worst, the work of the devil.

But CWM artists and worship leaders, like black gospel artists, had their own standards of suitability that focused on intentionality. Worship artist Paul Baloche, in a training video on how to execute guitar solos in worship, noted that a good soloist should serve the situation, not focus the attention on their own playing or "making it [their] moment."[42] In another video, Baloche pondered the fine line between performance and leading worship. "We don't want to make it sound like performing is all bad," Baloche explained, "[because] I think so much of it goes back to the posture of your heart, the condition of your heart."[43]

Imagery of the heart was central in the discourse of suitability in CWM, from Baloche's comments to Matt Redman's famous worship anthem, "The Heart of Worship." The defining borders of suitable worship music often fell on the landscape of the heart—what did the hearts of the worshipers look like? Or the heart of the worship leader? The true heart of worship focused the music on God—loving, worshiping, or praising God—and not just with lyrics but also with emotional states. For many worshipers, the lyrics and music of a song were made authentic and suitable by the emotional environment they created. That emotional environment, however, was created by far more than lyrics and musical conventions. These were two key components, but just as important was the affective disposition that worship leaders communicated in their performance style, body language and movement, vocal timbre, and facial expressions, or by the context, scenery, or atmosphere of a venue—manipulated by lighting, fog machines, stage props and acoustics. Still, even with an embrace of emotional states in its discourses of suitability, CWM had limits on the emotional experience of worship music. In a short film, author and speaker Brian McLaren warned against reducing worship to an emotional experience:

> It's just a rat race because I meet so many worship leaders who are paid to help people in this, but the people come like with their check list, "I didn't feel . . . you know, on a scale of zero to ten I only got the feeling to a six today . . . the Holy Spirit's not here." And they put all this pressure on the worship leader to deliver a certain experience and a certain high and it's just

---

42. Paul Baloche and Ben Gowell, in LucyjrAlyn, "Worship Guitar—What NOT to Do."

43. Paul Baloche • Leadworship, "Paul Baloche—Performance vs Worship Leading."

maddening because if the people start playing that game then they have to whip everybody into a frenzy... It becomes manipulation. It becomes propaganda.[44]

Thus suitability for CWM, like for black gospel, meant intentionality. But for both, intentionality involved more than lyrics or results. It involved creating affective dispositions that fused textual meaning with emotional states. Singing for the Lord was not enough. One had to present the right heart for worship, to provide an emotional response to God. And that emotional response had to remain the means, not the end.

Black gospel singer Sallie Martin fused all of these concerns over industrial authenticity, intentional lyrics, and suitable emotions nicely:

> I think the old songs were written out of some kind of burden. The old songs wasn't some song some person sat down and said, I'm gonna get me some kind of song together to make me some money... A song that carry a message got to have some kind of absolutely common sense, and a whole lot of songs sing about my mother's gone and my father's gone, well we don't need all of that. They're playing on emotions, that don't mean nothin'. They're not tellin' them you got to live right, and if you're not right, you need to get right, see.[45]

## Parallels of Practice

While the emergence of black gospel from Afro-Pentecostalism paralleled CWM in its development as a genre and in the subsequent growing pains found in discourses over authenticity and suitability, Afro-Pentecostalism— even early Pentecostalism at large—also paralleled CWM in its internal practices as well. The parallels emerged in three distinct practices: through an emphasis on participation, a penchant for "planned spontaneity," and most important, through the affective dispositions that Afro-Pentecostalism created and sustained.

### Participation

The liturgy of the Christian service has always meant "the work of the people." This was at the heart of early Afro-Pentecostal worship, where the congregants, particularly in their musical participation, performed hard,

---

44. McLaren in Graham, "The Worship Industry."
45. Heilbut, *Gospel Sound*, 17–18. Quoted in Sanders, *Saints in Exile*, 87.

bodily work. The hand clapping, foot stomping, wailing, "shouting" in the Spirit, tambourine playing, and even at times the song leading itself were all aspects of the work of the congregation. And this work was often highly democratized. Walter Hollenweger noted that at the Azusa Street Mission, everyone was a "potential contributor to the liturgy." The seats of the mission were all placed at the same level; there was no elevated front-platform or altar from which everyone would focus their attention on a pastor or preacher.[46] In this sense, early Pentecostalism at Azusa Street allowed for a "democratization of language through a dismantling of the privileges of abstract, rational and propositional systems," a democratization that celebrated the oral and bodily means of communication and participation that were so often deemphasized in other churches.[47]

Democratic participation also contributed to democratized authority. Cheryl Sanders used the term "song-testimonies" to describe the personalized fusion of speech and song that was common in early Afro-Pentecostal liturgies and in gospel music. Song-testimonies destabilized hierarchical authority and cultivated egalitarianism through their emphasis on the personal. That lower-class women and men received authoritative roles in the liturgy made these early pentecostal services participatory in a profound way.[48]

While CWM did not develop in the same liturgical space, it shared many of the same participatory qualities that made early Afro-Pentecostal music attractive to so many. Early CWM emerging from southern California rarely included foot stomping, wailing, or "Holy Ghost Singing," but it did occasionally include hand clapping and congregants leading songs. Chuck Fromm explained that at Calvary Chapel in the early 1970s, weeknight and Sunday evening services gave singers the authority to minister to the congregation through song.[49] The youth attending these services would often come to Chuck Smith and ask if they could share a new song, often so fresh that it had been written hours or days before. Congregants often saw their music as "given by the Lord," implying the prophetic and ministerial role of their songwriting craft, and that their music was meant to be a word for the congregation to hear.[50]

As CWM industrialized into a commercial culture that focused on recorded albums and "worship concerts," many of these original participatory

---

46. Hollenweger, *Pentecostalism*, 23.

47. Hollenweger, *Pentecostalism*, 35. Also see Albrecht, "Worshiping and the Spirit," 233.

48. Sanders, *Saints in Exile*, 84.

49. Fromm, "Textual Communities," 167.

50. Fromm, "Textual Communities," 181.

qualities faded. In fact, a consistent critique of CWM since the late 1990s has been that it is the opposite of participatory—a spectator's sport, another act of consumption in a consumer-oriented society. Theologian John Stackhouse Jr. contended that inherent to CWM was the "modern-day insistence that a few people at the front be the center of attention," which was accomplished "by making six band members louder than a room full of people" via amplification.[51] This was a far cry from Azusa Street's communal singing or even Calvary Chapel's Sunday evening service. "Worship is not a private practice," John Koessler tried to remind his audience in *Christianity Today's* March 2011 cover article.[52] Of course, much to Koessler's chagrin, it *was* a private practice for many.

But for all of the participatory elements that disappeared as CWM moved from a folk music culture to a commercial one in the late twentieth century, the personalized nature of the song lyrics and the affective dispositions they cultivated allowed individuals to "participate" in the music in a different way, one that many fans of CWM considered deeply meaningful. Worship songs often utilized first-person language to emphasize the personal nature of the love and intimacy between God and the believer. This characteristic of CWM has been documented and analyzed by several scholars,[53] but the point here is that these lyrics also provided a *participatory* element as they created a liturgical space for the worshiper to engage with God in a personal way. The lyrical focus was not on stating rational theological doctrines, or rarely ever on the communal reality of worship, but on the personal, intimate connection with God, which could even be couched in erotic language:

> Jesus take me as I am,
>
> I can come no other way.
>
> Take me deeper into you,
>
> Make my flesh life melt away . . .[54]

Participation, then, became the individual worshiper's ability to "lose themselves in worship," to abandon a reserved approach to singing and to open themselves up in an emotional response to God's presence. The resulting abandonment to God in worship paralleled the emotional fervor

---

51. Stackhouse, "Memo to Worship Bands," 50.

52. Koessler, "Trajectory of Worship," 21.

53. See Percy, "Sweet Rapture"; Woods and Walrath, *Message in the Music*, chs. 2 and 3; and Baker-Wright, "Intimacy and Orthodoxy."

54. Dave Bryant, "Jesus Take Me as I Am." Used with permission.

of a rock concert, but moved beyond its communal, liminal space. Instead of simply creating *communitas* (a liminal *social* space that allowed for intense feelings of togetherness and belong),[55] CWM also fostered an *individualized* liminal space between God and the individual believer, resulting in a setting that paralleled philosopher Charles Taylor's "social atomism."[56] Even though CWM took on the habits of consumption and spectatorship that were inherent in a rock concert, the music was still participatory in that it helped each individual believer commune with God in a time of individualized worship—yet all together, all at the same time.[57] It was, then, *atomized participation*.

## Planned Spontaneity

In his history of American Pentecostalism, historian Grant Wacker argued that early pentecostal worship at the turn of the 20th century "oscillated between antistructural and structural impulses," what he called "planned spontaneity." The spontaneity here was synonymous with the pursuit of authenticity in the early church—if the early church was spontaneous in its worship, then that was an authentic liturgical form. Any service marked by planning betrayed its nominal Christianity.[58] But Wacker explained that the creed of improvisation in early pentecostal worship eventually begat structure:

> To call it a prescribed order of worship would be an exaggeration. But singing, testimonies, prayer, sermon, and the call to come forward for salvation, healing, and baptism took a predictable sequence ... Yet the kind of explicit regularization represented only the tip of the berg. A little probing shows an array of devices, more instinctive than self-conscious, that imposed real order on apparent disorder.[59]

These instinctive devices or "implicit forms of regularization" came through the "disciplined use of ecstasy." Glossolalia and slaying in the spirit became

---

55. See Eurich, "Sociological Aspects and Ritual Similarities," or Ingersoll, "Thin Line." *Communitas* is a term popularized by anthropologist Victor Turner in the 1960s.

56. Taylor has noted that the modern culture of authenticity was wracked by "self-centered forms," which "tend to center fulfillment on the individual, making his or her affiliations purely instrumental; they push, in other words, to a social *atomism*," or foster a "radical anthropocentrism." See Taylor, *Ethics of Authenticity*, 58.

57. Cf. theologian Jeremy Begbie's note that most theorists of emotion understood emotion as "intrinsically social." See Begbie, "Faithful Feelings," 326.

58. Wacker, *Heaven Below*, 99.

59. Wacker, *Heaven Below*, 107.

ritual sacraments.[60] The result was, literally, a routinized form of charisma, or charismata, to be exact. Wacker described it in an early 20th century Church of God association meeting:

> At the founding meeting of a Church of God association in Alabama in 1911 (a precursor of the Assemblies of God), controversy erupted over the practice of praying with hands upturned while standing. Was it optional or required? Soon an interpreted tongues message settled the matter once and for all: it was required. Any reasonably impartial outsider surely saw what saints did not: that the Holy Spirit Himself had just turned a seemingly spontaneous act of praise into a prescribed ritual.[61]

While these prescribed rituals maintained an air of spontaneity, they were also tools to bring about order and regulate emotion. And no tool was more powerful than music. With music, "[leaders] could ratchet up the tempo until worshipers broke into ecstatic praise," Wacker explained, "or tone it down when things seemed to be getting out of hand." In other words, music gave pentecostal leaders a "ready means for managing the intensity of the service" and for "regularizing the expression of emotion."[62] While outsiders only saw emotional manipulation, for insiders, pentecostal music was more than it seemed: a vehicle that directed the saints through the emotional landscape of worship.

Pentecostalism's emphasis on spontaneity seeped into black gospel as well. Lawrence Levine highlighted the inherent improvisatory nature of gospel music, revealed in the fact that "gospel singers rarely sang a song precisely the same way twice and never sang it according to its exact musical notation." Instead, gospel singers developed "head arrangements," custom approaches to a song molded by the singers' emotions, "from the way in which 'the spirit' moved them at the time."[63] Even in publishing, this improvisatory nature was apparent, as composer Kenneth Morris explained:

> We don't write it too difficult by including all of the harmony. The people who play it are not interested in harmony. There is no attempt to include perfect cadences and the like. It's not written for trained musicians... A musician is a slave to notes. It's not written for that kind of person. It's written for a person who can get the melody and words and interpret the song for himself.[64]

60. Wacker, *Heaven Below*, 108.
61. Wacker, *Heaven Below*, 109.
62. Wacker, *Heaven Below*, 109.
63. Levine, *Black Culture and Black Consciousness*, 186.
64. Kenneth Morris, interview with George Robinson Ricks, 1956. Quoted in Levine, *Black Culture and Black Consciousness*, 186.

Morris's publishing strategy rang true for any twenty-first century Contemporary Praise & Worship leader, who got hold of most of their music via chord charts (a document that includes the chord progression running above the lyrics, providing the "musical skeleton" for a song) instead of scored music (which documents each and every note change, among other musical characteristics, like dynamics, providing a more "literal" rendering of a song). Even professional online worship music distribution and aggregation services, like CCLI's Song Select, *Worship Leader*'s Song Discovery, and Praisecharts.com all focused on chord charts instead of scored music, mirroring Morris's assertion that black gospel musicians primarily used the music as a base for improvisation, not as binding instructions.

Mellone Burnim argued that improvisation—"the expectation of individual interpretation or personalization of the performance"—lay at the heart of the black musical aesthetic. Yet the mechanics of delivering this improvisation were anything but spontaneous. Burnim explained that if "in the spirit," a singer could emphasize a certain word or line by repeating it several times, drawing the audience into an emotional response. Gospel singers and leaders also managed musical time for emotional effect by "extending the length of notes at climactic points." And though the leader would make these decisions on the fly, they were communicated to other musicians "by using a core of specialized signs and symbols." Even though the improvisations were then staged across the band, from the audience's perspective, the result was a projected spontaneity that marked the difference between a well-executed performance and one that was "inspired."[65] This was Wacker's "planned spontaneity" in good form: a pre-rehearsed sign language employed to communicate an expected improvisatory change that appeared as a spontaneous movement of the Spirit to the audience. Was there spontaneity in the Spirit? Sure. The conductor registered the emotional tenor of the moment and made the necessary changes on the fly. But the sign language then required to communicate that change to the band, all in a fashion that was hidden from the audience, was pre-meditated.

Burnim's observations still rang true for CWM in the twenty-first century. Worship music superstar Israel Houghton, for example, often gave "specialized signs" to signal a change to his band, either by quickly raising his strumming hand, kicking back his left foot, or giving a quick stomp in rhythm. The result was a synchronized cut, crescendo, or repeated chorus that was tailored to the emotional state of the audience, and that seemingly came out of nowhere.[66]

---

65. Burnim, "Black Gospel Music Tradition," 162–63.

66. I observed most of these while watching Israel Houghton live. Houghton's

As in black gospel, an improvisatory culture anchored the conception of authenticity within CWM. Carl Tuttle, one of the founding members of the Vineyard Fellowship and the first worship leader at the Anaheim Vineyard mother church, explained that in the early days of Vineyard worship, when they met as a small evening group, improvisation was key:

> I knew a handful of the choruses that came out of the Jesus Movement and in particular Maranatha Music, so we sang those. I didn't have a list; we didn't have lyrics. I just sang what came to mind and they all joined in. At first it was a few minutes, but over a few months, and as the group exploded, it would go on for at least 45 minutes. Again we had . . . no plan but to try to be sensitive to God and not get in the way.[67]

The core idea here was to "not get in the way" of what God was doing. In other words, like Wacker noted about early pentecostal worship, to avoid anything that looked like planning, anything that would "put God in a box." It was the equivalent of "tarrying in the Spirit," patiently waiting on God to show up and move the congregation to worship. In 1977, when the small evening group finally grew large enough for a Sunday morning service, Carl Tuttle, John Wimber, and others started Calvary Chapel Yorba Linda, and formed their first "worship team." But even with the added complexity of a worship team, Tuttle explained that the emphasis remained heavily on spontaneity and improvisation:

> Our approach didn't vary during this time; we would get together and tune our instruments, pray and then I would simply start a song and the guys would follow. In all that time we never rehearsed, never had a set list, never had any monitors and never provided lyrics for the congregation. The songs were all so simple back then and our repertoire was only about 30 songs, so if you stuck around you learned them pretty quickly.[68]

This was the pentecostal legacy of "planned spontaneity." The spontaneity came from the lack of rehearsal, lyrics, or set list. This pattern created an atmosphere where the Spirit could move as the Spirit saw fit. But the planning was also there, and it came in the form of the repertoire, which was small enough to memorize. In other words, there was a scripted "book

---

signals are readily evident in several YouTube videos of his performances. See, for example, jwill333, "Lakewood Church Worship—Israel Houghton."

67. Tuttle, "Vineyard Worship—The Early Years." Tuttle's Quaker background would have reinforced eschewing pre-planning.

68. Tuttle, "Vineyard Worship—The Early Years."

of common song," a generous and flexible structure—but structure nonetheless—that was a rehearsed (in that it was repeated every Sunday) and pre-meditated (in that it was a bounded set list) body of musical common knowledge that ordered the service. This repertoire provided room for improvisation within a planned structure.

Like Afro-Pentecostalism (and black gospel), CWM was more than it seemed to the casual observer. Critics saw bad music, sacrilegious entertainment, or emotional gimmicks. But for insiders, authenticity emerged within the cacophony of guitars and drums and the crescendos in volume and emotion. Here pentecostal musical sensibilities ran deep. CWM supporters desired an authentic experience that—like in Pentecostalism—demanded a spontaneity that elicited an emotional response. But they also, knowingly or not, sought these musical experiences as normative of proper worship. Prescribed experiences led to planned rituals and liturgies.

The age-old tension between ritual and improvisation that marked pentecostal worship also marked CWM. Torn between prescribing an emotionally moving experience in worship and knowing that an emotional state could not be forced, CWM developed rituals and performative strategies that elicited an emotional reaction from the congregation. Body motions and postures (like the raising of hands or the opening of palms), spoken word interludes over music, chorus repetitions or a bridge build with a slow crescendo toward a climax (often energized by the drums), a lighting strategy that put the front stage in the spotlight and the congregation in the dark, and instrumental cuts that allowed the congregation to hear itself as an *a cappella* instrument were all rituals and strategies that developed to regulate the emotional tenor of the service. And they were rituals and strategies that originated, historically, from a pentecostal sensibility, and as such were shared with black gospel.

## Theo-Affective Dispositions

The pursuit of spontaneity in Afro-Pentecostal music, black gospel, and CWM was a quest for authenticity. The assumption was that when spontaneous, the music was raw and fresh, prodded along by the trans-rational and uncontrolled movement of the Spirit. Thomas Dorsey, the father of black gospel music, understood this well:

> Every singer who performs, speaker also, preacher, anybody, you don't stick exactly to your script. You got to have something that comes from inside of you that Providence or something give to you while you are performing. Well now, we call that,

religiously, you call that the voice of God speaking through you. See you got to always be—everybody who performs or does anything, even talk—susceptible, openly susceptible for whatever comes in the heart or the mind or your ear.[69]

To be "openly susceptible" to the Spirit was also to be emotionally accessible. It was through the emotional tenor of a worship service that participants often found the Spirit moved. If the quest for authenticity was also a quest for an authentic encounter with God, then it often led to the emotions. The successful communication of emotion—both the proclamation of emotion from the gospel conductor, singer, or worship leader and the emotional response of the congregation that the music elicited—remained an integral part of what participants considered authentic music.

Mellonee Burnim explained that for black gospel, this communication of emotion often came from the visible personal involvement of the gospel singer: "the voice must transmit intensity, fullness, and the sense that tremendous energy is being expelled. The singer must convey complete and unequivocal absorption in the presentation, thereby compelling the audience to respond." When the gospel singer met the expectations of the congregation, the performer and congregation or audience united in "a sense of ethnic collectivity and spiritual unity." But Burnim also noted that the emotional communication was only "eloquently achieved through the manipulation of the principles of subtle shading and contrast." In other words, the gospel singer must "prepare the audience properly for musical and emotional climaxes by alternating peak phrases with periods of relaxation." This, Burnim argued, explained why gospel music often displayed sudden dynamic vocal contrasts and the juxtaposition of different vocal textures. It was through "a myriad of vocal sounds . . . yells, screams, shouts, moans, grunts" that gospel singers showed their total involvement in the performance and moved the audience from one emotional state to the next.[70]

No one knew this better than Thomas Dorsey. Johari Jabir noted that Dorsey was first attracted to Mahalia Jackson's vocal craft because "she possessed a way of eliciting physical responses" from her audience, an ability to move her audience emotionally into further participation with the music.[71] Both Jackson and Dorsey clearly understood the power of gospel music to draw an emotional response from a crowd. This focus on the emotional power of music also explained why Dorsey rejected the divide between

---

69. Thomas Dorsey, interview with Michael Harris, Jan 19, 1977. Quoted in Harris, *Rise of Gospel Blues*, 100.

70. Burnim, "Black Gospel Music Tradition," 156–58.

71. Jabir, "On Conjuring Mahalia," 651.

music labeled as "sacred" and "secular." For Dorsey, any musical genre could be used in worship because, at their core, each was simply a "vehicle for your feeling." Dorsey explained:

> If a woman has lost a man, a man has lost a woman, his feeling reacts to the blues; he feels like expressing it. The same thing acts for a gospel song. Now you're not singing blues; you're singing gospel, good news song, singing about the Creator; but it's the same feeling, a grasping of the heart.[72]

Dorsey's conception of music as a "vehicle for your feeling" was a wonderful description of the affective power of music. As the founder of "gospel blues," Dorsey was particularly attuned to the emotional character of the blues, and understood it as more than a musical structure: "blues is more than just *blues*. It's got to be that old low-down moan and the low-down feeling; you got to have feeling."[73] In the same interview, Dorsey explained why he could baptize the blues and transform it into gospel music:

> The only thing about all the music is the words are different, see. You use different words and then you take that blue moan and what they call the low-down feeling tunes and you shape them up and put them up here and make them serve the other purpose, the religious purpose. And then too, the [blues] lilt, tempo, expression, the feeling all go together to make gospel songs what they are and to make blues what they are.[74]

As Michael Harris explained, Dorsey understood that the blues was not just "a set of harmonic, melodic, and rhythmic configurations," but configurations "associated with a set of emotions and their attendant responses."[75] Each musical genre was associated with a set of emotions and the ways those emotions were communicated and received. This developed as a common language or currency within the cultural world of a genre. For the blues, it combined musical structures (melody, rhythm, vocal timbre, scales) to create an emotional disposition, that "blue moan" or "low-down feeling." But as Dorsey explained, the music could be transplanted into a new setting, a new musical culture, where the emotional disposition of the "blue moan" could be transformed to serve a sacred, even theological, purpose. In

---

72. Harris, *Rise of Gospel Blues*, 97.

73. Thomas Dorsey, interview with Michael Harris, Jan 19, 1977. Quoted in Harris, *Rise of Gospel Blues*, 98.

74. Thomas Dorsey, interview with Michael Harris, Jan 19, 1977. Quoted in Harris, *Rise of Gospel Blues*, 100.

75. Harris, *Rise of Gospel Blues*, 97.

other words, the affective resonance of the music was harnessed—hijacked even—to create a baptized affective disposition for gospel music, or, as we might call it, a "theo-affective disposition." The affective meaning that was culturally constructed, communicated and understood within the blues world was then used to fuel and funnel religious affection in gospel music. This hijacking was cultural translation, utilizing an affective language "in the world" in order to express a religious communion "not of the world." Why should the devil have all this good rhythm? But more importantly, why should the devil have all this affective power?

In their unique combinations of lyrical themes, musical structures, performative liturgies, and bodily responses, music genres created cultural worlds that communicated meaning via a host of affective channels. Meaning was not simply communicated from musician to audience, or via lyrics or beat alone. Instead, music was a two-way "broadband" connection that combined several channels to communicate affective meaning. The lyrics, the beat, the vocal timbre, the surging solo, the thumping bass, and the congregational responses and participation (and, more recently, the fog machine and lights) were all parts of a common language that registered emotional cues and elicited emotional reactions, creating a shared affective disposition. Pentecostal music inherently understood this, and black gospel, emerging from Pentecostalism, leveraged the affective language of blues, jazz, and the spirituals to baptize powerful affective dispositions for worship, dispositions that helped congregants celebrate the joy they found in the Lord.

Likewise, CWM appropriated the affective power of rock music in order to develop theo-affective dispositions for Contemporary Praise & Worship. Religious studies scholar Julie Ingersoll noted that one of CWM's major roles in a congregation was "to bind the members of the religious community together emotionally." "Church members [were] connected to each other," Ingersoll explained, "because they [shared] a musical language."[76] And that musical language connected congregants through affective dispositions that brought a theological interpretation and weight to a set of shared emotions. The early CWM that emerged from Calvary Chapel baptized the emotional resonances of the folk movement, leveraging the culture of activism and authenticity that was marked by acoustic guitars, long hair, the soft grain of the folk vibrato, and intricate vocal harmonies to move the congregation emotionally toward praising God and spreading the gospel. For Vineyard Music, worship leaders and songwriters turned to the emotional energy of the soft rock or adult contemporary love ballad and leveraged it to create

---

76. Ingersoll, "Contemporary Christian Worship Music," 123.

an atmosphere of meditative intimacy, where simple musical structures and lyrical repetition allowed congregants to memorize songs, close their eyes, and sing love songs to God within a structure of atomized participation. And with the rise of "modern worship" and its embrace of the sound, venues, and performative culture of arena rock, CWM adopted the transcendent spectacle of the large rock concert and leveraged the affective states induced by massive venues, massive sound (that often vibrated the interior of the body), the collective singing and rhythmic clapping of thousands of congregants, and the "emotional feedback loop" created by giant stadium screens filming leaders and audience members in emotional ecstasy.

## Conclusion: Revealing Parallels

Because of its Afro-Pentecostal roots, black gospel music often met resistance in the black church. Yet those same Afro-Pentecostal roots also led to its eventual widespread adoption among black congregations and its popularity beyond. The mesmerizing sound, the alluring work of musical participation, and the exhilarating affective power of early Afro-Pentecostal music not only rooted black gospel but also echoed through the development of CWM sixty years later. Even though it was more indirect and obscure in CWM, black gospel and CWM shared a common heritage of early pentecostal dispositions, one that gave voice to alternative instruments and musical styles and celebrated the emotional work performed in congregational singing. Further, early Afro-Pentecostal music, black gospel, and CWM shared a culture of participation (though conceived in a different ways), a penchant for "planned spontaneity," and theo-affective dispositions that both emerged from and empowered the musical experience of worship.

Black gospel and CWM were burgeoning worlds separated by time, space, and culture, where the "flora and fauna" looked drastically different. Yet when the organic veneer was peeled away, the topography carried deep similarities, revealing the power of shared tectonic forces just beneath the surface. And perhaps these tectonic forces not only marked the development of black gospel and CWM as influential musical worlds, but also twentieth century American Evangelicalism at large: the fear of corrupting, worldly culture; the eventual appropriation of said culture when justified by the right theological ends; and the allure of the pentecostal intuition for leveraging the theo-affective power of music in worship.

# Bibliography

Albrecht, Daniel E. "Worshiping and the Spirit: Transmuting Liturgy Pentecostally." In *The Spirit in Worship, Worship in the Spirit*, edited by Teresa Berger and Bryan D. Spinks, 223–44. Collegeville, MN: Liturgical, 2009.

Ayer, William Ward. "Jungle Madness in American Music." *Youth for Christ*, Nov 1956, 19–21.

Baker-Wright, Michelle K. "Intimacy and Orthodoxy: Evaluating Existing Paradigms of Contemporary Worship Music." *Missiology* 35 (2007) 169–78.

Begbie, Jeremy. "Faithful Feelings: Emotion and Music in Worship." In *Resonant Witness: Conversations between Music and Theology*, edited by Jeremy Begbie and Steven R. Guthrie, 323–54. Grand Rapids: Eerdmans, 2011.

Boyer, Horace Clarence. "A Comparative Analysis of Traditional and Contemporary Gospel Music." In *More than Dancing: Essays on Afro-American Music and Musicians*, edited by Irene V. Jackson, 127–46. Westport, CT: Greenwood, 1985.

———. *How Sweet the Sound: The Golden Age of Gospel*. Washington, DC: Elliott & Clark, 1995.

Bryant, Dave. "Jesus Take Me as I Am." Thankyou Music (PRS), admin. by Capitol CMG Publishing, 1978.

Burnim, Mellonee V. "The Black Gospel Music Tradition: A Complex of Ideology, Aesthetic, and Behavior." In *More than Dancing: Essays on Afro-American Music and Musicians*, edited by Irene V. Jackson, 147–68. Westport, CT: Greenwood, 1985.

Crawley, Ashon T. *Blackpentecostal Breath: The Aesthetics of Possibility*. New York: Fordham University Press, 2017.

Daniels, David D. "Navigating the Territory: Early Afro-Pentecostalism as a Movement within Black Civil Society." In *Afro-Pentecostalism: Black Pentecostal and Charismatic Christianity in History and Culture*, edited by Amos Yong and Estrelda Alexander, 43–64. New York: New York University Press, 2011.

Darden, Robert. *People Get Ready! A New History of Black Gospel Music*. New York: Continuum, 2005.

Day, Thomas. *Why Catholics Can't Sing: The Culture of Catholicism and the Triumph of Bad Taste*. New York: Crossroad, 1990.

Dorsey, Thomas A. "Gospel Music." In *Reflections on Afro-American Music*, edited by Dominique-René De Lerma, 189–95. Kent, OH: Kent State University Press, 1973.

Douglas, Kelly Brown. *Black Bodies and the Black Church: A Blues Slant*. New York: Palgrave Macmillan, 2014.

Eurich, Johannes. "Sociological Aspects and Ritual Similarities in the Relationship between Pop Music and Religion." *International Review of the Aesthetics and Sociology of Music* 34 (2003) 57–70.

Fromm, Charles E. "Textual Communities and New Song in the Multimedia Age: The Routinization of Charisma in the Jesus Movement." PhD diss., Fuller Theological Seminary, 2006.

Graham, Ted. "The Worship Industry." *YouTube*, May 10, 2007. https://youtu.be/RHGyHCm4jhA.

Hardman, Marlin "Butch." "The Real Scoop on Rock n' Roll." *Youth for Christ*, Oct 1959, 10–12.

Harris, Michael W. *The Rise of Gospel Blues: The Music of Thomas Andrew Dorsey in the Urban Church*. New York: Oxford University Press, 1992.

Harvey, Paul. *Through the Storm, through the Night: A History of African American Christianity*. Lanham, MD: Rowman & Littlefield, 2011.

Heilbut, Anthony. *The Gospel Sound: Good News and Bad Times*. New York: Simon and Schuster, 1971.

Hollenweger, Walter J. *Pentecostalism: Origins and Developments Worldwide*. Peabody, MA: Hendrickson, 1997.

Houghton, Israel. *A Deeper Level*. New Kensington, PA: Whitaker, 2007.

Ingersoll, Julie. "Contemporary Christian Worship Music." In *Religions of the United States in Practice*, edited by Colleen McDannell, 121–28. Princeton: Princeton University Press, 2001.

———. "The Thin Line Between Saturday Night and Sunday Morning: Meaning and Community among Jimmy Buffett's Parrotheads." In *God in the Details: American Religion in Popular Culture*, edited by Eric Michael Mazur and Kate McCarthy, 258–70. London: Routledge, 2011.

Jabir, Johari. "On Conjuring Mahalia: Mahalia Jackson, New Orleans, and the Sanctified Swing." *American Quarterly* 61 (2009) 649–69.

Jackson, Joyce Marie. "The Changing Nature of Gospel Music: A Southern Case Study." *African American Review* 29 (1995) 185–200.

Jackson, Mahalia, and Evan McLeod Wylie. *Movin' on Up*. New York: Hawthorn, 1966.

jwill333. "Lakewood Church Worship—Israel Houghton—Your Presence Is Heaven to Me 7.3.11." *YouTube*, Jul 13, 2011. https://youtu.be/mZx_799ftLc.

Koessler, John. "The Trajectory of Worship: What Is Really Happening When We Praise God in Song." *Christianity Today* 55 (2011) 18–21.

Lena, Jennifer C. *Banding Together: How Communities Create Genres in Popular Music*. Princeton: Princeton University Press, 2012.

Lena, Jennifer C., and Richard A. Peterson. "Classification as Culture: Types and Trajectories of Music Genres." *American Sociological Review* 73 (2008) 697–718.

Levine, Lawrence W. *Black Culture and Black Consciousness: Afro-American Folk Thought from Slavery to Freedom*. Oxford: Oxford University Press, 2007.

Lucarini, Dan. *Why I Left the Contemporary Christian Music Movement: Confessions of a Former Worship Leader*. Webster, NY: Evangelical Press, 2002.

LucyjrAlyn. "Worship Guitar—What NOT to Do When It Comes to Soloing—Paul Baloche and Ben Gowell." *YouTube*, Sept 12, 2011. https://youtu.be/Fklcr52NQdA.

Mashego, Shana, and Emmett G. Price. "Black Church Music—History." In *Encyclopedia of African American Music*, edited by Emmett George Price et al., 64–72. Santa Barbara, CA: Greenwood, 2011.

Mosher, Craig. "Ecstatic Sounds: The Influence of Pentecostalism on Rock and Roll." *Popular Music and Society* 31 (2008) 95–112.

Paul Baloche • Leadworship. "Paul Baloche—Performance vs Worship Leading." Video from the DVD "Modern Worship Series," produced by Paul Baloche. *YouTube*, Dec 13, 2007. https://youtu.be/1NTHzSTu_RQ.

Payne, Daniel Alexander. *Recollections of Seventy Years*. Nashville: A.M.E. Union, 1888.

Percy, Martyn. "Sweet Rapture: Subliminal Eroticism in Contemporary Charismatic Worship." *Theology & Sexuality: The Journal of the Institute for the Study of Christianity & Sexuality* 3 (1997) 71–106.

Rogers, Everett M. *Diffusion of Innovations*. New York: Free Press, 2003.

Sanders, Cheryl Jeanne. *Saints in Exile: The Holiness-Pentecostal Experience in African American Religion and Culture*. New York: Oxford University Press, 1996.

Smith, Willie "the Lion." *Music on My Mind: The Memoirs of an American Pianist*. London: MacGibbon & Kee, 1965.

Southern, Eileen. *The Music of Black Americans: A History*. New York: Norton, 1971.

Stackhouse, John G., Jr. "Memo to Worship Bands." *Christianity Today* 53 (2009) 50.

Swaggart, Jimmy, and Robert Paul Lamb. *Religious Rock 'N' Roll: A Wolf in Sheep's Clothing*. Baton Rough: Jimmy Swaggart Ministries, 1987.

Taylor, Charles. *The Ethics of Authenticity*. Cambridge, MA: Harvard University Press, 1992.

Tuttle, Carl. "Vineyard Worship—The Early Years—Part 1." CarlTuttle.com, January 30, 2009. http://www.carltuttle.com/wimber-years/2009/1/31/vineyard-worship-the-early-years-part-1.html.

Wacker, Grant. *Heaven Below: Early Pentecostals and American Culture*. Cambridge: Harvard University Press, 2001.

Williams-Jones, Pearl. "Afro-American Gospel Music: A Crystallization of the Black Aesthetic." *Ethnomusicology* 19 (1975) 373–85.

Woods, Robert, and Brian Walrath. *The Message in the Music: Studying Contemporary Praise and Worship*. Nashville: Abingdon, 2007.

Yong, Amos, and Estrelda Alexander. *Afro-Pentecostalism: Black Pentecostal and Charismatic Christianity in History and Culture*. New York: New York University Press, 2011.

# 7

## Nashville and Sydney Are Not the World

*The Transnational Migration of Sources for Chinese Contemporary Praise & Worship Songs*

— Lim Swee Hong —

> For the immigrant generation, religious ties were generally less important than ethnic ties. The second generation left the ethnic church because for them, assimilation into mainstream society was of utmost importance. The third generation, however, did not need to prove that they were American. They could practice and embrace their cultural beliefs and practices without the threat of being labeled "un-American." —Sharon Kim[1]

Most depictions of the sources of contemporary worship music for North American congregations, including those of Chinese Christian communities, portray a picture dominated by white songwriters and major companies based in a few centers of activity like Nashville, Tennessee or Sydney, Australia. While this portrayal has some truth, such a picture is neither exhaustive nor thorough. This essay will document alternative sources for contemporary worship music written in Chinese as well as the international reach of these sources as significant examples of the limits of emphasizing centers like Nashville or Sydney.

To enter into the world of Chinese contemporary worship songs, it is important to remember that the following description of Chinese sources for music remains overly simplified for a variety of reasons. For one thing, the Chinese language has two standard written character sets. While mainland China and Singapore have adopted 简体字 (*jiǎntǐzì*), the simplified

---

1. Kim, "Shifting Boundaries," 100.

script, the diaspora of Chinese communities throughout the world has retained 正體字/繁體字 (*zhèngtǐzì/fántǐzì*), the traditional script. Secondly, 華人 or the ethnic Chinese populace has a variety of spoken forms of Chinese.[2] In Hong Kong one would hear 廣東話 (*guangdonghua*), known more widely as Cantonese while in Taiwan one would hear 臺灣話 (*taiwanhua*), Taiwanese. Thirdly, spoken Chinese forms are tonally inflected. Mandarin has four tones, while there are nine tones in Cantonese and eight in Taiwanese. However, they all share a common written script. As a result, though the script may look the same, they can be quite illogical if one does not know which spoken Chinese readership it is intended for. Context, in this instance, is paramount.

To help organize the information about sources of contemporary worship music in Chinese it is useful to consider the different waves and direction of waves for the transnational migration of songs.

## The First Wave: From Europe and North America to Asia

Historically speaking, transnational migration of worship music is not a new phenomenon. With their missional aspiration and Christian empire building ethos, Euro-American missionaries enthusiastically proselytized other parts of the world. Music making efforts often accompanied this effort. Consider the following account of inaugural Methodist missionary work in nineteenth century Singapore:

> Immediately after landing [in Singapore], the town hall was secured and such advertisement as was possible was put out, calling the people together to hear Dr. Thoburn, who was at that time the best known missionary in Southern Asia. On the first evening a remarkable company gathered to hear the preacher . . . The town hall gathering included many different kinds of white men and women with a sprinkling of Tamils from India and Ceylon, a few Chinese from the coast of China, and one inquisitive English speaking Malay. Mrs. Thoburn led the singing. Young Oldham distributed the singing books, and Dr. Thoburn took charge of the service.[3]

---

2. For a summary of the relationship between Mandarin and other spoken Chinese, read Walker, "History of Mandarin Chinese." Read also Egerod, "Chinese languages." For a detailed explanation about the origin of Mandarin, read Coblin, "Brief History of Mandarin," 537–52.

3. Oldham, *Thoburn*, 131–32.

Subsequently, these missionary efforts would establish and support translation work of the Bible and worship music materials. A case in point is the establishment of the Methodist Publishing Press in Singapore. In time, Western hymns were paraphrased into the vernacular, enabling these songs to be sung to their original imported tunes by local believers. The conclusion of the Second World War in the mid-twentieth century ushered in a period of ecclesial changes. Congregations previously established by Euro-North American missionaries became autonomous. However, this clamor for self-determination did not significantly transform the inherited worship practice. Even now, in the twenty-first century, translated Western congregational songs remain dominant and continue to shape the spirituality of these congregations.[4]

In examining this first transnational migration of worship music resources from North America to Asia, it is apparent that its purpose was to provide and sustain the flowering of Christianity in missional lands. This work was primarily taken up by Western missionaries with some fluency in the vernacular. Not surprisingly, Western nuances infused these materials as vernacular texts were juxtaposed with Western tunes and arranged for European four-part singing. Here is a musical example from this era, George F. Root's "The Lord is in his Holy Temple":

WORDS: Habukuk 2:20  
MUSIC: George F. Root, 1820-1895

IRREGULAR  
QUAM DILECTA

---

4. Read Lim, "We're All 'Bananas and Coconuts,'" 136–56, and "Just Call Me by My Name," 502–15.

While this now public domain song has fallen out of favor in Western hymnals, singing it remains an essential worship act for most Chinese Christian faith communities. In many instances, it is sung at the start of worship. On the surface, it is an attempt to convey a pietistic approach in worship. However, more than this obvious reason, the song inscribes for the Chinese Christian community the memory of its missional heritage, a sentiment that is not without some positive interpretation on the part of the Chinese Christian community. With respect to our investigation, this song represents an artifact of the initial transnational migration of worship music.

With the development of Contemporary Praise & Worship in the mid-twentieth century and its unequivocal embrace by people across denominational and geographical boundaries, this transnational migration continues from non-Asian regions to Asia. The difference is that translated Western contemporary worship songs are now superseding Western hymns. Here are two video examples: first, Karen Lafferty's "Seek Ye First" in Cantonese[5] and in Mandarin[6] and, second, Chris Tomlin's more recent "How Great is Our God" in Cantonese[7] and in Mandarin.[8]

## The Second Wave: Worship Songs that Connected First Generation Immigrants

As they immigrated to North America, the diaspora of Chinese Christians established their congregations along linguistic lines. This migration was also accompanied by the next wave of transnational migration of worship music materials. Given the uniqueness of the spoken language cultures of the immigrants, newly established Chinese Christian communities could only rely on the resources imported from their homeland even when the received materials were vernacularly translated Western artifacts.[9] In time, however, Chinese Christian music groups in Hong Kong and Taiwan created songs that found their way to the Chinese Christian diaspora in North America. Noting this connection, Roger Brubaker noted that this phenomenon reflects the "shared collective identity constructed on bounded solidarity and an orientation toward a real or imagined ancestral homeland."[10]

---

5. andychan417, "先求祂的國."
6. 叶百合, "11. 先求神的国."
7. HosannaTheHighest ch, "神祢名尊貴 (How Great Is Our God)."
8. R P, "我神真偉大 How Great Is Our God CH."
9. See Brink, "Glimpses of Recent Chinese Hymnody," 8–24.
10. Brubaker, "The 'Diaspora' Diaspora," 5.

In her ethnomusicological research on Chinese American worship, Maria Chow described the choice of worship music materials and their use. She noted that Asia-originated hymnals including 生命聖詩 *Hymns of Life* (Hong Kong: China Alliance Press, 1986) are widely used by the churches in their multiple services every Sunday.[11] However, it is important to keep in mind that Chinese congregations have a tendency to draw on multiple sources for their worship music making. The adoption of a particular hymnal by the congregation does not preclude the church leadership from including worship music materials from other sources in their services. Often, this approach is driven by the needs of the multiple services organized by age group and socio-cultural consideration, e.g., new Mandarin speaking immigrants from mainland China *vis-à-vis* well established first generation Cantonese speaking (Hong Kong) Chinese-Americans or a second generation that is English speaking Chinese Americans. Wong observed,

> However, it seems that this practice of singing hymns and songs from various sources is also found at some of the Chinese services that do use service hymnals. Among the song collections often used for this kind of free selection, *New Songs Rising* 新歌頌揚 (Taipei, Taiwan: Elim Christian Book Store, 1992) deserves special attention. This is a collection of 400 translated contemporary American Christian songs in four volumes with English texts of the songs provided at the end of the songbooks.[12]

In this instance, translated Western contemporary worship songs that made an impact in Chinese congregations in Asia return to North America via Chinese-American congregations.

Equally significant, this second wave of music migration movement included locally composed original works. Connie Wong has traced the story of these locally composed materials in her dissertation as she described the development of the Contemporary Praise & Worship movement in Asia.[13] In the 1980s, she noted Asian Christian music organizations such as 香港基督音樂事工協會 (Hong Kong Association of Christian Music Ministry, ACM), and the Hong Kong Campus Crusade for Christ affiliated group, 敬拜者使團 TWS (The Worshipers TWS founded in 1994, subsequently renamed 同心圓, One Circle in 2008) were active in creating local worship songs. Eventually, these songs found their way to North America. An example of this resource is the 齊唱新歌 *Come and Sing* hymnal

---

11. For detailed description of Asian-based hymnal use in North America, read Chow, "Reflections on the Musical Diversity," 287–315.

12. Chow, "Reflections on the Musical Diversity," 292.

13. Wong, "Singing the Gospel Chinese Style," 70–120.

series.[14] Describing the songs in this collection, Chinese-Canadian church music scholar, Angelina Ng noted that

> These songs differ from songs in the traditional four-part harmonic style. Composed in folk-hymn style, they are characterized by pleasing arrangements and simple western harmonic chord progressions for accompaniment by piano and guitar, with easily memorized choruses. The content of the songs address personal spiritual experience and tend to be more emotional than the hymns of traditional hymnals about the attributes and activities of God.[15]

Joining in the northward migration of Hong Kong Chinese worship songs are the musical works produced by Taiwan-based 天音 (Tianyin, Heavenly Melody), the music performing arm of Overseas Radio and Television, Inc. that was established in 1960 and 約書亞樂團 (Joshua Band) that was established in 1998. These two organizations made available original worship music materials to Chinese (Mandarin and Taiwanese speaking) Christian communities in Asia and North America. Musical examples are readily available. From the Hong Kong Association of Christian Music Ministry comes 空空的墳墓 ("Empty Grave")[16] and 榮光普照 ("Your Glory Shines").[17] From Heavenly Melody come two other examples: 是愛 ("It's Love")[18] and 粒小種籽 ("Little Mustard Seed").[19]

## The Third Wave: Chinese Contemporary Worship Music Born in North America

In the mid-nineties, there was a proliferation of Chinese Christian music organizations in North America, particularly in California. These were established by Chinese who relocated earlier to the United States as young children or as international students. This burgeoning growth of organizations ushered in the next transnational migration of worship music materials. This time round, contemporary worship music materials were transmitting back to Asia. However, instead of being English-based as in the first migration movement, the lingua franca for this third wave was in Chinese,

14. 齊唱新歌 *Come and Sing*.
15. Ng, "From Tradition to Contextualization," 39.
16. HKACM Official 香港基督徒音樂事工協會, "空空的墳墓—ACM."
17. HKACM Official 香港基督徒音樂事工協會, "【榮光普照】'齊唱短歌4.'"
18. 天韻合唱團 Heavenly Melody, "【是愛】天韻合唱團."
19. 天韻合唱團 Heavenly Melody, "【一粒小種籽】天韻合唱團."

primarily Mandarin. Chief among these groups has been Los Angeles-based 讚美之泉音樂事工 (Stream of Praise Music Ministries [hereafter SOP]).[20] Two of their musical productions are 在這裡 ("You are Here")[21] and 只需要你 ("All I Need").[22]

Established by Taiwanese-American Rev. Sandy Yu (游智婷) in 1993, Stream of Praise Music Ministries, an inter-denominational Chinese Christian music organization, has been a dominant player in the field of Chinese Contemporary Praise & Worship music. Chinese Christian communities worldwide including congregations in mainland China affiliated with both the House Church Movement and the Three-Self Patriotic Movement Church widely use its repertoire. This breadth attests to its music's ability to cross theological and polity differences comparable to how the music of Maranatha! Music, Vineyard, Integrity Hosanna!, Hillsong, and others have been able to do so in the English-speaking world. In 2014, SOP launched its first Japanese Children's Praise and Worship Album, "小さな夢 (A Little Dream)," and begun its foray into Japanese-speaking communities as seen in this song: いつだってさんび ("When I Praise You, I'm Filled with Joy").[23]

To further its reach, SOP's website provides complimentary video tutorial worship team performance practice training for some of its songs. With minimal voiced instruction and video capture of various angles of individual and full worship band performances, this pedagogical approach provides an effective visual rote learning experience that overcomes the inherent spoken language barrier. Despite its obscurity to non-Chinese-speaking faith communities, Chinese-speaking Christian communities around the world, including those in China itself, regularly sing SOP's songs. Since, according to the report of the Council on Foreign Relations, China is on track to have the world's largest population of Christians by 2030, SOP is well placed to become one of the most significant international exporters of Chinese contemporary worship music, even if it is only reaching the Chinese (Mandarin) speaking populace.[24] Without a doubt, SOP's significant influence has profoundly shaped the spirituality of Chinese-speaking congregations globally, paralleling what Hillsong and other groups are doing in the English-speaking realm.

Another American-based exporter of Chinese worship music is San Diego-based 小羊敬拜音樂事工 (Lamb Music | Warrior Bride Worship

20. For a detailed description of SOP and its music-making practice, see Wong, "Singing the Gospel Chinese Style," 120–67.

21. 讚美之泉 Stream Of Praise Music Ministries, "讚美之泉 EP7."

22. 讚美之泉 Stream Of Praise Music Ministries, "讚美之泉 EP10."

23. 讚美之泉 Stream Of Praise Music Ministries, "01 いつだってさんび."

24. Albert and McPherson, "Christianity in China."

Ministry). Taiwanese-American 林婉容 (Lín Wǎnróng), an electrical engineer who wrote her first song in 1994, established this ministry in 1999.[25] By 2005, the organization was doing ministry in the United States and beyond. Aside from leading worship for congregations, it offered worship music leadership training and produced its own music. Two examples of their songs are 陪我走 ("Walk with Me")[26] and 詩篇 23 ("Psalm 23").[27]

Yet another Chinese Christian contemporary worship music organization is Los Angeles-based 我心旋律 (Melody of My Heart Music Ministry). A husband and wife team, Paul Yeh and Francy Shao, established it in 1997. Its primary mission is aimed at mainland China. In 2004, the founders visited Jerusalem, a pilgrimage which refined their sense of purpose. Subsequently, the organization has sought to use their music making efforts in helping "Chinese believers to know God's will in relation to Jerusalem."[28] This interest for Jewish-Chinese expression was reflected in the production of CDs and videos as found on its website. Though the website is still active, it has not featured any new worship materials since 2011.[29]

Established in 1997, Houston-based 新心音樂事工 (New Heart Music Ministries) also has a vision of "ushering people into the presence of God through music."[30] The distinctiveness of this Chinese Christian music organization is its emphasis on music education being on par with its worship music production rather than having the educational activity as an afterthought. Equally interesting is the fact that this group decided to have its second ministry center located in Singapore rather than Taiwan or Hong Kong, the traditional epicenters of Chinese Christianity. The Singapore location is perhaps due to the fact that one of its founders, 余遠淳 (Yenn Chwen Er), is originally from Singapore and knows the infrastructure context of the island. Musical examples from this organization include 呼喊! ("Shout!")[31] and 心的歸屬 ("Home Of My Heart").[32]

---

25. For a brief biography of the founder of Lamb Music, Wanrong Lin, see https://www.lambmusic.org/artists/sehlin.

26. Lyrics at http://songs.lambmusic.org/songs/m_walkwme.php.

27. Lyrics at http://songs.lambmusic.org/songs/m_psalm23.php.

28. Wong, "Singing the Gospel Chinese Style," 197.

29. For a detailed description of Melody of My Heart Music Ministry's music making, read Wong, "Singing the Gospel Chinese Style," 197–202.

30. See https://www.newheartmusic.org/t/Main.

31. NewHeartMusic, "呼喊! Shout!"

32. NewHeartMusic, "心的歸屬 Home of My Heart."

## Revitalization and Other Continuing Issues

One important aspect of the new outbound transnational migration of worship resources from North America to Asia is that composers use Mandarin as the standard language for lyrics. But why have these songwriters turned to Mandarin as the *lingua franca* instead of English or even another Chinese dialect? One obvious answer is that the majority of the creators of these worship music materials are Asian Americans who have competency in Mandarin. At the same time, Mandarin has increasingly become the *lingua franca* for ethnic Chinese communities regardless of where they are located. That is true also in Hong Kong, even if there is resistance to its use for Christian worship in that city.

However, these answers belie a deeper issue confronting Chinese Christian communities worldwide particularly in non-Chinese-speaking contexts, namely, the issue of how worship music facilitates revitalization (or not) in Chinese-speaking congregations in non-Chinese-speaking areas. For pastoral leaders, the need to strengthen vitality in worship practice and congregational numerical strength drives the decision to use different musical repertoires to supplement existing translated Western hymns. It is a commonly held opinion that worship practice in non-Chinese-speaking geographical regions is light years behind its Asian counterpart. Taking up this repertoire is seen as a panacea for this situation. This approach of expanding congregational song repertoire also offers the means for easier integration of new Chinese immigrants.

However, one issue that is less readily resolved is the relationship between the first generation of immigrants and the more culturally immersed subsequent generations that are drawn towards English-language-based contemporary worship music. Such socio-cultural differences manifest in the areas of ecclesial leadership and worship practice including song repertoire. These elements have a tendency of disrupting the stability of the congregation if not managed carefully.[33] Congregational schism and exodus of young adults are all too common realities for Chinese Christian communities in North America.[34]

As a result, Chinese churches in the non-Chinese-speaking region are likely to hold multiple-language-based services or make use of translations for significant church events: Cantonese or Taiwanese for congregants who immigrated from Hong Kong or Taiwan, Mandarin for recent arrivals from mainland China, and English for those who grew up or were born in North

---

33. See Settles, "Singing God's Truth," 17–25.

34. Sharon Kim in her research has uncovered similar concerns in Korean American congregations. See Kim, "Shifting Boundaries," 98–122.

America. The diversity of language used also influences music selection and their performance practice for the various services albeit still governed by the overall worship ethos of the church. Equally significant is that the songs from these Chinese-speaking, American-based organizations have as much—or more—use outside of the United States as they do within the country in invigorating Chinese Christianity worship.

Equally significant is that while 敬拜讚美 (*jingbaizanmei*) Praise and Worship (a decidedly pentecostal term in its origins) is the normative term used to describe the less formal type of worship practice, this nomenclature itself does not reflect the embrace of Pentecostalism by North American Chinese congregations. Chinese congregations are dominantly evangelical rather than pentecostal in theology and expression. Broadly speaking, the various congregations in the church with 敬拜讚美 (*jingbaizanmei*) Praise and Worship services are likely to be centered on lengthy expository preaching and less-than-embodied singing. These services are less likely to have a worship style that is a musically-driven pentecostal worship approach entailing exuberant visible physical worship expressions, profoundly intense prayer ministry, and speaking in tongues for an experiential encounter with God. Often, exuberance in these services is constrained. It is largely held in abeyance by the normative Chinese cultural trait of reservedness.

The continued success of the music organizations mentioned above is due to their ability to discern the Chinese psyche and to hold in tension the demands of being Chinese and American in their musical productions. In so doing, they have been able to create a hybrid musical genre that merges Chinese cultural sensitivities with popular musical styles. As a result, this music has become the heart song of Chinese Christian communities both in North America and in Asia, contributing to the revitalization of Chinese Christian spirituality.

SOP offers one striking example of holding together the tension well. In my recent conversation with Yu, she offered that SOP's concert programing is guided by various factors including prompting from the Holy Spirit, geographical location, and the audience's concerns.[35] For concerts in Asia, she asserts that the repertoire has a higher musical energy setting displaying stronger emotional demonstration and visible physical movement to connect with a youthful populace that has no qualm displaying their worship. 我有喜樂 ("A Joyful Song") is an example of this song type.[36]

In contrast, in North America SOP takes a less musically heightened approach by using a familiar and less physically exuberant repertoire to

35. Sandy Yu, Interview.
36. Patrick Lie, "Stream of Praise New MV" (time code 3:48–8:48).

connect with an older audience that is inherently reserved. Wong encountered this phenomenon while undertaking her participant-observer research with Stream of Praise in 2001.[37] A musical example of this approach is 恩典之路 ("The Path of Grace").[38]

To conclude, current scholarship about contemporary worship music has casually located its epicenters in Nashville and Sydney. At the same time, it has chronicled the dominance of white songwriting artists. However, in the world of Chinese contemporary worship music, the dominance of Nashville and Sydney is not the case. Rather, Chinese music creators elsewhere, artists who have competently filtered this worship expression through their own cultural lens, now dominate this field.

This lens was not created *ex nihilo* but came about through music making's waves of migration. The initial move of translated Western congregational song repertoire to Asia was generated by the need to nurture missional congregations. This work was taken up by Western missional organizations with local collaborators. In the mid to late 20th century, Asian Christian publishers and para-church organizations generated a musical wave back to North America to support and sustain Chinese-speaking church plants in North America and elsewhere. Bilingual hymnals and contemporary worship songbooks with translated Western songs as well as originally crafted songbooks by Asia-based organizations such as Hong Kong's ACM and One Circle and Taiwan's Heavenly Melody made their way to the Chinese Christian communities beyond Asia. By the 1990s, a new generation of Chinese Americans drew on their cultural heritage and initiated a new musical wave to Asia. This wave, largely dominated by Stream of Praise Music Ministry, became a worldwide phenomenon impacting all Chinese-speaking Christian communities in both Asia and North America.

This historiographical investigative approach to understanding the transnational migration of musical phenomena in Chinese contemporary worship music making can readily be used to examine similarly embedded ethnic communities in North America, such as the Koreans or other ethnic Christian communities. This approach can be used to uncover how a community's sense of ethnic identity can be reconciled with their practice of Christianity outside the socio-cultural conditions of the dominant culture.

Equally important, this transnational musical movement reveals the profound link between the worship music practice in the country of origin and the diasporic faith community. This relationship provides the means for the latter to be self-determining in its worship practice, minimizing influence

37. Wong, "Singing the Gospel Chinese Style," 144.
38. 86MoonLight, "赞美之泉 Stream of Praise SOP 恩典之路 The Path of Grace."

from the local socio-cultural milieu. Significantly speaking, this musicking approach purveys a transplanted faith community and sustains it. Yet in so doing, how might such faith communities see their role in fulfilling their mandate of loving God and neighbor or root itself culturally in the host country? Might this approach result in the unintended siloing of ethnic Christian worship, strengthening the ethnic Christian populace at the expense of exacerbating the insider-outsider divide? How valid then is the identity formed by this approach? For as cultural theorist Gordon Mathews reminds us,

> The choices each of us makes as to cultural identity are made not for ourselves but for performance for and in negotiation with others: we choose ourselves within the cultural supermarket with an eye to our social world. One's cultural identity is performed in that one must convince others as to its validity.[39]

Perhaps then, the way forward is to ensure this transnational movement of music is less of an indispensable umbilical cord but an inspirational source of developing local worship music expressions. Ultimately, congregations need to discover for themselves their distinctive practice of *lex cantandi est lex orandi* (the rule of singing is the rule of worship). Only then can their worship vitality be truly self-sustaining.

## Bibliography

86MoonLight. "赞美之泉 Stream of Praise SOP　恩典之路 The Path of Grace." *YouTube*, Jun 15, 2011. https://youtu.be/XrXlFpgWk_E.

叶百合. "11. 先求神的国." *YouTube*, Jan 3, 2011. https://youtu.be/9OlXdcaeRTM.

天韻合唱團 Heavenly Melody. "【是愛】天韻合唱團 Official MV." *YouTube*, Apr 25, 2016. https://youtu.be/2suta9Yft_E.

———. "【一粒小種籽】天韻合唱團 Official MV." *YouTube*, Apr 25, 2016. https://youtu.be/AmxHad1SuQ4.

讚美之泉 Stream Of Praise Music Ministries. "01 いつだってさんび【さんびの泉・SOPキッズワーシップ2陽はてるよ雲の上】讚美之泉." *YouTube*, Aug 8, 2017. https://youtu.be/gwgVm3VYc-4.

———. "讚美之泉《天堂敬拜　LIVE》第一季—EP7 官方HD ： 活著為要敬拜祢/ 在這裡/ 每一天我需要祢/ 帶我進入祢的同在/ 日日夜夜." *YouTube*, Feb 28, 2019. https://youtu.be/UtXpV2tNsnQ.

———. "讚美之泉《天堂敬拜　LIVE》第一季—EP10 官方HD ： 奔跑不放棄/ 只需要祢/ 三百六十五天/ 榮耀的呼召/ 一同起舞." *YouTube*, Mar 20, 2019. https://youtu.be/ypBg1oheO-M.

---

39. Mathews, *Global Culture*, 22.

齊唱新歌 *Come and Sing*. Hymnal series. Hong Kong: Hong Kong Association of Christian Music Ministry, 1982.

Albert, Eleanor, and Marisa McPherson. "Christianity in China." Council on Foreign Relations. Last modified Oct 11, 2018. https://www.cfr.org/backgrounder/christianity-china.

andychan417. "先求祂的國." *YouTube*, Dec 16, 2010. https://youtu.be/641MalrQjr0.

Brink, Emily R. "Glimpses of Recent Chinese Hymnody: Including a Review of the 2006 Edition of 'Hymns of Universal Praise.'" *The Hymn* 59 (2008) 8–24.

Brubaker, Rogers. "The 'Diaspora' Diaspora." *Ethnic and Racial Studies* 28 (2005) 1–19.

Chan, Samuel Sum-Yee. "Growing Chinese Boomer Churches in Toronto." DMin diss., Fuller Theological Seminary, 1991.

Chan, Sharon Wai-Man. "The Dynamics of Expansion of the Chinese Churches in the Los Angeles Basin." PhD diss., Fuller Theological Seminary, 1996.

Chong, Eric King Chung. "More than Praises: Cantonese Christian Worship Music and Hong Kong Immigrants in the Greater Toronto Area." MA thesis, York University, 2011.

Chow, Maria M. "Reflections on the Musical Diversity of Chinese Churches in the United States." In *Music in American Religious Experience*, edited by Philip V. Bohlman et al., 287–315. New York: Oxford University Press, 2005.

Coblin, W. South. "A Brief History of Mandarin." *Journal of the American Oriental Society* 120 (2000) 537–52.

Dumbauld, Ben. "Worship Music and Cultural Politics in the Chinese-American Church." *Ethnomusicology Review* 17 (2012) 1–13. https://ethnomusicologyreview.ucla.edu/journal/volume/17/piece/590.

Egerod, Søren Christian. "Chinese languages." Encyclopædia Britannica. https://www.britannica.com/topic/Chinese-languages.

HKACM Official香港基督徒音樂事工協會. "【榮光普照】'齊唱短歌4' Official Lyric Video—官方完整版." https://youtu.be/OAVJTUTAP2w.

———. "空空的墳墓—ACM 齊唱兒歌5 (官方完整CD版)." *YouTube*, Mar 19, 2019. https://youtu.be/MK5ZEm_58bU.

Ho, Vicky Wing-Ki. "Thirty Years of Contemporary Christian Music in Hong Kong: Interactions and Crossover Acts between a Religious Music Scene and the Pop Music Scene." *Journal of Creative Communications* 8 (2013) 65–75.

HosannaTheHighest ch. "神祢名尊貴 (How Great Is Our God)." *YouTube*, Feb 2, 2015. https://youtu.be/WOTFDOSd1Jw.

Jeung, Russell. "Asian American Pan-Ethnic Formation and Congregational Cultures." In *Religions in Asian America: Building Faith Communities*, edited by Pyong Gap Min and Jung Ha Kim, 215–43. Walnut Creek, CA: Altamira, 2002.

———. *Faithful Generations: Race and New Asian American Churches*. New Brunswick, NJ: Rutgers University Press, 2005

Kim, Sharon. "Shifting Boundaries within Second-Generation Korean American Churches." *Sociology of Religion* 71 (2010) 98–122.

Li, Qiang. "Ethnic Minority Churches: The Case of the Canadian Chinese Christian Churches in Ottawa." PhD diss., University of Ottawa, 2000.

Lim, Swee Hong. "Just Call Me by My Name: Worship Music in Asian Ecumenism." *The Ecumenical Review* 69 (2017) 502–15.

———. "We're All 'Bananas and Coconuts': Congregational Song in the Global South." *International Journal of Practical Theology* 23 (2019) 136–56.

Mathews, Gordon. *Global Culture/Individual Identity: Searching for Home in the Cultural Supermarket*. London: Routledge, 2000.

NewHeartMusic. "呼喊! Shout! (新心音樂事工)." *YouTube*, Aug 26, 2014. https://youtu.be/rqUTtwI46io.

———. "心的歸屬 Home of My Heart (新心音樂事工)." *YouTube*, Oct 6, 2015. https://youtu.be/d5yQadd-AaM.

Ng, Angelina. "From Tradition to Contextualization: Worship Music in the Cantonese Congregation of Richmond Hill Christian Community Church." ThM thesis, Emmanuel College, University of Toronto, 2019.

Oldham, William Fitzjames. *Thoburn—Called of God*. New York: Methodist Book Concern, 1918.

Patrick Lie. "Stream of Praise New MV." *YouTube*, Aug 3, 2013. https://youtu.be/4zxFKUfuDfs.

R P. "我神真偉大 How Great Is Our God CH." *YouTube*, Aug 3, 2012. https://youtu.be/_5RKtz-NcRI.

Settles, Pauline Chiu. "Singing God's Truth in the 1.5 Generation Chinese American Way." PhD diss., Fuller Theological Seminary, 2012.

Tölölian, Khachig. "The Nation-State and Its Others: In Lieu of a Preface." *Diaspora: A Journal of Transnational Studies* 1 (1991) 3–7.

Walker, Joanne. "History of Mandarin Chinese." Language Tutoring. http://www.languagetutoring.co.uk/HistoryofMandarinChinese.html.

Wong, Connie Oi-Yan. "Singing the Gospel Chinese Style: 'Praise and Worship' Music in the Asian Pacific." PhD diss., University of California, 2006.

Yu, Sandy. Interview by Lim Swee Hong, Sept 15, 2017.

# 8

## The Rise of the Worship Degree

*Pedagogical Changes in the Preparation of Church Musicians*

— Jonathan Ottaway —

In 2002, Margaret Brady defended her doctoral thesis exploring "The Use of Contemporary Congregational Music in Undergraduate Sacred Music Programs." At the time, Brady's thesis was the latest major study of the development of Christian music education (especially at the undergraduate level) and it provided a bleak analysis of the current situation. Following decades of decline, recent statistics gleaned from the National Association of Schools of Music (NASM) showed that enrollment in sacred music programs had decreased 25 percent in the ten years from 1982 to 1992. Even more alarming was the precipitous 40 percent decline in enrollment from 1990 to 2000 that had led to the closure of forty-five sacred music programs within that same period.[1] With falling enrollment and closing programs, the future of Christian music education[2] was in question, if not in peril.

For Brady, the decline of sacred music degrees was a symptom of a growing misalignment between the pedagogical goals of existing programs and the forms of music being used in the worship of many churches. Through a review of the literature of NASM proceedings and surveys

---

1. Brady, "Contemporary Congregational Music," 6.

2. In this chapter, "Christian music education" will be the term that I use to refer to all forms of undergraduate and graduate programs that train musicians or ministers for service within the worship of the church. As this chapter will show that these degree programs have shifted their nomenclature from "sacred music" to "worship" during the period under discussion, I intentionally sought a term that would encompass the full range of programs in their varying manifestations including, "sacred music," "worship," and "church music."

completed by member schools of the Council for Christian Colleges and Universities (CCCU), Brady argued that sacred music programs were reluctant to integrate Contemporary Praise & Worship music forms, which an increasing number of hiring churches expected their musicians to be skilled in.[3] Frequently, students perceived hostility in this reluctance toward forms of worship and music that were central to their experience and formation. Additionally, because programs were failing to prepare students for their future ministry contexts, students were encouraged away from undergraduate sacred music degrees (and toward music education programs or graduate programs in sacred music) in order to gain more marketable skills that would ensure a better likelihood of employment.[4]

Because of the existing misalignment, Brady concluded that it was the responsibility of sacred music programs to adapt if they were to survive. She pointed to "the acceptance of jazz into the music academy" as providing a corollary model for "the acceptance of contemporary congregational music into the undergraduate sacred music curriculum."[5] Like Contemporary Praise & Worship music, jazz had been a genre of music that had been excluded from the academy due to both a lack of desire and an inability among faculty members to integrate it. She envisioned the recent integration of jazz into the academic study of music as a widening of the study of music that nevertheless preserved the core aims and pedagogies of the discipline. Likewise, she advocated an "integrated approach" toward Contemporary Praise & Worship music that preserved the meta-structure of sacred music programs but widened its approach to include "a familiarity and appreciation for contemporary congregational music."[6]

However, even as Brady was formulating her solution to the problems of sacred music degree programs, a seismic shift in the landscape was already underway that would bring about a renaissance of Christian music education, reversing the decades of decline that had preceded it. This renaissance did not come about through the incremental changes to sacred music degrees that Brady advocated, though. Indeed, Brady's description

---

3. Brady, "Contemporary Congregational Music," 122.
4. Brady, "Contemporary Congregational Music," 63.
5. Brady, "Contemporary Congregational Music," 59.
6. Brady, "Contemporary Congregational Music," 125. It is perhaps illustrative of Brady's commitment to the traditional format of sacred music degrees (albeit with an incremental increase in contemporary styles of worship music) that her nomenclature for these programs remained "sacred music" even though this was an increasingly neglected term. Indeed, throughout her dissertation, Brady described all Christian music education degrees, which by the time of her defense already existed under a variety of terms, as "sacred music programs."

of the decline of sacred music programs would prove to be terminal. (In 2018, among member schools of the CCCU, only three schools still offered a sacred music degree.) Instead, a realignment of the pedagogy of Christian music education programs to the musical and liturgical practices of churches occurred through the inauguration and rise of an entirely new degree program: the worship degree. In this chapter, I will show how the worship degree rose to become the predominant form of undergraduate training for music ministry over the last two decades. Following a historical overview of the renaissance of Christian music education within this period and the role of the worship degree in this renaissance, I will describe the pedagogical shifts that have occurred as institutions have made the transition from the sacred music to the worship degree.

## Historical Development of the Worship Degree

By as early as 2000, a handful of schools throughout the United States were already forging a new approach to Christian music education through the introduction of new worship degree programs. The first of these worship programs were master's degrees, possibly because students in previous decades were increasingly encouraged to pursue training for music ministry at the graduate level. In 1997, Regent University became the first accredited institution to offer a worship studies concentration to their MA in Practical Theology, made possible through a partnership with the Christian record label, Integrity Music. Liberty University likewise introduced a similar program in 1998 (also in conjunction with Integrity Music).[7] In their partnership with these universities, Integrity Music's role was to provide staff and key worship leaders (such as Don Moen and Ron Kenoly) who could teach the core courses of these programs within the institutional framework of the universities.[8] While the link that these degrees had with Integrity Music implies that the curricula was influenced by pentecostal/charismatic theologies of Praise and Worship, other figures within American Evangelicalism were also exploring new forms of worship education. In particular, in 1999 Robert E. Webber began admitting students to his new program, the Institute for Worship Studies, to work toward a Doctor of Worship Studies degree.[9] Web-

---

7. Liberty University's MA of Religion in Worship Studies was launched through its Worship Institute. See Redman, "Expanding Your Worship Worldview," 20.

8. Redman, "Expanding Your Worship Worldview," 20.

9. Robert E. Webber Institute for Worship Studies, "History," https://iws.edu/about/unique/history/. See chapter 5 for more information on Robert Webber. Originally named the Institute for Worship Studies, after Webber's death in 2007 the school was renamed the Robert E. Webber Institute for Worship Studies.

ber designed his program to equip church musicians who already had master's degrees. This program distinguished itself from the degrees introduced by Regent and Liberty programs by its emphasis lying not in the equipping of students with new forms of praise music, but in the renewal of "a more historical and traditional approach to worship."[10]

The introduction of master's degrees in worship studies only briefly preceded the introduction of undergraduate programs in worship. By as early as 2000, both Judson College and Northwest Nazarene College were advertising degree majors in "Worship Arts" and "Worship Leadership" respectively.[11] Judson College, in particular, had introduced its Worship Arts degree in 1999, partly because institutional changes made restructuring necessary (the theater program had proved unsustainable as a standalone program), partly because prominent local ministries (such as Willow Creek Community Church) had successfully experimented with contemporary forms and were encouraging Judson to adopt new pedagogies, and partly because Judson recognized that students whose musical experience was based in less traditional forms of music-making were not being accommodated.[12]

During the next decade following the launch of these undergraduate degrees, the study of Christian music education underwent a transformation as it took up a renewed role at the center of the educational offerings of undergraduate institutions. Particularly illustrative is to track the way that programs which ostensibly trained musicians for ministry in the church were advertised to potential students in the annual education edition of *Campus Life*, a magazine produced by *Christianity Today* for older teenagers.[13] The annual college edition was an important source of information during this period that existed to help students make decisions about higher education through a presentation of Christian institutions and the degree majors they offered.[14] In 2000, only fifty-two schools (48 percent of

10. Redman, "Expanding Your Worship Worldview," 21.
11. "The 2000–2001 Christian College Directory."
12. Anderson, Interview.
13. In 2006, the magazine changed its name to *Ignite Your Faith*, which remained its title until the magazine's closure in 2009. *Christianity Today* still produces content for teenagers through its website (https://www.christianitytoday.com/iyf/), including producing an annual guide to Christian colleges that is hosted on the separate website, http://christiancollegeguide.net.
14. In constructing this narrative, I surveyed three representative years of *Campus Life*'s annual college edition (2000, 2005, and 2008). My choice of 2008 as a final year to include in the survey was driven by the magazine's closure in 2009. Using their college guide, I created a data table that listed institutions, region, denomination and degree programs (within Christian music education) offered. My quantitative analysis in the following paragraph is built upon this analysis. Using *Campus Life* to discern some of

all the schools included in this edition) advertised some form of Christian music education program.[15] In the 2005 edition of *Campus Life*, a dramatic upshift in the number of schools advertising a program is observable: 82 percent of all schools listed a Christian music education degree as available at their institution. Not only did the number of institutions offering a Christian music education program increase, but also there was a dramatic increase in the number of programs being offered. In 2000, with 108 schools advertising in *Campus Life*, there were sixty-seven degree programs advertised. By contrast, in 2005, with a reduced ninety-one schools advertising, 121 degree programs were offered.

|  | 2000 | 2005 | 2008 |
| --- | --- | --- | --- |
| No. of Schools Advertising | 108 | 91 | 72 |
| No. of Christian music education degrees advertised | 67 | 121 | 91 |
| No. of Christian music education degrees per school | 0.62 | 1.33 | 1.26 |

This reveals that a number of schools were diversifying their educational offering by advertising multiple programs in Christian music education. Forty-eight percent of schools who advertised in *Campus Life* in 2005 offered multiple programs (versus 27 percent in 2000). This trend toward a

---

the underlying trends in Christian music education does introduce some limitations to the methodology. First, the number of institutions that advertised in my sample years was not constant. This is likely driven by editorial decisions on the part of *Christianity Today* and decisions by colleges not to participate. Even more important to recognize though is that as a popular magazine whose task was to educate students on potential college choices, *Campus Life* had no obligation or aim to provide a holistic and comprehensive list of all programs available in the institutions that advertised in them. Therefore, my use of *Campus Life* will not approach this data as presenting an objective picture of all of the potential programs offered. However, with this caveat it can still be seen that colleges discerned a renewed interest in Christian music education throughout 2000–2008, and their response can be seen by the radical increase in number of Christian music education programs offered during this period.

15. Chief among the titles these programs were listed under were Sacred Music (30 percent), Christian Music (34 percent), Church Music (16 percent), and Organ (15 percent). One of the difficulties in using this data is the lack of attention paid to specific program names. *Campus Life* did not differentiate between different forms of Christian music education perhaps either on pragmatic grounds (simplicity of publication or ease of understanding for the reader) or because they failed to recognize that changes were occurring. For this reason, I have drawn no conclusions in this paper about the nature of worship education based upon the descriptions that *Campus Life* used.

higher concentration of degrees is continued in the 2008 edition of *Campus Life* where even though a reduced 61 percent of schools advertised a program in Christian music education, 39 percent of all schools advertising were offering multiple programs.

|  | 2000 | | 2005 | | 2008 | |
|---|---|---|---|---|---|---|
|  | # | % | # | % | # | % |
| Schools advertising | 108 | – | 91 | – | 72 | – |
| Schools advertising a Christian music education degree | 52 | 48% | 75 | 82% | 44 | 61% |
| Schools offering multiple Christian music education degrees | 14 | 13% | 36 | 40% | 28 | 39% |

The data from *Campus Life* reveals that Christian music education was experiencing growth across (predominantly) evangelical institutions in the early 2000s. Through their increasing advertisement of these programs, schools implicitly communicated their expectation that these programs were attractive to potential students. This data also suggests that schools were diversifying the range of programs that they offered in this area. The basis of the growth of Christian music education cannot be solely attributed to the inauguration of the worship degree. While the *Campus Life* data from 2005 shows a dramatic increase in the number of advertisements for Christian music education programs, the worship degree did not become established as a mainstream offering of Christian institutions until after 2005. In an interview about the Liberty University worship programs, Vernon Whaley notes, "When we started this program in 2005, there were only six other undergraduate colleges or universities offering a major in worship or any kind of worship related discipline. Today [in 2013], there are over 100 colleges or universities offering some type of worship degree."[16] This narrative alongside the *Campus Life* data suggests that the reenlivening of Christian music education briefly *preceded* the worship degree's establishment. However, the rapid expansion of worship degrees following 2005 indicates that the momentum of Christian music education became indelibly linked to this new degree program.

---

16. Vernon Whaley, quoted in Armstrong, "Liberty University," 16–17. Whaley's observation is borne out by the fact that in its 2005 college edition, *Campus Life* only advertised three degree programs that included the word "worship" in the title.

This timeline is supported by other sources that reveal both an increasing awareness of worship education's existence as well a gradual conversion to the argument that these programs provided significant resources for contemporary church musicians. For example, *Worship Leader,* the bimonthly magazine focused toward practitioners of praise and worship, introduced a new annual section in 2008 specifically designed to promote worship degrees. Initially, this section was a small, paid, advertisement section that largely promoted graduate education (nine out of sixteen programs in 2008 and seven out of thirteen programs in 2010 were graduate programs). In 2011, this annual section started to expand dramatically, becoming a glossy fifteen-page section that provided significant space to twelve schools to describe the nature and extent of their programs.[17] Not only did the paid advertisement sections that had become a regular feature of the September edition of *Worship Leader* expand (in 2014, multiple monthly editions featured lengthy advertisements sections), but arguments that contended for the benefits of worship education began to appear throughout the regular editorial content of the magazine as well. A culture was forming and being formed among evangelical and pentecostal churches that saw the need for their musicians to receive degree-level education as part of their training.[18] Worship leaders were increasingly being told they needed to be trained to be "thoroughly informed in the history of the church, holding close to the teachings of the Bible and the wisdom that has been passed down through the ages"[19] and that "a call [to worship ministry] without education does not honor the trust God has placed in you."[20]

While students and worship practitioners were being made aware of an increasingly broad diversity of programs, recognition was also growing at an institutional level that the working definitions of Christian music education were becoming antiquated in comparison to the new worship

---

17. "College Bound," 46–61. This expansion was continued in 2012 where twenty-two pages were devoted to advertising the worship programs at thirteen schools.

18. Parallel to this trend is the rise of church-based education programs in worship (outside of an accredited degree program). Church-based schools of worship have existed alongside university-based programs (and may even preexist the worship degree). The advertisement of their programs in periodicals like *Worship Leader* indicates that they have followed a similar historical trajectory as their accredited counterparts. For example, Christ for the Nations Institute advertised their "School of Worship and the Arts" as early as 2000; see *Worship Leader* 9, no.5 (2000).

Over the past decade, the number of these programs has increased dramatically, and they are often presented (especially in periodicals like *Worship Leader*) as equally viable ways of preparing oneself for worship leadership.

19. "College Bound," 46.

20. Cherry, "Open Letter," 58.

degrees being introduced. Brady notes that, within the NASM, pressure for reform of the accreditation of sacred music programs had been building since the 1980s.[21] After 2000, the main faculty voices calling for change came from evangelical institutions whose critiques of the current training of church musicians were presented at annual NASM proceedings. Their presentations addressed numerous different concerns, advocating for increased attention to how programs did or did not pastorally form church musicians,[22] presenting survey data that highlighted ongoing changes that were taking place in church music or sacred music degrees (particularly highlighting respondents' answers to concerns about Contemporary Praise & Worship),[23] and demonstrating how pedagogy for traditional music theory could be adapted to better speak to the experience and aims of current students (especially those who were immersed in churches who practiced Contemporary Praise & Worship).[24] By 2012, these voices within and without Christian music education were answered by the NASM's addition of a new accreditation rubric for a worship degree to coexist alongside the rubric for the sacred music degree.[25] With the introduction of this rubric, worship degrees received an important form of legitimacy through recognition from a wider body of music educators. This rubric was also significant because it is one of the first cross-institutional documents that established what a worship degree was. (This definition also provides a useful benchmark for distinguishing how worship degrees compare in emphasis and pedagogy to the sacred music degree.)

Nothing more indicates the radical change that has taken place in Christian music education than a survey of the degree programs offered across the member schools of the CCCU presently.[26] In 2018, 103 schools

21. Margaret Brady provides a useful overview of comments within the NASM proceedings in her dissertation. See Brady, "Contemporary Congregational Music," 23–39.

22. Uitermarkt, "Learning about Music."

23. Isensee, "A Brief Survey of NASM Schools."

24. Kinchen, "Toward Praxis Music Theory." In particular he writes, "since the music concepts and styles foundational to the four-part writing practices of the Baroque and early classical period are somewhat remote from the experience of the styles and practices these students will have in their ministry, it was decided that in addition to common-practice music principles, other more relevant concepts would be taught side-by-side, namely the Nashville Number system and Jazz theory" (Kinchen, "Toward Praxis Music Theory," 60).

25. These degree rubrics continue to exist in parallel to the present, offering two different options for preparation for music ministry.

26. In the following paragraphs, my data is compiled from the websites and undergraduate catalogs of all member institutions of the CCCU. (The list of CCCU schools was obtained from the CCCU website: "Our Institutions," https://www.cccu.

(out of 136) in the CCCU offered a degree program in Christian music (76 percent). Twenty-one schools (20 percent) offer multiple degrees at their school showing a continued presence but reduction in the number of concurrent offerings of degree programs.[27] The continued and robust presence of Christian music education at CCCU schools is not the most notable aspect of this data though. Instead, in the sixteen years following Brady's dissertation, the most significant change that has occurred is in the name under which most Christian music education is now carried out. Within the CCCU, only three schools still offered a degree in "Sacred Music"[28] while twenty-two continued to offer a degree in "Church Music"; 113 out of the 138 programs in Christian music education that are now offered contain the word "worship" (or "music ministry") within the degree title.

| Christian music education degree title | Number | Percent |
| --- | --- | --- |
| Sacred music | 3 | 2 percent |
| Church music | 22 | 16 percent |
| Worship (or music ministry) | 113 | 82 percent |
| Total | 138 | |

org/institutions/.) This information has additionally been cross-referenced against the institutional data that NASM makes available through their website. This information was gathered in March–April 2018 and so is correct for the academic year 2017–2018. In order to gain the most accurate picture about the nature of worship degree programs and their relationship to accreditation agencies, a number of methodological choices were made in how data was gathered about the CCCU schools. Although the CCCU includes graduate schools as well as a few universities and colleges located in Canada, these schools report to different accrediting agencies. Because the question of accreditation and centralized authority was key to my analysis, I excluded these schools from the data I gathered. I also only gathered information on programs pertaining to worship in a specifically Christian context. General music, music education, or degrees that were focused on the study of particular instruments were not included in my survey (despite the likely strong connections that would be made in some of those programs to the context of Christian ministry). Additionally, I limited my survey to traditional four-year bachelor's programs that required residential learning (as opposed to online study). The stated major needed to imply a strong connection to the worshiping life of the church. Programs that were included had titles like "Sacred music," "Worship," Worship Arts," and "Church Music."

27. Indeed, some schools such as North Central University and Ohio Christian University have four or five different programs in worship studies.

28. Sterling College, Tabor College, and Franciscan University of Steubenville.

This change at the level of terminology is accompanied by other underlying changes that indicate that broader pedagogical shifts have also occurred as schools have transitioned to the worship degree as the primary mode of Christian music education. First, the worship degree has brought about changes in the departments and faculties who offer those degrees. While 68 percent of worship degrees offered in 2018 continued to be housed in traditional music departments, 16 percent now resided in theology or ministry departments and 5 percent of programs were housed within a specialized worship department.[29] Inevitably, with departments offering degree programs that transcend their discipline, eleven CCCU colleges were offering simultaneous and competing worship degrees through different departments in 2018.[30]

A second major change is in the accreditation source for worship degrees. In 2018, the majority of worship programs offered through CCCU institutions were not listed as accredited with the NASM.[31] Within the CCCU, sixty-nine of the 136 member colleges have music departments that are accredited through the NASM. While fifty (72 percent) of these schools offer a worship degree, only seventeen (34 percent) of these worship degrees are listed by the NASM as accredited with them. In combination with the forty-seven CCCU schools who are not NASM-accredited institutions but who offer a worship degree, 84 percent of CCCU schools who offer a worship program do so without the accreditation of the NASM. This is despite the fact that the NASM has had an accreditation rubric for a worship degree since 2012. This has a further impact upon the actual degree that is conferred upon students. While twelve out of the seventeen NASM-accredited worship degrees are Bachelor of Music degrees, only six out of the remaining 113 worship degrees are. The overwhelming majority of programs in Christian music education have become Bachelor of Arts

---

29. The other 11 percent of degrees reside in broader, blended departments that could not be defined either as theology, music/fine arts, or worship. An example of this is Dordt College that listed a "Church Music" degree through their Music department and a "Worship Arts" degree through their Humanities department. Additionally, Lincoln Christian University does not differentiate between different departments at their college.

30. Dordt College, Emmanuel College, Mount Vernon Nazarene University, Northwestern College, Oklahoma Baptist University, Spring Arbor University, Sterling College, Nyack College, Moody Bible Institute, University of Mobile, Missouri Baptist University.

31. Data about the accreditation of worship degrees at CCCU institutions was compiled in 2018 from the NASM's list of accredited institutions that they make publicly available through their website. See https://nasm.arts-accredit.org/directory-lists/accredited-institutions/.

or Bachelor of Science degrees. This perhaps suggests that the worship degree is less commonly perceived of as a specialized music degree requiring centralized accreditation.

## Changes within the Pedagogy of Christian Music Education

Thus far my narrative has described the rise of the worship degree from its inception in the late 1990s to the position of dominance it holds today (eclipsing the sacred music degree as the principal form of preparation for music ministry). These two decades have seen a sharp reversal of fortunes for Christian music education in general. The study of Christian music has gone from a position of severe decline to become a nearly universal part of the educational offering at CCCU schools. This abrupt change in popularity alongside the concurrent rise of the new worship degree suggests that worship programs introduced broad pedagogical changes that realigned the *telos* of Christian music education with both the church's worship and the vocational aspirations of students. The worship degree is not the sacred music degree under new nomenclature. In the following section, I will describe these pedagogical shifts that occurred in the transition from the sacred music degree to the worship degree. Principally, this transition is revealed through the changing competencies required of worship students. Some proficiencies that were once central to the pedagogical content of sacred music programs have evolved or were relegated. In its place, new skills are emphasized that articulate a new vision of what the role of the church musician is today.

The realignment between the pedagogy of Christian music education programs and the church's worship is most clearly revealed through changes in the level of musical proficiency required of students in worship degrees. Although music remains a major component of most worship degrees, the transition to the worship degree is often accompanied by a reduction in the rigor of musical standards. For example, Glenn Koponen, a professor at Nyack College notes that their worship degree (unlike the former sacred music program) replaced four semesters of music history with one semester of music appreciation. In addition, it no longer requires a senior recital. And, finally, it offers students more elective space to tailor their worship degree to their interests.[32] Likewise, the NASM accreditation for worship degrees also

---

32. Koponen, Interview. Koponen described these changes as an accommodation to the students who are entering this degree program. In his experience, students are not graduating high school with the same level of musical proficiency that they had

reveals both a scaling back of focused musical proficiency while simultaneously increasing their requirements for a broader set of musical competencies. The former requirement in sacred music degrees to "perform, improvise, and conduct at the highest possible level as appropriate to the area of specialization" has become a requirement to perform at "a high level" while displaying a wider set of functional skills in piano and voice.[33]

While many programs have responded to the need for realignment of their pedagogy with the worship practices of the church by scaling musical proficiencies back, other programs have attempted to produce the realignment through a creative adaptation of their music pedagogy. Liberty University has been a particularly influential example of this sort of adaptation when John Kinchen developed a new methodological approach for teaching music theory through Contemporary Praise & Worship songs and the Nashville numbering system.[34] This methodology seeks to transform a potentially abstract skillset into a valuable applied aptitude that is intelligible to a new generation of students and that has clear links to the musical practice of the church. The popularity of this approach can be seen by the rapid growth and expansion of the worship degree offering at Liberty. Eight years after the launch of their worship degree in 2005, Liberty's program had grown from eighty-nine students to serving over one thousand graduate and undergraduate students in fifteen distinct worship degree tracks.[35]

Not only is the proficiency in established areas of Christian music pedagogy evolving to meet the changing practices of churches, but new skillsets are also being required to prepare students for the ministry marketplace. While previous stricter requirements for proven musical proficiency has broadly been relaxed in worship degrees, one of the most universal changes is an inverse rise in the number of required theology and biblical studies courses as part of the major.[36] This undoubtedly illustrates the increased role

---

previously. Accordingly, in their worship degree, Nyack have felt a need to downgrade their requirements to better meet the skills and experience that their students possess. As a longstanding faculty member, Koponen felt this gap was a point of continuing tension in the dynamic interplay between the discipline of Christian music education and the student.

33. National Association of Schools of Music, *Handbook 2017–18*. The language of the 2018 Handbook is identical to the language of the 2013 Handbook where the worship degree accrediting standards were first introduced.

34. Kinchen, "Towards Praxis Music Theory." Armenio Suzano, in an e-mail message to the author (June 1, 2018), noted that this approach has been the cornerstone of Liberty University's program that other institutions are using as the roadmap for their programs.

35. Armstrong, "Liberty University," 16–17.

36. Koponen, Interview; Brian Walrath, e-mail message to author, Dec. 7, 2018;

of the worship leader in the Free Church context as a pastoral presence who has wide-ranging responsibilities in shaping liturgical practices within the church.[37] Moreover, since the 1990s, as churches have become reliant upon electronic technology in worship, musicians have become increasingly responsible for the management and integration of these technologies.[38] Thus, a new competency of employing "media and technologies in developing and producing music and worship experiences"[39] has become a key distinctive of the NASM accreditation standard for worship degrees. Finally, professional experience in worship through internships has become an indispensable component of the degree content. This both increases the students' employability (by helping them establish ecclesial networks and proven professional experience) but also serves the interest of the degree program itself whose work and methodologies are exposed "to an ever-renewing source of prospective students from these very churches."[40]

The above description has shown that in the transition to the worship degree, the competencies required of students are less specialized than in sacred music degrees. Conversely, through the broader competencies required in worship programs, graduates are empowered to function in a broader and different capacity in ministry contexts. However, in the transition to the worship degree a more fundamental change has occurred that transcends the changed competencies that are required of students. There has been a more elemental evolution in the nature of the Christian music education degree *as* a qualification. Whereas through the sacred music degree, musicians sought a degree that would provide a focused but narrow skillset that was confirmed through an accredited professional qualification, the worship degree does not confer that same professional qualification.

---

Anderson, Interview. These professors noted that this was one of the primary changes introduced in their schools in the transition into worship degree programs.

37. Nelson Cowan notes the increasingly common pastoral role of the "worship leader." He argues, "worship leaders are prophets insofar as they are bearers of charisma whose presentation of self and performance has an effect on the gathered assembly. Worship leaders are priests because the worship leader makes important liturgical structuring decisions and mediates content like musical dynamics, lyrical curation and dissemination, and transitional elements." Cf. Cowan, "Lay-Prophet-Priest," 24–31.

38. Lim and Ruth, *Lovin' on Jesus*, 46–51. Lim and Ruth note that while churches practicing Contemporary Praise & Worship in the 1980s usually employed electronic technology through simple sound systems, technological developments in the late 1980s and early 1990s especially in movie theater sound systems became increasingly taken up by churches looking to replicate that quality.

39. National Association of Schools of Music, *Handbook 2017–18*. While most of the accrediting standards for the worship and sacred music degrees are similar, this requirement has no corollary in the sacred music degree.

40. Suzano, e-mail message to author, June 1, 2018.

Indeed, the NASM requires accredited schools to inform incoming students that worship degrees do not meet the requirements of a professional degree (unlike sacred music).[41] If students are aware of this distinction between the two degrees, this has not dampened their enthusiasm for the degree. In turn, this suggests that professional qualifications are not significant to their vocational contexts. The decreased emphasis on the worship degree as a professional qualification also indicates why a relatively low number of worship degrees within CCCU schools seek accreditation through the NASM[42] or why the movement away from offering Bachelor of Music degrees has not caused a decrease in worship programs.

## The Worship Degree: Completed Revolution or Continuing Evolution?

Brady's 2002 diagnosis of the collapse of the sacred music degree provided a solution that preserved the content, aims, and pedagogy of existing programs while seeking to become open to the experience of students and churches. However, this diagnosis and any resulting pedagogical changes came too late and was too conservative. While it would go too far to describe the rise of the worship degree as a *revolution* in Christian music education, it is far from the gentle *evolution* that Brady envisioned. Instead of a centralized conversation among scholars and theologians about the nature of Christian music education leading to incremental and mature changes, the worship degree arose out of the experimentation of numerous individual colleges whose new programs proved a large demand for this educational offering existed. Because the worship degree developed at the periphery and moved to the center of Christian music education, the content, aims, and pedagogy that Brady sought to preserve became subjected to an external reenvisioning, affecting both the skills that the programs impart and the nature of the qualification that the program provides.

However, the realignment of the pedagogy of Christian music to the worship of the church is still in flux today. From the ecclesial standpoint, the relationship between churches and the schools who provide their ministers will always be dynamic because the worship and liturgy of the church is always evolving and that creates a changing set of musical needs. From the institutional direction, schools are caught in a dynamic interplay as they

---

41. Koponen, Interview.

42. Lack of accreditation with NASM does not mean that the program is unaccredited. NASM recognition is generally additional to the school's accreditation that it gains from regional authorities.

both seek to serve the needs of the church while also playing a prescriptive (and prophetic) role in defining the worship of the church (and maintaining the orthodoxy of their academic discipline). The institutional position is doubly difficult as they try to provide a stable and rigorous definition of what preparedness for music ministry means while also attracting students to enroll in their programs (who are, themselves, subject to market concerns of cost, duration, difficulty etc.).[43] While this ongoing dynamism can be a source of tension among faculties and churches, the tension itself is generative as it continues to fuel dialogue between stakeholders about how music relates to the life of the church. While the rise of the worship degree has brought about significant changes in the pedagogical landscape of Christian music education (with correlative gains and losses), it has extended the life of a conversation that was dying out.

## Bibliography

"The 2000–2001 Christian College Directory." Christianity Today's *Campus Life* 59 (2000) 120–40.
"The 2005–2006 Christian College Directory." Christianity Today's *Campus Life* 64 (2005) 102–31.
"The 2008–2009 Christian College Directory." Christianity Today's *Ignite Your Faith* (2008).
Anderson, Warren. Interview by Jonathan Ottaway, Jun 13, 2018.
Armstrong, Jeremy. "Liberty University School of Music with Dr. Vernon M. Whaley." *Worship Leader* 22 (2013) 16–17.
"Back to School." *Worship Leader* 21 (2012) 48–70.
Brady, Margaret M. "An Investigation of the Use of Contemporary Congregational Music in Undergraduate Sacred Music Programs." EdD diss., Northern Illinois University, 2002.
Cherry, Constance. "An Open Letter in the Spirit of Paul." *Worship Leader* 23 (2014) 58.
"College Bound." *Worship Leader* 20 (2011) 46–61.
Cowan, Nelson "Lay-Prophet-Priest: The Not-So-Fledgling 'Office' of the Worship Leader." *Liturgy* 32 (2017) 24–31.
Isensee, Paul. "A Brief Survey of NASM Schools Offering a Curriculum in Sacred/Church Music with Special Attention to Internships." *Proceedings of the 83rd Annual Meeting of the National Association of Schools of Music* 96 (2008) 153–60.

---

43. Brian Walrath, e-mail message to author, Dec. 7, 2018. Walrath described this particular problem at Spring Arbor University. The theology department introduced a worship degree as a form of pre-divinity program. This program had a lower musical requirement than the music department's worship degree with the expectation that further study would complete the student's education. However, Walrath notes that students have proved adept at using this program to gain their worship qualification with the minimum amount of proven musical proficiency *and* without pursuing further study.

Kinchen, John D. "Toward Praxis Music Theory." *Proceedings of the 87th Annual Meeting of the National Association of Schools of Music* 99 (2011) 59–68.

Koponen, Glenn. Interview by Jonathan Ottaway, May 31, 2018.

Lim, Swee Hong, and Lester Ruth. *Lovin' on Jesus: A Concise History of Contemporary Worship*. Nashville: Abingdon, 2017.

National Association of Schools of Music. *Handbook 2012–13*. https://nasm.arts-accredit.org/accreditation/standards-guidelines/archive/.

———. *Handbook 2017–18*. https://nasm.arts-accredit.org/accreditation/standards-guidelines/archive/.

Redman, Robb. "Expanding Your Worship Worldview: Education and Training for Worship Leaders." *Worship Leader* 9 (2000) 18–21.

Uitermarkt, Cynthia. "Learning about Music Isn't Enough! Educating Future Church Musicians Who Succeed." *Proceedings of the 78th Annual Meeting of the National Association of Schools of Music* 91 (2003) 256–57.

# 9

## Methodological Insights for the Historiography of Contemporary Praise & Worship

— Lester Ruth —

Anyone who has farmed or gardened can tell you the difference between working a well-developed plot of land, one that has been carefully maintained and cultivated over the years, and a virgin field. The former needs only to be reawakened and rejuvenated in order to tease out of it a bountiful harvest. The latter, however, takes a different kind of work as the soil is cleared, turned over, and made ready to see what it can yield.

This same difference applies to studying and writing about the history of Contemporary Praise & Worship. Since the nineteenth century, liturgical historiography as a general field has developed a mature body of literature on antecedent historical periods and on the main features of worship across a wide range of Christian traditions in those earlier centuries. One can find compelling studies on a range of eras and topics: reflections on the development of baptism and the Eucharist in the early church, works that detail the specifics in the development of the early Byzantine rite, studies in the performed aspects of worship in the Middle Ages, accounts of the major shifts brought out by the Protestant Reformation, and even reflections on the impact of Vatican II on the Roman Catholic Church and beyond. Although liturgical history is itself a relatively new academic field—at least compared to the study of church history generally—it is no longer virgin territory overall.

The same cannot be said for the study of Contemporary Praise & Worship. It is still pristine. A few sociologists have taken their spades to a few corners of this field. Others with more pointed liturgical interests have dabbled in a few sections. A few folks who reside in the middle of the field have written popular, non-scholarly accounts of what an amazing place God has made it. The most sustained and serious attempts at systematically turning over this soil have come from musicologists, but even they have only begun to scratch the surface. Indeed, as compared to other topics in liturgical history, the study of this recent phenomenon is one through which the plow (or rototiller as the case may be) has gone through the plot only very recently and, even in that case, not through the entire field.

The freshness of the field is both refreshing and challenging. It is exciting—even exhilarating—to be discovering new facts and writing new accounts never before published. What lurks in that next undulation in the ground? What mysteries will be uncovered by traveling just a bit further? These are questions that greet the researcher approaching this topic currently.

But it is also deeply challenging in that, because of how little the entire field has been documented and mapped, there remains to be done much basic gathering and organizing of materials that can open up this history. In other words, discussing the appropriate method for writing the history of Contemporary Praise & Worship must include discussion of bibliographic development itself.

That emphasis upon bibliography provides a contrast to older, better-researched areas of church history. In that historiography, advancement is often made not in the discovery of new primary materials (i.e., materials from the historical figures and churches themselves) but in raising new methods of interpretation of already-established bodies of materials.[1] Historians in these better-documented areas refine the history by asking new questions and bringing new grids of analysis to established bodies of primary materials.

However, that situation is not the case in writing the history of Contemporary Praise & Worship. Here the first challenge is still the hunt for primary material: What sources are available to tell this history? Which are most critical? How might they be organized to tell a coherent story? And, most critically, have we gathered enough of them to be able to write a full and accurate history? (One can miss telling an accurate history not only by including misinformation but also by failing to account for significant aspects of that history.) Not surprisingly, many of the methodological points I will discuss below will deal with bibliographic development of primary materials. The question of interpretation of these materials follows the development of primary materials. Sometimes this sequence is theoretical since in actual practice the historian is constantly trying to make some sense of all

---

1. Cf. Taft, "Structural Analysis," 190.

new data. The key for a researcher is not to allow too hasty an interpretation to shut off the search for more information. As one of my former professors once told me, it is easy to prove your point when you ignore all evidence to the contrary. The goal in balancing the gathering of primary materials and their interpretation is to delay pulling the trigger on interpretation so quickly that one quits looking for possible contrary evidence.

The issue of the proper sequence between bibliographic development and interpretation leads to the first of my methodological principles for studying Contemporary Praise & Worship.

## Methodological Principles

### Principle One: Bibliography is everything, and methodology is the other half.[2]

As just noted, bibliographic development is indispensable to proper research in this field. As I have argued elsewhere,[3] many prior studies of Contemporary Praise & Worship have been derailed from accurately portraying the history of the phenomenon by cutting short their accumulation of primary materials and then jumping too quickly to an interpretive scheme to make some polemical point—pro or con—about this liturgical phenomenon. For some this defect produced a positive account of how this way of worship was a result of God's movement. Only primary material that reinforced that narrative was referenced. In contrast, others threatened by this approach to worship only highlighted historical details that could be used to offer a critique.

Significant developments, figures, and underlying theologies were overlooked in both cases. Authors have not done the sustained, systemic, and comprehensive bibliographic development that would have allowed for a more thorough, accurate history. This root deficiency likewise corrupted sound methodology by setting up a problematic answer to the most fundamental of methodological questions: what is the researcher looking at? By having a limited bibliography the researcher struggles to answer the next two methodological questions (i.e., What questions is the researcher asking of the material? What presumptions did the researcher bring to the

---

2. I apologize for the Yogi Berra–type statement to begin the discussion of key methodological principles, but this sort of overstatement does justice to the criticalness of this first point. Yogi Berra was a famous professional baseball player who also gained notoriety for his ability to speak in what have been called Yogi-isms. My first principle is similar to his statement that "90 percent of baseball is mental; the other half is physical."

3. Ruth, "Divine, Human, or Devilish?" 290–310.

material?) with enough objectivity to write a thorough, accurate history. Limited bibliography means an inferior history as one scholar has succinctly put it: "A historical argument is never stronger than the evidence on which it is based."[4]

This utter necessity for bibliographic development means the researcher needs to be creative and relentless in locating primary materials. James White's assertion that to write Protestant worship history liturgical historians need to go beyond the liturgical text to look at a variety of issues (piety, time, place, prayer, preaching, and music)[5] is amplified in documenting this phenomenon. Because the materials are "popular" in nature and often not in published form, a researcher will not find them in research libraries but more likely will find them in online used book sites. Examples would be the writings of popular, influential pentecostal authors like Judson Cornwall, Kevin Conner, or Bob Sorge. Moreover, because of the propensity for extemporaneity in worship, sound and visual recordings of different sorts are critical. Even here, however, creative zeal for discovery is needed since few of these recordings have been cataloged as part of library holdings.

The researcher's zeal must lead to unconventionality, at least as it relates to the sorts of materials liturgical historians normally pursue. Magazines aimed for worshipers and worship leaders are critical, including better-known magazines like *Christianity Today* or *Worship Leader*, or lesser known like *The Psalmist* or *Worship Times*. Segment-specific magazines as in the case of technology-related journals (*Church Production, Technologies for Worship Ministries*) or denomination-specific (Vineyard's *First Fruits*) can likewise be important sources for information. Beyond magazines, researchers can make use of church supply catalogs of various sorts not to mention publisher's trade catalogs to see what books were offered when. In addition, perhaps one of the biggest sources of information little explored (so far) are the educational materials for worship leaders (guidebooks, workbooks, and media) that exploded in quantity starting in the 1980s.

The unconventionality should extend to online resources, too. The Google Ngram Viewer, for example, is an online search engine that allows one to get a sense of the frequency of publication by time period for particular words or phrases. Other online resources are invaluable including YouTube for videos of past services, Netflix for documentaries that include scenes from worship services, and data from Christian Copyright Licensing International's websites.

---

4. McKenzie, *Little Book*, 59.
5. White, *Protestant Worship*, 14–21.

Perhaps the biggest example of unconventionality for liturgical historians is in the use of interviews. While those in social sciences might be used to relying upon talking to people as a source for information, historians often are not. However, because many participants are still living and because their information has been documented in few secondary sources, anyone wanting to write the history of Contemporary Praise & Worship must speak to those who lived and made the history.

If possible, the researcher should try to find video or sound recordings of past services. The feel of a service is not necessarily reproducible or transferable in a written description. When researching the early worship of the Anaheim Vineyard congregation, for example,[6] I discovered my sense of what the worship was like increased significantly after I was able to hear my first audio recording of a 1982 service. Unfortunately, like popular literature, such recordings are not likely to be found in research archives but still reside with individuals. Sometimes a historian can find recordings on YouTube or other online sites or for purchase on online sites dealing with previously owned materials.

Regardless of the particular source of primary material, a researcher in this field must be careful not to cut off bibliographic development prematurely. To do so places greater strain on other methodological concerns if one hopes to be able to tell a full, accurate history.

## Principle Two: The researcher must go beyond the better known, most obvious, or most easily accessible; the researcher must not think these aspects tell the whole story.

Having a bibliography prematurely stillborn can lead to a related methodological flaw: the propensity to focus on the better known, most obvious, and most easily accessible. As I like to tell my students, if one is mesmerized by window dressings, it is easy to overlook the foundation. In other words, if one's eye is only drawn to the most conspicuous, it will be difficult to tell the full story.

The "window dressings" can be either topical (like music) or human (like a significant person or church). There are multiple reasons why the researcher's eye (or ear, as the case may be) would be drawn to conspicuousness. One key reason is that, because this field is a new one and not yet well documented, the researcher will naturally seek to find cases or issues from which larger extrapolations can be deduced. The researcher will seek to find some manageable bit from which they can draw larger conclusions about the

---

6. Park et al., *Worshiping with the Anaheim Vineyard*.

wider phenomenon. Part of that attraction will come, perhaps, from the fact that more prominent figures or topics leave a larger trail of evidence and thus are easier to document.[7] Part of that attraction, perhaps, comes from another reason why our eyes and ears or drawn to the most noticeable: the subtle influence of our own Western culture to make us think that the most glamorous, the most charismatic, or the largest have the most influence.

But a window dressing may not have had the most influence. Neither might it be the best case to make universal claims.[8] For example, take the historians who were mesmerized by a certain kind of megachurch of the 1980s and 1990s (usually Willow Creek Community Church) that pursued and promoted some form of Contemporary Worship for tactical reasons: to attract the unchurched and evangelize more effectively. Narrow the focus to this sort of example and one kind of story emerges: this way of worship had been foisted on mainline congregations who have sold out their liturgical birthright for the promise of numerical growth.

In actuality, as a more thorough review of a range of primary materials would show, this story is only one narrative that occurred. Being fascinated by Willow Creek Community Church means overlooking critical developments in pentecostal churches large and small, in a variety of stands of Pentecostalism,[9] which will shape the nature of the whole phenomenon. It also means neglecting other megachurches who adopted this way of worship for entirely different reasons. And, as interviews with early mainline adopters would actually show, implementing Contemporary Worship emerged from a variety of motivations—some of which included satisfying the deep, unfulfilled hungers of their already existing members who had been touched by a renewal movement of some sort like charismatic renewal—and with a variety of applications reflecting the hybrid state of what churches with fewer resources could develop.

---

7. For an example, see Christerson and Flory, *The Rise of Network Christianity*, or Lee and Sinitiere, *Holy Mavericks*.

8. My critique on this point is a variation of Paul Bradshaw's critique of historians who are "lumpers" with respect to the history of the worship in the early church. As Bradshaw finds fault in the method of historians who overlook variety and divergent details in order to portray a simpler, more homogeneous picture of worship in the early church, similarly I am arguing for the avoidance of lumping with respect to the worship history of the last half century. See Bradshaw, *Search for the Origins*, especially ix–x.

9. To lump all Pentecostals together is a common tendency in liturgical historians who come from Roman Catholic or sacramental Protestant liturgical traditions like Anglican or Lutheran. Such lumping shows a lack of real familiarity with the divisions within the pentecostal approach to worship and, unfortunately, contributes to overlooking significant develops within these divisions.

It is also problematic to focus entirely on the topic of music in order to tell the history of Contemporary Praise & Worship. While music has been and remains an extremely critical part of this phenomenon and while all of us owe much to the musicologists who have advanced the knowledge of this topic beyond that of other possible topics, music is not the entire story.[10] In some strands of the development of contemporary ways of worship, other issues have been just as critical. In the liturgical experimentation in mainline congregations in the 1960s and 1970s, for example, updating the language away from archaic King James Bible English and focusing the service on issues of immediate relevance to people's lives were just as important as music in making services "contemporary." Moreover, even in the strands from which many of the major musical developments came, much energy also was poured into the development of biblical theologies of worship and establishing solid biblical preaching. To tell a full story all of these dimensions must be taken into account. To focus on musical structures, institutions, and performance practices is to risk overlooking other critical dimensions in this history.

Indeed, the problem with focusing on music as the key element in the history of Contemporary Praise & Worship can lead a researcher to think that the history started when there was a change in the music. However, before there were significant changes in the sort of music people used in worship, there were significant changes in other liturgical areas including, especially, the development of a new theology of worship focused on praise and God's presence.

Lesser known does not always mean insignificant. In interviewing participants in the phenomenon, it becomes quite apparent, for instance, that often the critical people who made initial, groundbreaking, or behind-the-scenes steps are folks who do not today immediately come to mind or, perhaps, never achieved widespread conspicuousness. For example, John Wimber is widely seen as the shaping force behind early Vineyard worship but also critical was Kenn Gulliksen, the original Vineyard church planter who installed a notion of intimacy in worship from the beginning years. Eddie Espinosa, too, was important by bringing his biblical theology of worship learned in other pentecostal circles into conversation with Wimber and Vineyard sensibilities in order to have a critical hand in developing what would be taught as the Vineyard phases of worship. Or take Don Moen, who in the 1980s and 1990s especially, was *the* voice of Integrity Hosanna! Praise

---

10. While music is not the entirety of the story, a researcher in this field must be aware that many sources collapse the terms "worship" and "music." In assessing primary material the historian must be aware of whether the source has made the terms synonymous or is meaning "worship" as a broader term.

and Worship recordings. But who knows the story of the influence on Moen of the evangelist Terry Law and the educational conferences known as the International Worship Symposiums? (See chapter 4.) Or, perhaps even more at the headwaters of the entire river, who remembers Reg Layzell, the 1940s pentecostal minister whose teaching connecting God's presence with the church praising God seems to be the theological fount that undergirds the phenomenon's whole development?[11]

Thorough bibliographic development of primary material will show that the most prominent people are neither always the best source of information nor the critical figures in earlier developments. Part of that comes about because prominent people often learn to focus the story around themselves as they repeatedly have been asked for information. In other words, prominence sometimes undercuts the sort of bird's eye view that allows an interviewee to highlight truly significant events, dates, and developments. That same can apply even if a researcher is trying to extrapolate from case studies of large, prominent churches. It may be that the researcher will find that the more mundane and obscure the case, the more likely it can be universalized to draw conclusions about congregations more generally. (See also principle four below.)

## Principle Three: Prescriptive liturgical material may actually be descriptive.

This principle stands in contrast to a methodological principle accepted by liturgical historians working in other historical periods, namely, materials that prescribe a certain liturgical practice may actually be stronger evidence for opposite practices than for the thing prescribed. The acceptance of this principle, especially for the study of worship in the early church, can be attributed to liturgical historian Paul Bradshaw.[12] Wanting to counter an earlier method that took such prescriptions at face value as evidence of actual practice and thus usable to provide a description of what worship was like at a particular period, Bradshaw instead argued that prescriptive statements and legislation showed what was hoped for. Thus, they are actually a corrective to existing practices, not evidence of those practices.

---

11. Similarly, the movement of which Reg Layzell was a part, the Latter Rain movement, is overlooked as a major influencer of worship since, as other historians have noted, it seems not to have made any major institutional or structural impact on Pentecostalism. See Faupel, "New Order of the Latter Rain," 259, and Riss, *Latter Rain*, 144. Yet if one wants to look at how thousands upon thousands of congregations worship, this movement has made a huge impact.

12. Bradshaw, *Search for the Origins*, 17–19.

Bradshaw's presumption is that prescriptions do not try to reinforce what already exists in terms of worship but to bring about something hoped for, with varying degrees of success.

A much different cultural context for the emergence of Contemporary Praise & Worship shifts the nature of prescriptive material within this phenomenon, however. Instead of being evidence of what does not exist, prescriptive Contemporary Praise & Worship material can show what is already being done, at least in some locales. And it can serve as a predictor of what other churches are likely to adopt as standard practice.

The different cultural context for Contemporary Praise & Worship as compared to previous historical phenomenon is the post-Enlightenment sensibilities of democracy, pragmatism, and capitalism. The combination of these three sensibilities creates a different atmosphere so that prescriptive Contemporary Praise & Worship material may actually be descriptive.

Imagine curious participants at a Contemporary Praise & Worship teaching conference in the 1980s.[13] As our interviews with such people have often indicated, such persons arrived with some attraction to this new way of worship and were eager to learn more—especially with respect to the details of liturgical practices—in order to implement them when returning to their home church. Their innate pragmatism naturally led them to want to imitate whatever liturgical practices and perspectives the instructor described and prescribed. Thus the session's worksheets and handouts, typically written in a prescriptive form, were likely to indicate actual practice, especially in the instructor's home context and likely in the learners' churches. Of course, as any of us who have been one of those eager-to-learn-and-implement conference participants can attest, actual implementation of what was learned at the conference could vary from church to church. Everything the teacher taught may not actually have been everything the teacher got as the participants adopted and implemented in their home settings. This limitation adds a degree of cautiousness in taking the prescriptions of Contemporary Praise & Worship teaching materials as universals, but it adds only a *degree* of cautiousness, not a complete rejection of those materials as a source for understanding how churches are worshiping.

---

13. Beyond the different cultural contexts between the late patristic period and the late twentieth century, one should take into account that the different sources for liturgical prescriptions. Bradshaw mainly considers prescriptions emerging from legislative councils trying to correct errors and create more uniform practices. Historians of Contemporary Praise & Worship, on the other hand, are much more likely to deal with prescriptive teaching materials intentionally generated for a body of receptive learners eager to adopt and implement them.

How a post-Enlightenment, democratic culture vests authority to speak and teach on worship in a prescriptive way reinforces our ability to use prescriptive primary materials to assess actual practice. Consider the instructor mentioned above. In all likelihood, such teachers were chosen not because of some kind of formal credential but because they had proved to be successful practitioners of things that they then prescribed in their teaching. Their expertise was not granted merely by formal means but was developed in grassroots practice. Their authority to speak in such settings presumes that the practices that they prescribed already had some degree of implementation, at least in their home settings.

More broadly, prescriptive materials in published form like books, tapes, and DVDs may likely be descriptive. For one thing, the authors of such materials often had the same sort of vested authority that speakers at conferences had. Potential adopters were eager to read, listen to, and watch materials from successful practitioners. Acquisition editors at publishers could turn that eagerness into sales, and prescriptions sold easily turn into prescriptions adopted. Buyers purchased such prescriptive materials not to reject the content but to implement it.

In this way, published prescriptions can indicate trends. Even if the published material was the leading edge of actual practice, the fact that it was a leading edge can indicate where actual practices were going. In the current cultural context, novelty and practicality were two elements in prescriptive Contemporary Praise & Worship materials that generated interest and sales.

## Principle Four: Reliance upon only one label for the phenomenon is misplaced.

Because this liturgical phenomenon is so large—crossing a range of denominations, traditions, and liturgical spiritualities, with two main originating impulses—it has never had a single name. Consequently, historians who limit themselves to a single term risk overlooking significant persons, churches, events, and developments. Because all of the people and churches that practice some form of this phenomenon do not all use a common term for it, researchers must look for shared qualities so as to discern the phenomenon, regardless of how it is labeled, and see its breadth and complexity.[14]

14. Lim Swee Hong and I have identified the defining qualities of worship within this phenomenon. See Lim and Ruth, *Lovin' on Jesus*, 2–7. A researcher should realize, however, that different strands within the larger phenomenon might have relatively different weightings for the nine qualities we list. For example, a concern for nonarchaic English was slow arriving for most pentecostal expressions of the phenomenon.

By settling for an easier path of relying upon one term or label, a historian will tell a story that is partial at best and misleading at worst. For example, liturgical historians—mainly white and from mainline denominations—often have locked on the term that is the predominant one for white, mainline congregations, i.e., "Contemporary Worship." In doing so, such historians overlooked pentecostal developments since Pentecostals mainly use other terms, usually "Praise and Worship" or simply "worship." Even if these historians did not completely overlook Pentecostals, they will give the pentecostal strand of the phenomenon a cursory treatment. Either approach is devastating for a solid historiographical approach because not handling the pentecostal dimension in depth will leave critical issues unexplored, especially the key theological commitments that drove the motivation for pursuing a new way of worship. In one major strand of development in the phenomenon, the premise that God associates God's presence with the corporate act of praising was the underlying foundation for pursuing extended times of congregational singing dedicated first to praising and then adoring God. Therefore, if one only focuses on those using the term "Contemporary Worship," one will overlook this critical theological commitment since this biblically-derived theology is absent in the mainline materials that promoted this way of worship.

Moreover, as just implied, locking in on a single term can have particularly catastrophic effects on a historian wishing to explore the full ethnic and global breadth of the story. Outside of the United States and outside of white, mainline congregations, the overwhelming term is "Praise and Worship" or whatever the equivalent would be in that region's language.

Similarly, only looking for "Contemporary Worship" or "Praise and Worship" could cause a researcher to overlook some important terms used in certain white strands of the phenomenon. The two most important would be "Modern Worship" and "Emerging Worship."[15] Moreover, to insist upon finding a church using a technical term before recognizing that that church was worshiping within the larger phenomenon would mean that historians could neglect some churches. Perhaps the most striking examples would be early Vineyard congregations that have tended only to speak of "worship."

In order to find a term with enough breadth to cover the entire phenomenon, I suggest a synthetic term: Contemporary Praise & Worship. I have found in my use of the term so far that it has enough familiarity that people know to what I am referring. However, by it being a new term—thus neither strictly "Contemporary Worship" nor "Praise and Worship"—I do

---

15. For a discussion of the origin of "Modern Worship," see Ingalls, "Transnational Connections," 425–48. "Emerging Worship" was a term with an even smaller circumference of use. For an example of use, see Kimball, *Emerging Worship*.

not have to choose between which of those two most common terms and risk excluding worshipers who use the other.

## Principle Five: Those who experienced the history may not know the history.

This methodological principle is a caution about utilizing information from interviewees and writers who have been part of this liturgical phenomenon. Those who know the facts and have experienced events in this phenomenon's development do not always see the bigger picture and larger connections. Gathering information from those who have experienced the history can be like the parable of the men trying to describe an elephant but can only describe the part of the animal they are touching; their localized knowledge may be true and invaluable but their globalized knowledge can be limited or erroneous. This limitation applies to both interviews and written materials. (The limitation also applies to the perspective of interviewers if they assume their own personal experience of the phenomenon is exhaustive or representative.) The limitation has multiple facets.

Some of the limitation is unintentional or even natural. It is easy, for instance, for someone's proximity to events to accentuate their distinctiveness. One's participation in something heightens its importance in that person's mind. This emphasis seems even more true when the events are closest to the present time. One's lack of familiarity or information about prior events can mute those events' importance and domesticate the character of the actual happenings.

Combine the tendency to emphasize events in which one participated with the tendency to universalize one's own awareness and it becomes possible to distort the actual history. For example, ask most people when multi-media worship began and I suspect many will say that it emerged at the time they first became aware of it. However, as historian Eileen Crowley has shown, forms of multi-media worship began in the early twentieth century almost as soon as the technology was available, not to mention the surge in multi-media experimentation in the 1960s.[16]

Another easy, unintentional distortion arises when a researcher does not take into account that over time a historical figure's thoughts and teaching can become more systematized and less messy. Just as historians of other eras and long past historical figures need to be careful not to read back a later or "mature" form into earlier periods, historians of Contemporary Praise & Worship need to make sure they do not make the same mistake. An example

16. Crowley-Horak, "Testing the Fruits," 22–46.

is one I myself have struggled with: reading back the developed Vineyard teaching on the phases of worship into the first years of Vineyard congregations.[17] Moreover, researchers need to be attentive to when historical figures are doing their own reading back of their mature thought.

As mentioned above, historians working with those who have been better-known figures should be aware of the natural tendencies that often occur with such figures. Their standing has often given them the chance to tell their story. Consequently, not only do they tend toward presenting a smooth story without some of the texture that allows for a richer history, but also they often focus the story around themselves. Sometimes better, richer information can be found with folks who have not been eminent, as noted above.[18] They can have the ability to describe what was going on around them or behind the scenes, which sometimes is exactly the information that has never appeared before and can provide the crucial links to enable an enriched historiography. What is amazing is that lesser-known people often feel as if what they experienced and the historical artifacts they possess are not that important. It is easy for people to conflate popular celebrity with historical significance, but celebrity status and significance are not synonymous.

Beyond the natural limitations of a single individual's perspective, I have discovered another reason for a participant's restricted horizon of information, namely, a lack of awareness brought on by the separateness of the two main branches of development. As discussed in the introduction to this book, there have been two main branches of development, one largely pentecostal, focusing on new worship as a gift from God supported by a certain biblical theology of worship, and one largely mainline or evangelical, driven a desire to be relevant and accessible to people in a changing culture. Although both are necessary to document the entire phenomenon, participants in one strand or the other tend to know the details, persons, and events associated with their strand and not the other. For example, I recently was interviewing a pentecostal minister who had been involved with praise and worship services for over twenty years and was considering starting a second Sunday morning service in order to be able to offer people multiple services differentiated by style. He was astounded when I told him that what he was describing was standard practice in mainline congregations. He certainly is not the only one with a limited perspective brought about by worshiping within a particular part of the wider phenomenon.

17. Park et al., *Worshiping with the Anaheim Vineyard*, 117–20. Compare Samuel, *Holy Spirit in Worship Music*, 60–62.

18. And sometimes such folks, because they lack prominence, are easier for a researcher to access. That has proved especially true in trying to connect with currently prominent folks.

Consequently, if anyone wishes to write a full history, gathering information from across the breadth is absolutely necessary.

A longstanding tendency inherent in the piety of those who worship in Contemporary Praise & Worship is a final facet to why those who have experienced the history may not know the history. Most (almost all?) of those who worship in contemporary services are part of a larger liturgical spirituality of Pietism that is mesmerized by personal experience in worship. Consequently, their firsthand descriptions, whether found in writing or by interview, will tend to speak about their own personal experiences as shaped by what they value in worship (usually an encounter with God in the inward realm of affections or emotions). Their accounts will emphasize this affective encounter and shape the details to that end.[19] What their accounts typically will not emphasize are those concrete details that allow a historian to visualize the whole service and describe it for others. To compensate the historian must make sure large amounts of firsthand accounts are used, synthesizing them judiciously, in order to come up with a composite picture. Alternatively, some other form of corroborating primary material should be found.

There is a parallel need when using popular pentecostal literature. Authors of this literature are not careful about citing their sources for information or influences on their thinking. Their piety instead leads them to attribute ideas to divine inspiration. Therefore, a historian needs a wide collection of pentecostal material in order to ascertain developments over time and to see potential lines of influence between individual authors and teachers.

Similarly, popular materials from mainline authors can frustrate a historical researcher. While these authors tend not to make the same sort of appeal to direct inspiration for their ideas, nonetheless they often repeat information from each other without citation. A glaring example is the widely spread—but false—notion that Martin Luther or Charles Wesley intentionally appropriated music from bars/pubs as the main source for their musical innovations. Likewise, the tendency of Church Growth sources to cite unnamed studies for their broad descriptions of people can be frustrating to a researcher wanting to track lines of influence and development across sources.

---

19. I first noticed this tendency when researching the worship of early American Methodists. See Ruth, *A Little Heaven Below*.

## Principle Six: Realize that there is not always a direct line of causation.

Having named our natural—and necessary—desire to discover lines of influence for ideas and practices, historians should accept that there is not always a direct causation. It may be that, when something appears in close time proximity in two places or persons, this proximity is entirely coincidental. It may be that similar conditions with similar persons can result in similar developments without there being direct causation. I once was pursuing, for instance, the development of a line of thought among two pentecostal authors in the late 1970s and early 1980s, one in the United States and one in New Zealand. I was struck by the similarity of their thought and so prematurely concluded that there must be some direct line of influence one way or the other. Eventually I interviewed both and discovered that there had not been, a fact confirmed by one of the interviewees who had been struck by the similarity, too, and had asked the other person about influence of that person's thought when they eventually met. There proved to be no direct linkage.

## Principle Seven: Hold off on theological assessments.

As I have argued more extensively elsewhere,[20] many of the currently available histories of this phenomenon present an abbreviated history because they too quickly theologically assess Contemporary Praise & Worship. The histories from pentecostal and evangelical authors, for example, often portrayed the phenomenon as being of God and due to divine activity and referenced only those historical facts that contribute to that portrayal. In contrast, many liturgical historians, who were influenced by the concerns of the Liturgical Movement as well as by the historiographical categories of James F. White with respect to non-sacramental Protestant liturgical traditions, have tended to depict the phenomenon as a bad thing, a recurrence of theologically suspect tendencies in American approaches to worship.[21] Not surprisingly, these historians narrowed their historiography to elements that contributed to that judgement.

Thus, although both bodies of literature portray the phenomenon in diametrically opposed judgments with respect to theological appraisal, they share a common trait. For both bodies of literature the rush to theological

---

20. Ruth, "Divine, Human, or Devilish?" 290–310.

21. The US-centrism of this perspective should also call this historiography into question, given the global spread of Contemporary Praise & Worship.

appraisal meant the historians did not give enough effort to developing a breadth of primary materials to tell a broader, fuller, and more accurate history. Neither did the historians give themselves enough distance from Contemporary Praise & Worship to see its complexity as I have stated elsewhere:

> [The two theological approaches] lack attention to contemporary worship's multiple points of origin, the reasons for its origins, attentiveness to the developments in specific practices over time, awareness of shifting theological explanations, and the evolution of roles of leadership and popular participation, among other possible topics.[22]

We offer the essays in this current volume to help fill these lacunae.

Of course, there are more objective histories, largely from those who use methods of ethnomusicology or sociology, which have utilized a better breadth of materials with a more rigorous method.[23] However, these histories, too, share a limitation in that they are not concerned with telling a broad history featuring the range of topics in a fuller liturgical history. Specifically, they tend not to study the theological and biblical motivations of those who originated and developed Contemporary Praise & Worship.

Thus, we are back to principle one discussed above: bibliography is everything, and methodology is the other half. Gaining the patience and harnessing the drive needed to study this phenomenon legitimately are the necessary conditions for bibliographical development. What is needed for this historical task is what is needed for all good historiography: cultivating puzzlement (to use the terms of Sam Wineburg)[24] as historians "hold their initial impressions lightly as they continue to listen and think and probe and evaluate."[25] Jumping to theological evaluations prematurely is a sure way to undercut both patience and drive. It may be that a historian will eventually want to bring theological assessment to the phenomenon (and those who teach liturgy classes for future practitioners should do so), but to be fair to Contemporary Praise & Worship and to write sound history the historian must first attend to bibliography and method.

Let us devote ourselves to that task.

---

22. Ruth, "Divine, Human, or Devilish?" 302.
23. For a review of these histories, see Ruth, "Divine, Human, or Devilish?" 303–7.
24. Wineburg, *Historical Thinking*, 21.
25. McKenzie, *Little Book*, 79.

# Bibliography

Bradshaw, Paul F. *The Search for the Origins of Christian Worship: Sources and Methods for the Study of Early Liturgy*. 2nd ed. Oxford: Oxford University Press, 2002.

Christerson, Brad, and Richard W. Flory. *The Rise of Network Christianity: How Independent Leaders Are Changing the Religious Landscape*. Oxford: Oxford University Press, 2017.

Crowley-Horak, Eileen. "Testing the Fruits: Aesthetics as Applied to Liturgical Media Art." PhD diss., Union Theological Seminary, 2002.

Faupel, D. William. "The New Order of the Latter Rain: Restoration or Renewal?" In *Winds from the North: Canadian Contributions to the Pentecostal Movement*, edited by Michael Wilkinson and Peter Althouse, 239–63. Leiden: Brill, 2010.

Ingalls, Monique. "Transnational Connections, Musical Meaning, and the 1990s 'British Invasion' of North American Evangelical Worship Music." In *The Oxford Handbook of Music and World Christianities*, edited by Suzel Reily and Jonathan Dueck, 425–48. Oxford: Oxford University Press, 2016.

Kimball, Dan. *Emerging Worship: Creating Worship Gatherings for New Generations*. Grand Rapids: Zondervan, 2004.

Lee, Shayne, and Phillip Luke Sinitiere. *Holy Mavericks: Evangelical Innovators and the Spiritual Marketplace*. New York: New York University Press, 2009.

Lim, Swee Hong, and Lester Ruth. *Lovin' on Jesus: A Concise History of Contemporary Worship*. Nashville: Abingdon, 2017.

McKenzie, Robert Tracy. *A Little Book for New Historians: Why and How to Study History*. Downers Grove: IVP Academic, 2019.

Park, Andy, et al. *Worshiping with the Anaheim Vineyard: The Emergence of Contemporary Worship*. Grand Rapids: Eerdmans, 2017.

Riss, Richard M. *Latter Rain: The Latter Rain Movement of 1948 and the Mid-Twentieth Century Evangelical Awakening*. Mississauga, ON: Honeycomb Visual Productions, 1987.

Ruth, Lester. "Divine, Human, or Devilish? The State of the Question on the Writing of the History of Contemporary Worship." *Worship* 88 (2014) 290–310.

———. *A Little Heaven Below: Worship at Early Methodist Quarterly Meetings*. Nashville: Kingswood, 2000.

Samuel, Josh P. S. *The Holy Spirit in Worship Music, Preaching, and the Altar: Renewing Pentecostal Corporate Worship*. Cleveland, TN: CPT, 2018.

Taft, Robert F. "The Structural Analysis of Liturgical Units: An Essay in Methodology." In *Beyond East and West: Problems in Liturgical Understanding*, 187–202. 2nd ed. Rome: Pontifical Oriental Institute, 2001.

White, James F. *Protestant Worship: Traditions in Transition*. Louisville: Westminster John Knox, 1989.

Wineburg, Sam. *Historical Thinking and Other Unnatural Acts: Charting the Future of Teaching the Past*. Philadelphia: Temple University Press, 2001.

www.ingramcontent.com/pod-product-compliance
Lightning Source LLC
Chambersburg PA
CBHW051741230426
43670CB00012B/2112